D1168623

Minding the Store

Stanley Marcus, 1997

Stanley Marcus

Minding the Store

A MEMOIR

Facsimile Edition for

NeimanMarcus 90 years

University of North Texas Press
Denton, Texas

© 1974 by Stanley Marcus
All rights reserved.
© 1997 Facsimile Edition
Printed in the United States of America
5 4 3 2 1
Requests for permission to reproduce material from this work should be sent to
Permissions
University of North Texas Press
Post Office Box 311336
Denton, Texas 76203-1336

The paper used in this book meets the minimum requirements of the American National Standard for Permanence of Paper for Printed Library Materials, z39.48.1984. Binding materials have been chosen for durability.

The author is grateful to the following publishers and authors for permission to reprint previously copyrighted materials:

Fortune magazine, for an excerpt from the article "Dallas in Wonderland" by Louis Kronenberger, as published in its November 1937 issue, copyright © 1937 Time Inc.; and for an excerpt from the article "America Is in Fashion" by Stanley Marcus, as published in its November 1939 issue, copyright © 1939 by Time Inc.

North American Newspaper Alliance and the Bell syndicate, for the column "Pitching Horseshoes" by Billie Rose, published in the *Dallas Times Herald*, December 5, 1949.

Women's Wear Daily, for the article "From Where I Sit" by Samuel Feinberg, as published in its December 15, 1967, issue, copyright © 1967, Fairchild Publications, Inc.; and for one paragraph from the editorial "Industry Owes Appreciation for Fashion Understanding in Rulings of L-85" by Winnifred J. Ovitte, as published in its April 8, 1942, issue, copyright ©1942, Fairchild Publications, Inc.

Selma Robinson, for an excerpt from her article "Texas Tells 'Em," as published in *Collier's* September 16, 1939.

United Press International, for a portion of an interview by Robert Musel, as published in the *Dallas Morning News*, March 7, 1971.

Newsday, for an excerpt from the column "Despite Defensive Front, Dallas Is Doing Penance" by Marguerite Higgins, as published in the *Chicago Daily News*, January 7, 1964. copyright © 1964, Newsday, Inc.

Paul Crume, for one of his "Big D" columns as published in the *Dallas Morning News*, December 6, 1959.

Library of Congress Cataloging-in-Publication Data

Marcus, Stanley, 1905–
    Minding the store : a memoir / by Stanley Marcus.
      p.   cm.
    Includes index.
    ISBN 1-57441-039-3 (cloth : alk. paper)
    1. Marcus, Stanley, 1905–   . 2. Businesspeople—
      Biography
  I. Title.
  HF5429.5.D2M37   1997
  381'.14'092–dc21
  [B]   97-13287
                                            CIP

Dedicated to
My Father Who Was
and to
My Son Who Is

An Appreciation

T HANKS AND GRATITUDE go to my mother, whose vivid memory of incidents and people has been an invaluable source of knowledge and inspiration; to my wife, who has lived through the gestation period of this book with patience and understanding, sound criticism and encouragement; to my administrative assistant, Alice Snavely, who, in addition to doing painstaking research, has proofread my drafts and supplied answers and documentation to hundreds of questions; to Pat Acheson, Hortense Spitz, Julia Sweeney, and Linda Robinson, who have combed the newspaper and magazine files for verification of names and dates; to Beth Bailey, Margaret Bradley, Linda Grenadier, Nancy Collins, and Julie Travis, who have lent helping hands when needed to make deadlines; to Zula McCauley, for her chronicle of the store, *The First Forty Years;* and to all of my associates at Neiman-Marcus, past and present, who have had a part in the building of the institution.

— S.M.

Dallas, Texas
April 1974

Foreword

Neiman Marcus 90th Anniversary Edition

THIS BOOK, FIRST published in 1974, was my initial attempt at writing anything of greater length than an occasional magazine piece for the *Atlantic Monthly*, the *Saturday Evening Post*, or *Fortune*. I had considered writing a full-length book but I was uncertain of my ability to sustain a nonfictional story for several hundred pages. Above all, I didn't want to bore readers with tales of my retail experiences or, in writing a personal memoir, to appear pompous and self-opinionated. Besides which, I was already working a ten-hour day and taking a sack of mail and reports home almost every evening.

Actually the book came about as a result of a bit of serendipity involving a stranger sitting next to me on a flight to El Paso on the occasion of the launching of a book by my friend, Tom Lea. In the course of the flight, my seat companion introduced himself as Ned Bradford, senior editor of Little Brown, the prestigious Boston publisher. We had a pleasant conversation en route to El Paso where he, too, was going for the publication party of *The King Ranch* book which Tom Lea had written and illustrated.

He queried me about how the store functioned and my role in it. I related some anecdotes, many of which appear in this book, and as we landed he said, "I think you've got a good book in you. Have you ever thought of writing it?" I replied that I was so busy minding the store that I didn't see how I could find time to do justice to both. He handed me his card saying, "If you ever find the time and decide to write that book, I'd like to publish it."

I was flattered and promised to send him some magazine pieces I had written, but concluded by telling him that it was highly unlikely that I could take on anything else at that time. Just then, the plane landed and we both made our way to a bus that was standing by to take us to Juarez for the luncheon.

On my return to Dallas, I sent him the *Saturday Evening Post* article together with the *Atlantic Monthly* piece and several others. Shortly thereafter, I received a letter from him:

> Dear Stanley:
>
> Thanks for your letter and for the *Saturday Evening Post* article. It's fine—and should reassure you if you've had any doubts about your ability to venture beyond speech writing. To determine this, why don't you put down a very informal outline of the general subjects you want to cover in more or less depth, roughly in chronological order? Or is there actually all that much more material still lying around in your memory and files to make a full length book?
>
> Best regards as ever.
> Yours,
> Ned Bradford

When I had digested the letter I filed it and went on about my business of running a growing, fine quality specialty store that was expanding rapidly. With plans to build one store a year for the next dozen years, I was having a ball, so I gave no more than fleeting attention to his invitation.

The serendipity continued even on a business trip to New York. I arrived in the city on an evening in November of 1972 about 8:30 P.M. Whenever I got in at that hour, I usually checked into the hotel and then took a walk down Fifth Avenue to see what the New York competition was displaying in its show windows. As I was examining a presentation of Scottish cashmere sweaters, I felt a tap on my shoulder while a voice said, "It's later than you think! When are you going to write that book?" I spun around expecting to be mugged. Instead I found it was Ned Bradford. The first thing I could think to reply was, "As soon as some enterprising publisher gives me a sufficiently attractive advance and a contract, I'll write the book."

"In that case," he replied, "you'll have it on your office desk in the morning." He did as he promised, and I signed the contract after putting the check in an escrow account, just in case I was unable to deliver the manuscript on time.

It took a couple of weeks for the magnitude of what I, as an occasional magazine article writer, had done by signing a contract to deliver a book of some 350 pages. My wife and I went to Jamaica on a winter holiday for a couple of weeks during which I spent most of my time in bed trying to recuperate from a bad cold. Since I was immobilized, I decided to get started on the book. Before we left Jamaica, I had typed out the first two chapters and, even more important, I had completed the outline for the entire book. This, of course, was accomplished with no competition from any other time demands such as a store or social activities.

Once home I made the decision that the only way I could write a book and also meet my responsibilities as CEO of Neiman Marcus was to establish a rigid writing schedule to which I could adhere. So I dedicated the hours of 8:00 P.M. to midnight on weekdays and 8:00 A.M. until 10:00 P.M. on Saturdays and Sundays. My wife cooperated by declining all social invitations for a nine-month period, enabling me to concentrate on the book. At the conclusion of that time, I finished it and turned the manuscript in to the publisher. Only then did I feel free to cash the advance check that Ned Bradford had given me. Ned had assigned an editor to whom I sent finished chapters as they were produced to be sure that I wasn't straying from the subject. I received approval with a few minor exceptions.

During these months, Ned Bradford took ill and died, but he had provided me not only with the encouragement to write *Minding the Store*, but with an invaluable sense of direction. He wrote,

If I may say so, to me the most interesting books of an autobiographical nature are those in which the writer reveals in one way or another not only what he has done, but what he has learned, and I would hope that will be at the very least one of your important themes.

The business will loom large throughout, of course, but what I as a reader would like to know is what merchandising has taught you and, in fact, what being and working in Texas has taught you, if the region has influenced you, uniquely I suppose. Such a book would have much more than a regional sale, and I can't help thinking that its creation would give you a great personal satisfaction.

This comment proved invaluable, for it kept me on course and contributed greatly to the success of *Minding the Store* for which I remain eternally appreciative.

In the course of its celebration of the nintieth birthday of Neiman Marcus, the company has seen fit to encourage the republication of this book in this hard back edition. Since I was a participant in a good many of the ninety years of the existence of Neiman Marcus, I am pleased to be a contributor to this milestone celebration.

Stanley Marcus
May 14, 1997
Dallas, Texas

Contents

Illustrations

1

Genesis

THERE IS NEVER a good *sale* for Neiman-Marcus unless it's a good *buy* for the customer."

That was one of the first declarations of business philosophy I heard my father, Herbert Marcus, make soon after I came to work at Neiman-Marcus in 1926. It was reiterated so many times that it became established as an article of faith in my mind, and on numerous occasions he demonstrated his enforcement of this principle even when it meant lost sales and profits. He explained that there was a right customer for every piece of merchandise, and that part of a merchant's job was not only to bring the two together, but also to prevent the customer from making the wrong choice.

Some may regard this as sheer idealism, but having worked with my father for twenty-four years, I consider it a doctrine of idealistic pragmatism. First of all, he enjoyed doing business that way, and second, he recognized that there was no advertisement as potent as a satisfied customer. This was his way of practicing the Golden Rule, and now, almost seventy years since the founding of Neiman-Marcus, the same policy prevails.

Although every new employee goes through an orientation class, I have made it a custom, now carried on by my son, to meet with groups of them at a morning coffee to explain some of the background and ideals of the founders. I start by telling them that Neiman-Marcus was established as a result of the bad judgment of its founders, my father, Herbert Marcus, his younger sister, Carrie Marcus Neiman, and her husband, Al Neiman. This statement usually distracts my listeners from their coffee cups. I go on to explain that my father, who at twenty-five was a buyer of boys' clothing at Sanger Brothers, the leading store of the Southwest, and his sister Carrie, who at the tender age of twenty-one was the blouse buyer and top saleswoman at A. Harris & Company, another local store, were persuaded by her husband Al to leave their jobs and go with him to Atlanta, Georgia, to establish a sales promotion business. I was then six months old and, since my recall doesn't extend back that far, I am forced to rely on hearsay for what happened during the first half-dozen years of my life, and some of that may be apocryphal.

The partnership they set up was directed towards helping country merchants in Georgia raise cash by staging special sales, with flamboyant signs, banners strung up across the streets, and band music to lure the crowds. They were so successful that at the end of two years they had had two offers to sell out, and here is where the bad judgment came in. One offer was for $25,000 in cash, and the other was the franchise for the state of Missouri or Kansas for a relatively new product called "Coca-Cola." They apparently were too smart to be taken in by this unknown soft drink, so they took the $25,000 in cash instead, returning to Dallas to start a business of their own, to be run in a manner they had dreamed about when they were employees of Sanger Brothers and A. Harris & Company. In retrospect, if their judgment had been better, they would have taken the Coca-Cola franchise and Neiman-Marcus would have become a famous name in Missouri or Kansas as bottlers of Coca-Cola, with a fraction of the effort required to build a fashion institution of world renown.

They came back to Dallas with their $25,000, which, combined with their savings and with funds from the sale of some minority shares to other members of their family, provided them with barely sufficient capital to pay for the fixtures, carpets and merchandise for their new fifty-foot storefront in a building in the heart of the retail district. At that time, Sanger Brothers dominated Texas retail distribution, much as Marshall Field & Company did in the Midwest. Alex Sanger, the president of the Sanger business, had offered my father a raise of $1.87½ a month to keep him from going to Atlanta, and when he heard of the proposed new venture, he urged my father to give up his foolish dream and return to the Sanger fold, where a bright and secure future could be assured.

Nonetheless, the three young hopefuls were determined to go into business for themselves and to run it in the way they felt a fashion store should be operated. It was not unusual for three young people to leave secure positions to go into business for themselves. Young people have been, and still are, venturesome enough to want to try it on their own. Of course, it took courage to come into the same town dominated by Sanger Brothers. But courage they didn't lack, nor were they bashful or overly modest in their evaluation of their own standards of good taste and fashion. On Sunday, September 8, 1907, a full-page advertisement appeared in the *Dallas Morning News* announcing "the opening of the New and Exclusive Shopping Place for Fashionable Women, devoted to the selling of Ready-to-Wear Apparel" and labeling Neiman-Marcus as "The Outer-Garment Shop." It went on to state that "Tuesday, September tenth, marks the advent of a new shopping place in Dallas — a store of Quality, a Specialty store — the only store in the City whose stocks are strictly confined to Ladies' Outer-Garments and Millinery, and presenting wider varieties and more exclusive lines than any other store in the South." It editorialized,

Our decision to conduct a store in Dallas was not reached on impulse. We studied the field thoroughly and saw there was a real necessity for such a shopping place as ours. Our preparations have not been

5

hasty. We have spent months in planning the interior, which is without equal in the South.

We Will Improve Ready-to-Wear Merchandising. A store can be bettered by specialized attention. Knowledge applied to one thing insures best results. We began our intended innovation at the very foundation; that is to say, with the builders of Women's Garments. We have secured exclusive lines which have never been shown in Texas before, garments that stand in a class alone as to character and fit.

Our Styles. All the pages of all the fashion journals, American and Foreign, can suggest no more than the open book of realism now here, composed of Suits, Dresses and Wraps of every favored style. The selection will meet every taste, every occasion and every price.

Our Qualities and Values. As well as the Store of Fashions we will be known as the Store of Quality and Superior Values. We shall be hypercritical in our selections. Only the finest productions of the best garment makers are good enough for us. Every article of apparel shown will bear evidence, in its touches of exclusiveness, in its chic and grace and splendid finish, to the most skillful and thorough workmanship.

The advertisement concluded with the offer of a gift: "As a memento of the occasion we will present a handsome Souvenir to visitors on opening day. These Souvenirs will be worthy of the offerings of the new store." The gift was a chromo-lithographed tin plate decorated with a classical figure in a style which, in subsequent years, they recognized as pure kitsch, causing them no end of embarrassment.

The customers attending the opening were greeted by Mr. Neiman alone, for Carrie had undergone surgery several weeks prior to the opening, and my father was seriously ill with typhoid fever. As an economic sidelight, within a month of the opening the economy of the country was jarred by the money panic of 1907, which created a cyclical dip in the business of the nation and the region. Nevertheless, the new store met with instantaneous acceptance, and Mr. Neiman and the buyer, a bright-eyed Irish girl in her early twenties, Moira Cullen from Worcester, Massachusetts, were forced to return to New York to replenish the stock. The gentlewomen of Dallas and its environs were impressed indeed by the taste displayed in the selection of gowns and suits offered them, and they were charmed by the quality of the service rendered by the sales staff.

It might be well at this point to take a glimpse into the background and qualifications of these three partners who proclaimed the virtues of their new enterprise with such self-assurance. None of them had gone through high school. Abraham Lincoln Neiman, always known as Al, was born in Chicago in 1880 and brought up in a Cleveland orphanage. He had been in the merchandise brokerage and sales promotion businesses. He was an aggressive business-getter, but at the beginning he relied on his wife's and brother-in-law's taste in merchandise selection, the fitting qualities of garments, and in all matters of an aesthetic nature. His wife, Carrie, a tall, slim brunette with a somewhat mystical look in her eyes, was born in Louisville, Kentucky, in 1883, and was twenty-four years of age on the opening day. She was the essence of kindness and gentleness, with a reserved manner which caused many of her friends to wonder how she could have been attracted to the flamboyant and egotistical Al Neiman. She and my father and their brother, Theo, and their sisters, Minnie and Celia, were born of immigrant parents, who had come from Europe and had met in Louisville, where they were married. My grandmother Marcus was born in Hanau, Germany, and my grandfather, Jacob Marcus, in Wronke, a town on the shifting German-Polish border.

My father, Herbert Marcus, born in Louisville in 1878, was twenty-nine years old when the store that he had planned and envisioned was opened on September the tenth. It was three months before he was well enough to make his first inspection tour. He hadn't finished high school, for financial reasons, so he proceeded to educate himself by exposure to those who did have learning and by voracious reading. Gibbon's *Decline and Fall of the Roman Empire* and Plutarch's *Lives* were two of his favorite works which

7

he reread constantly, finding parallels and solutions to contemporary problems. He had come to Hillsboro, Texas, to join his older brother, Theo, who had preceded him there. My father, who was then fifteen, found a job in a country store where he swept the floors, wrapped packages, and sold when everyone else was busy. I suspect he proved to be a better seller than a sweeper, for physical exertion was never his predilection.

Hillsboro was just sixty-three miles from Dallas, and it didn't take long for my father to decide that city life had more to offer than a country town, even though Dallas was hardly a cosmopolitan center. He started to work there by selling life insurance, and it is fairly easy to understand why a nineteen-year-old newcomer would find the going pretty rough. He switched from insurance to the wholesale selling of men's pants without achieving the financial rewards he had anticipated. While he was on the road, he met a kindly older man, I. C. Biesenthal, who was so impressed with his ability that he offered him a job selling "Buster Brown" boys' clothes, named after a then-popular comic strip character. One of his accounts was Sanger Brothers, to whom he made such a good sales presentation that he was offered a position as a women's shoe salesman. He accepted the job with alacrity, for by this time he had met Minnie Lichtenstein, a native of Dallas, and one of the most popular young Jewish girls in town. He felt he could protect and promote his interests better by being on the scene rather than on the road.

For a young man from a poor family, with limited formal education and a restricted exposure to the way wealthy people lived, he had nonetheless developed very expensive tastes, investing almost all his earnings in his personal wardrobe. He was tall, handsome, and clean-cut, a good dancer, an interesting conversationalist, and even though he hadn't held on to any money, he was welcomed into Jewish society by the mothers of all of the unmarried daughters. True, some regarded him as a big talker who was always telling about what he was going to do; others perhaps regarded him as too much of a dreamer to ever accomplish much. Parties were fun and fine, but he wanted to get married and the one he wanted to marry was Minnie Lichtenstein, whose family, while by no means affluent, was well established in the community and had more material assets than the newly arrived Marcuses.

My maternal grandmother, Hattie Mittenthal, born in Russia, came to Peoria, Illinois, when she was four years old. In 1878, the Mittenthal clan, a large one, moved to Dallas. It was in Dallas she met and married Meyer Lichtenstein, an immigrant from the Russian-German border town of Koenigsberg. The Lichtensteins weren't too excited by the prospect of this "dreamer" as a husband for their younger daughter. Besides, Minnie was having much too good a time in the social whirl to want to get married and settle down at the age of nineteen.

On the other side, the Marcus family did not take too warmly to the idea of their young son and brother marrying a girl, nice enough as she was, but from a family of Russian origin. But determination was one of Herbert Marcus's strongest characteristics, and since he had made up his mind to marry Minnie Lichtenstein, he wouldn't permit his family's reservations, her family's misgivings, my mother's reluctance, or the fact that he had to borrow money to go on their honeymoon deter him from insisting on marriage. That was in 1902.

Herbert Marcus fortunately caught the eye of Philip Sanger, one of the Sanger brothers, who was impressed by his selling ability, ambitions, and appearance, and promoted him to the post of buyer for the boys' department. Mr. Sanger, a keen judge of talent, believed he had discovered a "comer." One observer commented that if Philip Sanger had only lived longer, there never would have been a Neiman-Marcus. He wouldn't have let Herbert Marcus get away.

Armed with a new job and an increased income, he pressed his courtship and overwhelmed Minnie with his self-confidence. She consented to marry him on the condition that he promise to save

$500 the first year they were married. He did, and that was the first money he ever saved, but only after borrowing $200 to go on their honeymoon. When mother was pregnant with me, he applied for an increase in salary. He was dissatisfied with the $1.87½ per month offered him and it was then that he yielded to the persuasions of his brother-in-law to join him in the sales-promotion effort in Atlanta. It was Al's idea that he and Aunt Carrie would set up a branch office in New York, while my father would manage the head office in Atlanta. Dad did extremely well in his operation, but apparently New York wasn't ready for Al Neiman at that point, so he closed the New York office and moved to Atlanta and joined forces. The Neimans had no children, and they lavished love and affection on me as virtually their own son.

Aunt Carrie was an extraordinary woman. She was not only kind and gracious, as I have described her, but she possessed a queenly quality which she carried as if to the manner born. She was devoted to her family, each and every member. She had elegance, but she never asked a maid to do something she wouldn't do herself. She was modest, but not self-deprecating. She and my father were born with an appreciation for beauty and fine quality that their home environment and education didn't provide. They were both perfectionists early in their lives, and concurred with Oscar Wilde's declaration, "I have the simplest tastes. I am easily satisfied with the best."

So this is a capsuled background of the trio, whose ages averaged twenty-six and a half years, whose credo was described so well in the opening newspaper announcement, whose self-assurance encouraged them to use advertising hyperbole to proclaim the virtues of their wares and buying skills. No one ever reported the Sanger reaction to that opening ad, but I suspect that one of the Sangers must have fallen back on that most expressive Yiddish word and commented, "Some chutzpah!"

That opening advertisement has always intrigued me, and I've read and quoted from it innumerable times. It was a declaration of principles in which they believed, and to the enactment of which they were willing to dedicate their careers. Actually, in their youthful unsophistication they did what every business school preaches today as the predicate for starting a new business: they set forth their ideals and objectives clearly on paper, they predetermined the market to which they would appeal, they proceeded to follow their principles through good times and bad. They succeeded. And what's more, they left an invaluable blueprint for those of us who followed them.

To fully understand the significance of their concepts, I should like to analyze a few of them. First and probably most important of all, they recognized the significance of "ready-to-wear," which in 1907 was an idea as new as the horseless buggy operated by a storage battery. Prior to the turn of the century, fine clothes for women were all made to order. If a woman had enough money, she went to Europe to have her clothes made; if she didn't have that much, she had them made in New York; if she didn't have *that* much, she went to the local dressmaker. They foresaw that fine ready-to-wear was here to stay and that it would eventually replace custom-made apparel. There was no fine-quality garment industry; there were a handful of custom apparel makers who had risen from the ranks of tailors and dressmakers who wanted to make good clothes, but they had not mastered the techniques of accurate size gradations, which would make possible the production of garments that would fit properly without extensive alterations. They lacked an understanding of what the American woman wanted, and there were few store buyers who knew enough to give them guidance. Aunt Carrie and Moira Cullen *thought* they knew, and had the courage to express their opinions and help the manufacturers to become more proficient producers. The customers liked the results, for they bought the clothes, expressing their appreciation for "the best ready-made clothes we've ever found in any store."

Why did they select Dallas as the place to go into business?

Why not St. Louis, or Chicago, or New York? That's a question often asked, and I'm not sure of the answer. However, I think two of the three partners considered themselves Southerners, they felt at home in Dallas, and I surmise that after two years in Atlanta they were homesick for their families, to whom they were deeply devoted. If Sanger and A. Harris could fare so well with department stores, didn't that indicate that a specialty store might do equally well? Dallas in 1907 was a thriving metropolis of some 84,000 inhabitants, the center of the then–all important cotton distribution industry. The wealth of the Dallas Establishment was land-oriented, either in the direction of cotton or cattle. The wealthy had cotton farms, or gins, or compresses, or warehouses, or sold insurance and services to those who were so engaged. To the west were the great cattle ranches, which needed saddles and materials, supplied by the Dallas distributors.

Many have erroneously explained the early success of Neiman-Marcus by crediting it to the fact that there was oil in Texas. True, there was oil, but nobody knew much about it — certainly not the founders. As a matter of fact, there was a discovery well in Petrolia, a town some one hundred and thirty miles from Dallas, in the same year as the opening of the store, but the local press considered it so unimportant that they reported this find in a curt two-inch story. After all, what was the importance of oil in a horse-and-buggy world? In later years, oil did play a very vital part in the growth of the business, but the knowledge of its existence was in no way a factor in the decision to locate in Dallas.

As the first specialty store in Texas, and in the South for that matter, it was not difficult for them to tie up the best lines of fine-quality merchandise on an exclusive representation basis. When they stated, "We shall be hypercritical in our selections," they meant just that. As perfectionists, I can attest to the fact that, in their eyes, nothing was ever perfect. They could always find some way in which anything could have been done better. They used a radical new approach in the manufacturing markets. They offered

12

to pay more to improve the product, an attitude makers had never encountered previously, for the traditional buyer's approach had always been to try to knock the price down. They were confident the customer would be willing to pay more if she got more. One of Neiman-Marcus's suppliers from the early days commented, "Neiman-Marcus was *always for better*."

In addition to their assurances of bringing the latest and best fashions to Dallas, they underscored the fact that "we will be known as the Store of Quality and Superior Values." They priced their merchandise with a reasonable profit, but they never took what my father described as a predatory markup. "If we make a good buy, pass it on to the customer. Let her go out and tell her friends what a bargain she got at Neiman-Marcus." They were never snobs about prices; they weren't impressed because an article was expensive, nor would they reject it because it was of low cost. They simply expected the expensive article to be worth its price and the inexpensive one to meet the same test. In one of my early experiences in the store, I saw my father extol the beauty of a $3,500 evening gown and the next moment, with equal pride, a copy of a Vionnet pure silk dress with handmade faggoting for $29.50, of which some two thousand pieces were sold.

Not expressed in the original advertisement were several other concepts somewhat new to retailing of that period, and to which the founders adhered tenaciously throughout their lives. These principles were imparted to my brothers and me upon our entries into the business, and they form an important part of my coffee talks to new employees. In 1907, retailing was just beginning to emerge from the doctrine of *caveat emptor* — let the buyer beware. This was particularly true in Texas, with its tradition of horse trading, in which it was the buyer's responsibility to examine the animal for any possible defects before purchasing it. Anything that showed up after cash had passed hands became the sole problem of the buyer, not the seller.

The founders didn't want to do business this way, so they instructed their new sales force, "We want to sell satisfaction, not just merchandise. We propose to sell the satisfaction which the uninitiated customer thinks she should receive, even though we, as professionals in our field, know she's expecting too much. This may prove expensive to us, and a few may take advantage of this policy unfairly, but we are convinced that adherence to this idea will cement our customers' loyalty to Neiman-Marcus." One might very well question whether this was just an expression of youthful idealism or a shrewd bit of business sagacity. A merchant in Philadelphia, John Wanamaker, had enunciated a similar idea when he declared, "The customer is always right"; and a retailer in Chicago, Marshall Field, advised his staff to "give the lady what she wants." This was before the days of Better Business Bureau or Federal Trade Commission regulations designed to protect the consumer. These were instances where enlightened business leadership paved the way to a new era of retail corporate responsibility.

Somewhat aghast at a few of the unreasonable complaints and demands which I encountered in my first years in the business, I asked my father, "How can we afford to replace a garment which the customer has clearly abused?" I was referring to a handmade lace ball gown a customer returned after one wearing. "She should have known it was fragile." My father replied, "Yes, she should have, but since this is the first fine garment she's ever bought, she didn't. Explain to her that we will replace it, and tactfully call her attention to the fact that a delicate handmade lace will wear less well than a coarser machine-made lace. She'll know better next time." Unconvinced, I asked, "How can we afford to take such a loss? The manufacturer won't assume any of the cost." He replied very patiently, "She's not doing business with the manufacturer, she's doing business with us. It costs us over $200 to get a new customer of this woman's buying potential, and I'm not going to lose her for the $175 this dress cost us." And then he added,

"When you tell her, do it with a smile." Over the years, this woman spent over $500,000 with us. I had learned one of the most important lessons in my retail career.

On the opening day, Al Neiman met and greeted every customer who came into the store. Later, when Aunt Carrie recuperated and my father had recovered, the three of them alternated between welcoming customers and assisting them with their purchases. They arranged different luncheon hours, so that there would always be one principal on hand and in evidence. So intent were they on practicing what they had preached about customer satisfaction, they frequently killed a sale when they didn't think the garment was appropriate or becoming. Aunt Carrie would say, "No, Mrs. Cleaver, this is the wrong color for you. Let me order it in a different shade of pink"; or my father would say, "I am not satisfied with the way this coat fits you. I want to get one especially made which will be better for you." This was a new experience for some of the salesladies who had never been accustomed to this exacting type of selling. They had been led to believe that "a bird in the hand is better than one in the bush." The owners' attitude was particularly remarkable when one realizes that they were operating on limited capital and every special order put additional strains on their financial capability. Customers, of course, were delighted with this type of personalized service which they had not experienced previously in any other stores, and it became another of the ties which bound them to Neiman-Marcus. The word spread quickly, and within a year the store had built a clientele of satisfied customers who spread the news of this unique store to all of their friends in the area.

"Equity" was one of my father's favorite words. He conceived that equity must be practiced with all who did business with Neiman-Marcus — employees, customers, vendors alike. This was another way of saying, "Let's practice the Golden Rule in all of our dealings." To this day we carry this message to all new employees as the *one* inviolable rule of operation. No one has ever had the temerity to disagree with it, but on occasion we have to issue a reminder to a backslider.

Neiman-Marcus showed a profit in its first year of operation, a remarkable achievement for a business undercapitalized and operated by three young people with high ideals, an intensity of purpose, a willingness to work hard and long hours, and only limited experience in business administration, merchandising control, and buying.

My father and mother spent many of their evenings with Aunt Carrie and Uncle Al, Grandfather Marcus, and other members of the Marcus clan, all of whom shared the interest and excitement of the new venture. Over the dinner table they discussed the events of the day, how one or the other had made a great sale, the weaknesses of the stock, or of salespeople. Like many Jewish families, they felt a personal responsibility for the welfare of the other members of the family, so when one of the brothers-in-law or nieces or nephews couldn't get a job, they found one for them at the store. Sometimes the relations made a contribution, sometimes not, but no member of the family was ever fired. What they may not have had in talent, they repaid with devotion and honesty. My grandfather Marcus, a retired cotton merchant, was given a seat of honor at the front door, where he greeted customers cheerfully and supplied any accompanying children with candy from his coat pocket.

While the store was growing up, so was I. My parents couldn't afford a maid, so when my mother went downtown to visit the store she deposited me in the department where ladies' dresses were altered, where I played on the floor and made toy carts from empty thread boxes and spools. Thus my experience at Neiman-Marcus literally started at the age of two and "from the floor up."

Early childhood memories consist of a series of fleeting impressions of trains and blocks and rocking horses supplied by my fond aunts, frequent illnesses relieved by my father stroking my feverish brow and singing "My Old Kentucky Home" to put me to sleep, falling out of the front seat of an affluent uncle's new Pierce Arrow, startled but unhurt. I recall my mother as the family disciplinarian, using the back of her hairbrush to enforce the domestic law, my grandmother Lichtenstein's constant admonition that my "conscience" was my most important attribute to cultivate, Uncle Leon Lichtenstein playing "catch" with me and taking me to see my first baseball game, and the terrible pangs of homesickness on the day my mother first deposited me at school. The smell of paper lunch bags containing hard-boiled eggs, sandwiches, and bananas is still unforgettable. Streetcar rides were a great thrill, particularly if you were fortunate enough to catch an open trolley and could go to the end of the line. A maternal aunt had one of the first electrics in town and sometimes she would take me for a ride; once she even let me steer while she kept a protective hand on the steering bar. An even greater treat was to be taken for a ride out to the country in an uncle's automobile to buy fresh country eggs and butter, a trip that was always marked by at least two or three tire "blowouts," as they were called.

The birth of my first brother, Edward, didn't bother me. I was four when he was born and I can recall no sense of jealousy or disturbance. Mother was meticulous in showing no favoritism or permitting any other member of the family to do so. She always equalized gifts, even after her four sons were grown and married. Years later when one of her friends would compliment her about one of her sons, she would immediately start to extol the virtues of one of her other boys. I can't honestly say that Dad ever showed any preference among us. He recognized that each of us had our individual strengths and weaknesses, and despite his strong sense of perfectionism, he tolerated the latter. He was a most affectionate father, who liked to kiss us when we were young, who wrestled with us, and who recounted the most marvelous stories, some of which he had read and others that he concocted from his own vivid imagination.

In his youth he had never been exposed to athletics and had had no opportunity to participate in sports. He was a graceful man in the way he moved, but he was awkward when he tried to throw a baseball or drive a golf ball; consequently he was never greatly concerned with our physical development, other than encouraging us from time to time to take boxing lessons. It was much more important to read books and understand arithmetic and know your geography. Mother supervised our homework, with the exception of arithmetic and later algebra, which she delegated to my father, who was impatient with my lack of comprehension of the mathematical world.

Mother didn't have much feeling for the importance of sports, either, but she was most insistent that I take "elocution" lessons and learn how to speak on my feet, for which I shall be eternally grateful. Every Saturday morning I went to Mrs. Woodrow's Elocution Studio where I declaimed from the stage the speech that I had committed to memory the week before. My enunciation, my articulation, my projection, my gestures, were all subject to the criticism of Mrs. Woodrow. I lost all timidity of speaking in public and I'm positive those elocution lessons served me better in my business life than all the years of math.

I was in a hurry to grow up. Everything I wanted to do was being done by people older than I. Playing with other children or participating in their games never really interested me. I wasn't a large child and I wasn't strong; I couldn't keep up with my peers, much less surpass them. When I was ten I wanted to be sixteen; when I was sixteen I wanted to be twenty-one. Consequently, my choice of companions led me to those three or five years older. I lied about my age to girls and boasted of fictitious accomplishments and deeds to document my age, but I doubt if my performance was overconvincing. In retrospect, I guess I must have been a lonely and moody child, for I can't recall having had any good friends of my own age until much later in my adolescence.

2

Exodus

On a Sunday morning, may 11, 1913, a devastating fire destroyed the Neiman-Marcus store, five and a half years after it had opened. I had just returned from Sunday school and was greeted by my mother, "The store has just burned down." We took the streetcar to town to meet the family, which had gathered there as in a wake, mourning the total loss of what had been The Store. The next day the partners counted up the monies that would be coming in from the insurance, took stock of their savings, canvassed the family for additional funds, and decided that they would rebuild in a different location. It would take time to find the proper site, so they leased temporary quarters and fixtures and dispatched the buyers to New York to buy new stocks of merchandise. In seventeen days they reopened for business. My father, who still wrote the advertisements, had this to say: "Rather pretty temporary home, comfortable and cool; clean, with good air circulating around and around; refreshing roominess."

As long as they were forced to move, the partners decided to be venturesome by going "uptown," opposite Titche-Goettinger's department store and seven long blocks from Sanger's. Dad, the "dreamer," persuaded his partners to build a larger store on the basis of the Neiman-Marcus experience and to add additional departments to better serve the clientele. Their available funds weren't adequate to build, fixture, and merchandise the new store, so Uncle Al went to New York to sell stock to some of the store's leading suppliers.

Uncle Theo, the most affluent member of the Marcus family, having made his money as a cotton merchant, was a conservative, politically and financially; he was the direct opposite of his brother Herbert, the perennial optimist who never saw problems, only opportunities. Uncle Theo opposed the move uptown on the grounds of the high rent ($2,000 per month on a ninety-nine-year lease with gradual escalation) and the cost of building, which he felt confident would exceed his brother's estimates. He predicted failure, and urged my father to sell the store and salvage whatever he could. While Dad respected Uncle Theo's financial judgment and counseled with him frequently, he refused to take his advice, and proceeded with the plans for the new store. When Uncle Theo realized his recommendations were being ignored, he not only bought additional stock himself, but persuaded one of his cotton merchant associates in New Orleans, E. V. Benjamin, to invest as well. Such was the solidarity of the Marcus family.

World War I began in August of 1914, and Neiman-Marcus opened its forty-thousand-square-foot building on September 15. From an "outer-garment shop" at Elm and Murphy, it became a "specialty shop" at Main and Ervay, with the addition of accessories, lingerie and corsets, infants, girls, and boys wear, and a moderately priced apparel department called "the Misses Shop." The four-story building was faced with red brick and had two elevators, which were supposed to have elaborate bronze doors on the first two floors. Unfortunately, the money ran out just before the opening, and the "tour de force" doors had to be abandoned for plain ordinary warehouse doors, all they could afford.

With the outbreak of the war, the English, French, and German mill representatives who bought cotton in Dallas were forced to return home, unable to ship Texas cotton across the submarine-infested Atlantic. Cotton dropped to ten cents a pound and glutted the market. It was a common sight to see bales of cotton on the sidewalks of the main streets, as merchants and other businessmen joined the "buy a bale of cotton" movement to help the nearly bankrupt cotton farmers. Texas was hit hard during the early days of the war.

All of this had not been foreseen in the spring of 1914, for the United States had no precedent for a military involvement in Europe. On February 22, my father forecast the store to come by writing an editorial advertisement, of which he was so fond, because it gave him the opportunity to sell and resell the concepts of Neiman-Marcus to its public. He reviewed the history of the store to date, "Its impetus found six years ago led by spare means but unlimited ambitions . . . Its leaders were beset with the usual tribulations of a new business and a stormy financial gale, but were determined to succeed beyond all peradventure of doubt . . . A disastrous fire drove the ship from its moorings and nearly set it adrift . . . but the clouds soon gave way to sunshine." To demonstrate his confidence and optimism he added, "The foundations of the new building, driven to solid rock, will carry, when needed, six more floors." He was convinced throughout his life that he never built big enough. His foresight in providing foundations adequate for expansion was appreciated some years later when two floors, and then an additional one, were added.

In the advertisement on September 15, he wrote, "We heartily invite your attendance at the opening of the GREATER STORE, today at ten o'clock . . . for your inspection and approval . . . the last word in modern store structure — filled with a stock of merchandise that would reflect credit on the largest city in the land." Later, in a New Year's message on January 1, 1915, he commented on the store's growth into "twenty-five specialty shops in one building" and expressed heartfelt thanks to the loyal customers who had supported the store from its inception. He concluded by observing, "We have undertaken large affairs for these particular times; we have presented in Dallas one of America's finest shops, built upon ideals of service and quality."

Coincident with the opening, they must have been faced with many problems: the economic condition of the region, the expenses of running a larger operation, the addition of new departments with the necessity of delegating authority to new buyers, the invasion of new markets in which they had less expertise. Delegation of authority was particularly difficult for them, since their entire operational experience, up to this time, had been limited to a small shop in which all three partners did everything. Aunt Carrie bought and sold; Uncle Al bought, sold, and shared in administration; my father participated in some of the buying, he wrote the advertising, he supervised the extension of credit, he handled employment, arranged for credit lines at the banks, and still found time to meet customers and assist them with their purchases.

Now, with a store instead of a shop, they were forced to learn to be merchants rather than shopkeepers. Miss Cullen moved to New York to act as a daily market representative and to take care of reorders, special orders, and interim purchases. Uncle Al concentrated his efforts on the buying of coats and suits and the supervision of the buying of the newly added misses department. Aunt Carrie devoted her complete attention to the better gown salon and its discriminating customers, many of whom wouldn't buy a garment unless she was in the fitting room advising them; my father merchandised the entire store including the new girls and boys departments and the new accessory division.

The store continued to make modest profits during the sluggish economy induced by the European war, but it wasn't until 1918, about a year after the United States entered the war, that business began to pick up. Simultaneously, the discovery of the West Texas oil fields around Ranger, Burkburnett, and Wichita Falls brought a new stream of wealth into the Texas economy, and for the first time diversification of income sources freed the state from its complete dependence on the products of the land. The products from under the land created not only new wealth, but a new breed of customer. They were people who had made their money in a hurry, and they were in an equal hurry to spend it on some of the luxuries they had heard about all their lives. They put their confidence in Neiman-Marcus, for the reputation of the store carried a guarantee of good taste.

Actually, Dallas had little justification for being anything more than another small-town American city. It was located on a relatively flat piece of topography that was scorchingly hot in the long summer months, cold and raw in the winter. It had no surrounding lakes, no mountain views in the background, no pictorial waterfalls, or any historic tradition, as did some of the other Texas cities. In short, there was little or no reason for anyone to want to come to Dallas to visit or to take up residence, except for its geographical location as the hub of the entire southwestern region. Dallas was roughly equidistant from Houston and San Antonio to the south, El Paso to the west, Oklahoma City and Tulsa to the north, and New Orleans to the east. Thus it was an ideal central point from which to distribute farm machinery, dry goods, and other commodities to the area. Railroad transportation provided adequate service for both passengers and goods. Much of this would characterize Fort Worth, a mere forty miles to the west, except for the fact that the land on which it was built offered the relief of rolling hills. Both towns had about the same opportunity to emerge as the larger community. Fort Worth didn't; Dallas did.

Without going into a deep sociological analysis of the differences between the families that settled in the two places, I have the impression that the business leaders of Dallas in the first quarter of this century recognized their problems and exercised some farsighted judgment in finding the solutions. They envisioned a metropolis, and they spent time, effort, and money to compensate for the lack of natural attractions. At that point in Dallas's history, there was no single wealthy individual who dominated the city, as Amon Carter did in Fort Worth and Jesse Jones in Houston; instead there was a large group of bankers, insurance company presidents, cotton-oriented industrialists, and retail merchants who banded together to supply the vitality for attracting conventions, establishing new industries, and making Dallas a better place in which to live.

My father plunged wholeheartedly into these activities, for he was keenly aware that the future of Neiman-Marcus was directly related to the speed with which Dallas would grow. A larger population meant more customers for Neiman-Marcus. Those were the days before a tax deduction was allowed for philanthropic contributions, but he always maintained a liberal policy in the support of any worthwhile public endeavor, for, as he often told me, "It's not enough to take out of the community, you must put back as well." When I queried him once about why he was making a contribution to a particular cause in which I knew he had no interest, he replied, "It takes many things to build a great city; many people have many different areas of interest. You need opera and art, golf matches and marching bands, to meet the needs of all the people." He brought the Chicago Civic Opera Company to perform annually in Dallas on a southwestern-exclusive basis, and he personally pounded the pavements calling on fellow businessmen to get them to share in the underwriting of the necessary guarantees. He and his company had limited financial resources, but they supported civic endeavors to the best of their ability. What he couldn't give in money, he donated in time and leadership effort. He was an effective money-raiser and a convincing speaker, so his talents were utilized by the established business leaders. He was an important fund-raiser for the new university being established in Dallas by the Methodist church. He and his associates had chosen Dallas as the place in which to build their store; now it was necessary to help build Dallas into a metropolis big enough to support the ambitions of the Neiman-Marcus founders. They, having had so little education, knew better than most what improved educational facilities could mean for the future of Dallas.

About the time the new store was being built, my father decided that his family needed a larger and better home, which was completed just about the time a third child was born. It was a boy, again, and he was named Herbert Marcus, Jr., somewhat contrary to the desires of my mother, who felt that a "Junior" lost something of his own personal identity.

I was sent to a public grammar school, many of whose students came from a rough and tough adjoining area, and many a day I was run home by a gang of schoolmates shouting, "Ikey, Ikey, little Jew-boy." This was my first experience with any form of anti-Semitism, but I was too young for it to make any deep impression, other than half-scaring me to death. My mother would pay a prompt visit to the school principal in protest; he would lecture my tormentors, and they would lay off me for a while. Finally I made my peace with them, and while I never had many friends at school, I no longer went with fear and trepidation.

I had the good fortune in elementary school to have an inspiring English teacher who stimulated and encouraged me in my studies. She was always concerned that I was constantly fidgeting, moving my hands. She admonished me that I was wasting vital energy and that I would lose years of my life unless I learned to conserve my strength. I have never been able to find any scientific substantiation for this warning, but to this day, when I notice myself toying with a pencil or a rubber band, I think back on Miss Edmiston's warning.

Report card day was always an important one in our home. Good grades were expected, superior grades commended, poor grades reprimanded. I was never a brilliant student at any period of my education, but I always responded to the teacher who could kindle my curiosity, and I was lucky enough to run into one in grammar school, one in high school, and several at college. My brothers and I were given private tutoring when the need was indicated, and we took private German lessons at home from a *fraulein* until the advent of the war, which made the study of German unpopular, if not downright unpatriotic. Very early I became an avid reader, jumping from Tom Swift and the Rover Boys to Dickens and Sir Walter Scott.

My evidenced lack of ability to make friends with my school-mates prompted my parents, with some financial aid from Aunt Carrie and Uncle Al, to send me to a boys' camp in Maine in the summer of 1918. It was my first major separation from my family and I suffered the miseries of homesickness for the first few weeks. I was a poor athlete, a poor craftsman, a poor camper, and I vowed I'd never go back. Two years later, I was persuaded by one of my former tentmates to go to another camp, which he claimed was much better than the one we had attended previously. I decided to go, but what was most important was that I made up my mind in advance I was going to enjoy it by being a good camper. I resolved to go out for every sporting event, whether I was any good or not, to play the game as hard as possible, to be a good loser and a good camp citizen. My athletic prowess hadn't improved, but my efforts were noticeable, and by early August I was awarded the camp's top camper award. This was probably my first overwhelming success in any endeavor for which I alone was responsible. This experience proved to me that I was the master of my own destiny to a great extent, and that I could accomplish any reasonable goal I might set.

During my high school days in a public high school, I profited from my camp experience by becoming an active participant in a number of activities, including selling advertising space for the school annual, being a member of the debating team, and by play-ing the saxophone in the school orchestra, which, I must admit, I did very badly. Despite an ambition to be a saxophone virtuoso, I possessed not one whit of musical talent, or even aptitude. I lugged my saxophone case with me on all my travels, enjoying the prestige which the carriage of such an instrument brought with it, but finally in my junior year at college I was hard up for cash preceding my junior class dance, so I hocked it, and with it, my aspirations.

I was a member of the high school cadet corps of the ROTC, but my interests in military affairs were as limited as my interests in sports, so after four years of service, the best I could do was to achieve the rank of corporal. My English teacher, a Miss Myra Brown, led me through *Lorna Doone, Wuthering Heights,* and a host of other English classics, and served as the faculty adviser to the debating society. She was a good critic in the latter capacity and a stimulus in the former. In my senior year, I received the dubious honor of being voted by my classmates "The Ugliest Boy" in the class. When my mother heard of this aspersion cast on her oldest child, she immediately paid a visit to the principal, Mr. Parker, and protested so vigorously that he persuaded the class to change the title of the award to "The Most Natural Boy." Mother, not completely satisfied, decided she could live with it, particularly after Mr. Parker explained that this was just the class's way of paying honor to me. I never considered myself handsome, but I didn't think I was ugly, so it never really bothered me.

Except for my two summers at camp, I spent my summer holidays working at the store. My father and mother both regarded idleness as one of the cardinal sins, so as soon as school was out I went to work, first as a messenger boy carrying packages from the selling floors to the basement, then as a cashier, and finally as a junior floorwalker. I usually had lunch with my father and my cousin Hervin, a lovable, happy-go-lucky fellow, who showed no talent for retailing, but to whom my father gave a job since he was a member of the family, and because he found him to be such an amusing companion, as well as a good driver. Uncle Al was usually at the market during the summer months, so I rarely had the opportunity to lunch with him. However, during the school year when I came down to work on Saturdays, Uncle Al was always most generous, invariably slipping me a few dollars in addition to my regular pay. He was a mercurial man, subject to unreasonable outbursts of anger if something occurred in the store that he didn't like. He would run down four flights of stairs, yelling all the way for Joe Berlinger, the store superintendent, if a special delivery had failed to reach a customer at the promised time. On such occasions, no elevator was fast enough to carry him to his victim. After laying out poor Mr. Berlinger in merciless terms, he'd then revert to his normal charming manner. He would scold a sales-person on the selling floor until she burst into tears; an hour later he would send her a box of candy. I soon learned to stay out of his way during moments of crisis.

He was, to a great extent, the victim of his marriage. Aunt Carrie, who possessed most of the human virtues, had one great weakness, and that was her utter devotion to all the members of her family. He must have known that at the time they were married, but I suppose it didn't seem too important to him then. When they returned from the Atlanta experience, they went to live with Aunt Carrie's older sister, Minnie Rosenbaum, and her husband, Abe, who had a little money. Later on, when Uncle Al started making money, the Rosenbaum family lived with the Neimans. Aunt Carrie wouldn't go out at night unless Aunt Minnie and Uncle Abe went with them. Whenever Aunt Carrie went to New York, she wanted to take Aunt Minnie with her. In the summer, when the Neimans had to spend most of the time buying the fall lines, she and Uncle Al would rent a large house on Long Island, and one of the requirements was that it had to be large enough to accommodate not only the Rosenbaums, but her sister Celia and Joe, her husband, their children and grandchildren, older brother Theo and his wife and daughter, and of course, her younger brother and partner, my father, and my mother and usually three of the four sons — the fourth and final son, Lawrence, was born in 1917. There were always twenty to twenty-five members of the Marcus family in residence. This Aunt Carrie considered her duty — and her pleasure. No wonder Al eventually got fed up with the Marcuses!

Business started to boom, my father began having his shirts custom-made at Sulka's, and mother took me to see my first opera performance, *Pagliacci*. Dallas County voted dry two years before national prohibition was enacted, and skirts became shockingly short — fifteen inches from the floor. My parents could now afford to send me to an eastern college, but apparently they had given little thought to my preparation in the local high school. When I failed the college entrance examinations in the spring of 1921, their immediate reaction was to find a prep school in the East that would prepare me for Harvard, the college of my choice. Why I had chosen Harvard, I don't know, for there were no local boys who had been there or alumni to influence me.

My father took me to New York with him, and we made a tour of a number of schools in New Jersey, Connecticut, and Massachusetts. Some were already completely filled, others indicated that they didn't have room for Jewish boys. I had grown up in a community where I associated with Jews and Christians, and aside from the one incident in grammar school, I was totally unprepared, at the age of sixteen, to meet this new reality of life. We had visited a school on Cape Cod, and on our return to Boston, my father thought it would be nice to go see Robert Maynard, the president of R. H. Stearns & Company, the leading women's specialty store in New England. Miss Cullen, our New York buyer, had worked for Stearns's at one time, and had familiarized Mr. Maynard with my father and the store. He greeted us very warmly and inquired the purpose of our trip. When he was told that we were in search of a prep school, he responded by declaring, "It's ridiculous to send your boy to a prep school after graduating from high school. Why don't you send him to Amherst?" Neither my father nor I knew much about Amherst, but Mr. Maynard assured us that it was one of the finest small colleges in New

England and informed us that Frank Waterman Stearns, chairman of the board of R. H. Stearns & Company, was chairman of Amherst's Board of Trustees. We indicated our willingness to consider his suggestion, whereupon he picked up the phone and called the president. "This is Robert Maynard. I've got a boy here in my office I want you to take in for the fall term next month. Fine! Just send him an application blank." So delighted was I at the prospect of getting into college so unexpectedly that I failed to ask him where it was located.

We returned to the Long Island headquarters where the entire family shared our elation. Uncle Al insisted that I must go to a tailor in New York whom he knew and have a couple of suits made to measure to take to college. He gave me some of his Sulka ties, and by the time he and my father got through dressing me up, I had all of the wrong clothes for a boy going off to an eastern college. It took me no more than two days after my arrival to recognize the mistakes in my wardrobe. My first call home was a request for extra money with which to buy a lilac tweed suit with plus-fours, the prevalent fashion on the Amherst campus. When I came down to New York to spend Thanksgiving with Aunt Carrie and Uncle Al at the Waldorf-Astoria, they bought me a raccoon coat, another necessity for an eastern college student.

The year at Amherst proved to be a most unhappy year for me, and at the same time, it was probably one of the most valuable experiences of my life. On the day of my arrival, I was met at the station by a group of rushers for the various fraternities, all of whom gave me their cards and extended invitations for me to visit their houses. After lunch, I proceeded on the rounds, knowing very little about fraternities in general and nothing about any of them in particular. I had some vague idea that some fraternities practiced religious discrimination, and when I was asked to pledge one of them, I said I'd be glad to, but I thought that they should know I was a Jew. Upon this disclosure, they thanked me very much and said in that circumstance they would have to withdraw their invitation, but that I should feel free to drop in and visit them anytime. Two days later when all the new students had been pledged, I found myself a member of a group of six "barbarians" including two other Jews, one Chinese, and two blacks. Since all of the social life at Amherst at that time revolved around the fraternity houses, including daily meals and weekend dances, my social circle was restricted to my fellow "barbarians." The fraternity members were quite nice in classes, but when it came to social events, we were frozen out completely.

I roomed with another Jewish student, a sophomore, who was the son of a friend of the Neimans. He was from Brooklyn, and took great delight in nagging me about my southern background, my southern prejudices, and my southern accent, to all of which, in my innocence, I thought I was entitled. He challenged my religious convictions, he argued long into the night about a whole group of philosophic concepts — he made me reexamine everything. To answer him I was forced to read a lot, and in so doing had my eyes opened. I ended up much wiser, but loathing him as much as the "Greeks." His harassment and my fraternity experience contributed to a severe homesickness, and I begged my parents to let me come home and transfer to the University of Texas. They wisely refused my request and told me I had to stick it out.

My homesickness subsided, and after the Christmas holidays at home I returned to Amherst with a new idea. Since I couldn't get into one of the existing fraternities, I decided to organize a chapter of one of the leading Jewish fraternities. About this time I received word from Harvard that they would accept me as a transfer student the next fall. I thereupon abandoned my fraternity plan and concentrated on my grades, so that there could be no hitch in transferring to the college of my first choice. President Alexander Meiklejohn and I left Amherst at the end of the spring term, he under fire from his board of trustees, and I in dissatisfaction with a discriminatory social system.

33

Harvard turned out to be everything I had dreamed it would be. There they had clubs which practiced discrimination, but they in no way dominated the social life of the college community. Harvard was so large and indifferent, there was room for everybody. I was excited by my classes and the famous professors who taught my courses, by the variety of people I met, and by the diversity of cultural opportunities which Boston provided. I did join a Jewish fraternity, which provided both eating and living facilities, and in my last year I became its president. As a transfer student I had missed my freshman year in the Yard, where most Harvard friendships begin, and since the college had no dormitory space for me, I lived alone in rented quarters during my first year. The fraternity had a wonderful group of members whose companionship I enjoyed fully, but I am confident that if I had got a place in the dorms, I would never have segregated myself into a fraternity.

I took a survey course in English literature given by the great Bliss Perry, another under the equally great but less well-known John Livingston Lowes, and Shakespeare II given by the renowned Shakespearean scholar George Lyman Kittredge, who would stride into class with his hat on, his traditional Harvard green bag slung over his shoulder, and his cane in hand, which he would use to impale a newspaper an unwary student might be in the act of reading. Perry taught me to love literature in general; Kittredge taught me how to read and understand Shakespeare; Lowes, who gave a course in nineteenth-century English poetry, started back in the twelfth century, so that we could understand the extent and basis of knowledge the nineteenth-century writers possessed. I would emerge from every one of his lectures with notes of at least a half-dozen books to read and a score of ideas to pursue. The greatest thing that can happen to any student — and some don't have such good fortune — is to encounter a teacher who unlocks the massive doors of knowledge, suggests the paths of curiosity,

34

and extends an invitation to enter. That John Livingston Lowes did for me.

My grades at Harvard were nothing sensational. My field of concentration was English literature, and I ended up with about a C-plus average. I had met my mathematical requirements at Amherst, so I was free to take almost any course that caught my fancy. One day I learned of a seminar given without credit, "The History of the Printed Book," conducted by George Parker Winship, librarian of the Harry Elkins Widener collection, which was held on Tuesday afternoons in the Widener Room itself. Surrounded by the first editions in leather slipcases collected by young Widener, who went down on the *Titanic*, we studied the genesis and development of printing from the time of Gutenberg to the twentieth century and America's foremost printers, Daniel Updike and Bruce Rogers. Examples of books printed by Aldus, Coster, Fust and Schoeffer, Caxton, and on through, to the handsome volumes produced by William Morris at the Kelmscott Press, were pulled off the shelves for us to examine and touch. This was my first exposure to the idea of collecting, and I felt the spark of ignition that started me into an avocation which became a consuming side interest. The thrill of handling a copy of the first book printed from movable type, the Gutenberg Bible, is one I can still recall. I had always liked books, but until then I had never really known anything about their construction; the word "incunabulum" had been meaningless. Excited by my newfound knowledge, I decided I wanted to become involved professionally in some form of the book business, either as a printer, publisher, or dealer.

I started haunting the used-book dealers' shops on Cornhill, buying modern press books as well as eighteenth- and nineteenth-century sets of the noted British authors. All too soon I discovered my allowance was inadequate to cover the costs of book acquisition and the expenses of my social life, and not wanting to importune my father for more money, I decided to start a mail-order book service to produce additional income to cover my increased financial needs. When I was ten years old, I had sold the *Saturday Evening Post;* during some of my summertime work at the store, I had sold ladies' shoes; and I had been exposed firsthand to the selling techniques of one of the greatest salesmen of the time, my father, all of which gave me some preparation for selling my book-scouting services to friends who lacked the opportunities I had for searching for out-of-print books.

I set up what I called "The Book Collector's Service Bureau," which I operated from my college residence with no out-of-pocket cost other than the mailing of my solicitation letters. I built in a certain snob appeal in my opening sentence which I hoped would be a "stopper." Not until later did I learn that this was a standard advertising device.

To the One Hundred People Who Will Receive Copies of This Letter:

Do BOOKS mean anything to you? If not, then throw this letter into your basket without further perusal. If they do, then read carefully, for it will inform you of a new and valuable service which has been opened for book lovers and collectors.

Being in the heart of the book market, in Boston and New York, I naturally have the advantage of being in closer touch with unusual books than are those who live in other parts of the country. Many fine old libraries go on auction every week in Boston, and I am able to secure handsome sets and rarities at exceedingly low figures.

It is my purpose to offer my patrons a service which will be of inestimable value to them in locating scarce books at the lowest possible prices. I have a thorough knowledge of the stocks of the leading book stores and second-hand shops, and I am well acquainted with bindings, first editions, pirated editions, out of print books, and their prices. Here is your chance to get the books you have long sought — that copy of "Poetica Erotica" now out of print for ten years, or Mencken's "Heliogabalus" which is so valuable a collector's item. Or perhaps you have desired a leather-bound set of Scott, Oscar Wilde, Balzac, Swift, or Fielding — I can find them for you.

I shall undertake to locate any book and quote prices to you. Please specify (where possible) the edition, binding, and approximate price you wish to pay. Any favors you can confer upon me by notifying your friends of this unusual service will be appreciated.

Yours very sincerely,

H. STANLEY MARCUS

The response was encouraging, and soon I was clearing fifty to two hundred dollars a month, which I promptly invested in books for my personal library. My father became one of my best customers, indicating an unexpressed delight in my commercial venture. My moderate success through selling by letter proved to me that a letter was a very potent selling tool, if written interestingly and with a psychological understanding of its potential readers. Later, in my retail career, I used letters to sell millions of dollars of furs, jewels, books, golf balls, and antiquities through the mail.

During my years at Harvard I encountered only one instance of obvious religious discrimination. Jews at that time didn't expect to be invited to join one of the "waiting" clubs or Hasty Pudding unless they were outstanding athletes or were scions of an outstandingly wealthy New York Jewish family. When you tried out for an open competitive office, though, you expected fair play. Others of my associates tried out for assistant managers' jobs on the various athletic teams; I competed for the advertising manager's position of the Harvard Dramatic Society, the sole criterion for which was the sale of advertising space in the society's theater programs. I capitalized on my acquaintance with some of the Boston retailers, and spent many an afternoon on the other side of the river selling space, not only to them, but to other Boston institutions to whom they directed me. My *Saturday Evening Post* selling experience as a youngster was good preparation for selling advertising, and I set an all-time record of producing the most advertising space sales in the history of the Harvard Dramatic Society. When the election was held, I was not elected. Later, the advertising manager, a good friend from New Mexico, told me confidentially, "Those goddamned blue bloods from Boston wouldn't elect you because you're a Jew." I was hurt, but by that time I had learned to live with this kind of situation. I mention this incident, as well as my experiences at Amherst, to illustrate both the climate of the times and some of the minor obstacles a Jewish student had to learn to hurdle. Times have changed at both institutions, and today both religious and racial discriminations are not likely to occur.

During one of my summer vacations, my father decided that I needed to get some retail selling experience, so he assigned me to Mr. Griffith, the ladies' shoe buyer, who taught me how to fit and sell shoes, and how to do stockwork by consolidating the broken sizes of various styles into a specified section of shelving. Mr. Griffith was a very profit-oriented buyer, with a profound dislike for customers who insisted on being fitted incorrectly and who would then bring the shoes back for credit on the claim that they had been misfitted. In the case of such customers, he required that the shoe salesman fill in a card with the customer's name, her correct size, and the size she had demanded. Normally we slipped the card into the vamp of the shoe, which the cashier would retrieve and place in Mr. Griffith's files. One morning I received a summons to my father's office, where I found him and Mr. Griffith awaiting me. "Did you sell a pair of black suede oxfords to a Mrs. E. A. Richardson?" he asked. I admitted to the sale, and he continued, "We've just had a visit from her husband, who was most indignant because his wife found this notation in the vamp of her shoe." He handed me the slip on which I had written "Pair of black oxford shoes sold to Mrs. E. A. Richardson after forty minutes of agonizing. The old crank measured for a size 5B but insisted on taking a 4½AAA." The cashier had failed to pull the slip. My father, trying to look very stern but obviously greatly amused by the incident, said, "Let this be a lesson to you. Never be guilty of writing or speaking unkind things about our customers," and then, turning to Mr. Griffith, "I understand why you put this system in, but you've just had a demonstration of its hazards. Even though you may get hooked by an unfair adjustment occasionally, I don't want to take a chance on a repetition. Please discontinue it."

Mr. Griffith did eliminate the system, but nothing could change his attitude toward the customer whom he regarded as a professional chiseler. One day a customer, who was a well-known complainer, came into the department. She could always be counted on to bring back her shoes after she had worn them for about three months and ask for a replacement. When Mr. Griffith saw her, he came over and asked if she had been waited on. She replied that her shoes were too small. "Weren't the last pair you bought too big, and didn't the ones before that have heels too high?" he asked. "Yes," she said, "I have bad luck with your shoes. I want my money back." With that he stooped down, took off both her shoes, wrote a refund slip, and told her she could cash it at the main cashier's office on the fourth floor. "How am I to get home barefooted?" she cried. "That's your problem, madam," he replied. "You asked for your money back and I have met your request. All I ask is that you don't come back here to buy your shoes." Bill Griffith was incurable when his sense of commercial injustice was aroused.

Selling shoes was a good training ground for me. I learned what every good shoe salesman knows, and that is: you have to learn to fit the mind as well as the foot. From this selling experience, I recognized that knowledge of the product, enthusiasm, perceptiveness, and politeness produced sales.

As graduation from college became imminent, I started having serious discussions with my father about what my life's work would be. While I was debating the various aspects of the book business, my father had no doubts at all that I was going to enter Neiman-Marcus. This was a foregone conclusion with him, and he told me very frankly he expected me and my brothers to follow in his footsteps. I remonstrated that I didn't like the restrictions which retailing might put on my rights of self-expression in political and other matters, for it was generally believed that retailers should shy away from controversial subjects, lest they offend some of their customers with contrary points of view. My father then made a bargain with me. "I will assure you that you will always have the privilege of speaking out in behalf of the political party you are supporting without any fear of suppression — as long as it's a legitimate party." He, like many others, was concerned with the menace of the "Bolsheviks," who did not constitute a legitimate party. As a final clincher he added, "If you want to build a library, you'll make more money in retailing than you will in the book business, and you'll have your library sooner." I capitulated. He kept his word, and never attempted to prevent me from free expression, even when we did get letters of protest from some of our good customers. He and I disagreed on many political matters, but he was essentially a moderate conservative, while I regarded myself as a liberal.

He was a remarkable man in that he represented the combination of so many antithetical forces: he had the tenderness of a woman and the sternness of a commanding general; the courage of a lion and the wariness of a panther; he was religious but a nonbeliever; he was a visionary but at the same time a pragmatist; he was un-educated but had an appreciation of all that was fine and beautiful; he was understanding of the personal problems of a stockboy, but not of his wife's inability to balance her checkbook. He could argue in behalf of a given proposition and then reverse positions and argue effectively against it. He was a constant optimist with the determination and will towards success, yet he was compassionate to those who had been vitiated by their life's struggles. He was a great merchant, but a poor delegator. He was right so much of the time it seemed difficult to believe he could ever be wrong.

He had great faith in the basic honesty of people, as illustrated by the incident of a young girl who finished college and got a job teaching school in a little West Texas town. As she prepared to go, she found it very difficult to get her mind on such things as Latin and arithmetic. She had heard through the grapevine that her new town contained a good many eligible bachelors and that they'd all be down to the depot to give the new schoolmarm the once-over. Like any other girl, she wanted them to look more than once. So she wrote Neiman-Marcus a letter:

Dear Mr. Herbert Marcus,

I have just graduated from normal college, and I'd like to have a fall suit. I spent all my money getting a diploma. I cannot even make a deposit because my pocketbook is empty and my family hasn't got any cash to spare. Could you possibly send me a suit in dark blue serge in the latest style? I'm young, so it shouldn't be old-ladyish. Send something with a lot of zip, but not too fussy either.

He sent her two suits, one the blue serge she asked for, the second a blue wool poplin. The second was a good deal "zippier" than the first; it was also more expensive. He told her to choose the one she liked. He received the blue serge by return mail. After she'd been teaching in her new town for a little while, he had some news of her:

The blue wool poplin set my heart palpitating. It was just right. When I put it on to board the train, I felt as though it were my armor — blue wool poplin with a Neiman-Marcus label. Sure enough, when I got to the station, there was the promised phalanx of local swains along the depot wall. But I had my confidence. I faced up to them like a queen. Soon, I had more dates than a strict superintendent would allow . . .

So the schoolteacher made a hit. She paid slowly and regularly, and when the bill was all done, we lost track of her for a good many years. Then one day she wrote to a national fashion magazine in the East. She said that reading about fashions always made her think of Neiman-Marcus and the experience she'd had with us twenty years before. The editor sent her letter along to us, and we've always kept it. It ended:

41

I know they are smart merchandisers there, people who know where the big money is. But I just want to tell you that to a poor West Texas schoolteacher, long ago, Neiman-Marcus was Santa Claus.

One of the turning points in the Neiman-Marcus history occurred in 1926 when the ailing Sanger Brothers business was sold to a Kansas City retailer. The new management came in, took inventory of both its merchandise and its personnel, and decided to slash both. Over a weekend, twenty-five saleswomen, fitters, and floormen were released because of salaries and age. The following Monday morning they were all employed by Neiman-Marcus, bringing with them the bulk of their established clientele. One salesperson, alone, sold over $200,000 her first year at the store. Loyal customers of Sanger's were incensed by the ruthless treatment of employees who had given years of faithful service, and they switched to Neiman-Marcus in appreciation.

When I agreed to go into the store, I was peripherally aware of my father's qualities, but I got to know them intimately in the years of our association, and I guess I really came of age when I discovered that great as he was, he wasn't always right.

It was decided that I would go to the Harvard Graduate School of Business Administration following my graduation from the College, to prepare me for a business career. As a graduation present, my father took me on a buying trip to Europe, the first for both of us. I accompanied him daily to our foreign buying office, where he looked at and bought leather gloves, silk lingerie, corsets, costume jewelry, blouses, handbags, dresses, and christening gowns, a job which today would be done by a dozen buyers. I was hitting the nightlife of Paris and getting very little sleep, so I found it very difficult to keep up with his pace. My most difficult responsibility, though, was to keep him entertained at night to quell his homesickness for my mother, who had remained at home to take care of my three younger brothers. Several times I feared that he would decide to catch the next boat home. I would dine with him and, after he went to bed, I'd go out on the town. On this trip he took the opportunity to buy some works of art, and gave me the privilege of making some purchases on my own. Up to that date, my sole acquisition had been an oil painting I'd bought in Province-town. My knowledge of contemporary French art was limited, but by good luck I bought a colored lithograph and a watercolor by Marie Laurencin which she inscribed to me, and three etchings by a young Japanese artist, who had recently come to Paris, named Foujita.

We met numerous Americans in Paris and Switzerland, and I noticed that my father had the habit of asking the women what they had bought on the trip and where they made their purchases. They would give him the name of a small dressmaker or an un-known bagmaker or a blouse designer, and he would have our commissionaire summon them to the offices with their lines. "Why are you always asking these women where they are buying? Doesn't the office already know all of the best sources of merchandise in Paris?" I asked. His answer taught me the most valuable lesson of the trip: "Don't ever underestimate the critical judgment of wealthy American women of discrimination. They are never satisfied with less than the best, nor am I."

The Business School was an interesting experience, with the exposure it gave me to a wide range of subjects, such as accounting, statistics, advertising, and finance. But my attention was distracted by an announcement that appeared in the *Dallas Morning News* in a Neiman-Marcus advertisement, "We are dreaming of expansion." Never content, never satisfied, my father dreamed of an enlarge-ment which would double the floor space of our building. An opportunity had come along to lease the corner directly behind our building, on which he proposed to build a duplicate of the original structure, tear down the intervening wall, and redecorate the entire store. If this was going to happen, I thought, I'd better

43

get down there and enter the store before the new organization jelled. I had reached the point where I wanted to do as well as to learn. My father agreed with my reasoning, and in June I said farewell to Cambridge and returned to Dallas. I was ready to go to work.

3

Crisis

Busy as they were in planning for the enlargement, evidently little thought had been given to my induction into the business. Any discussions my father may have had with Uncle Al must have been minimal, or at the best not exhaustive, for I was given no specific assignment or responsibility other than to stay on the better apparel floor and learn how to greet customers. In my summertime work in previous years I had done this sort of thing, as well as having sold ladies' shoes, so my first job didn't come up to the expectations of a college graduate with a year's business school experience. I yearned for any type of responsibility, however insignificant, in the performance of which I could be judged. I was eager to apply some of my new knowledge of statistics and advertising to Neiman-Marcus, but at that moment they weren't ready for my college expertise. I reported to my father and to Uncle Al jointly, though the latter, at that particular moment, was willing to leave me in my father's hands.

During the hot non-air-conditioned summer months, it was difficult to persuade customers to come downtown to shop. The Baker Hotel had recently opened a roof garden dining-dancing facility, the Peacock Terrace, and it had gained great cachet with fashionable Dallas. The idea occurred to me to produce a weekly fashion show at luncheon, using the hotel's big-name band for background music. First, I went to the hotel's management to see if they would like to increase their luncheon business, and if they would permit us to put on the show without charge to us. They readily agreed. I then went back to my father and told him what I had accomplished, and urged him to let me put on the weekly show and do the fashion commentary. The shows proved to be an immediate success, both in the size of the audiences they brought and in the aftershow business we did in the store. We had created an occasion for women to come to town, and when they did, and saw beautiful clothes that they liked, they bought. This was the beginning of the first weekly retail fashion show in the country, later copied by many, and its success kept it running every week continuously for some twenty-eight years.

My elocution lessons paid off again, for I felt no shyness in getting up before an audience of some four hundred women, with Ted Weems's music playing softly behind me, and commenting, recommending, and editorializing about the fashions of the day. I found that I had enough "ham" in me to make the job enjoyable, and the fact that I could actually influence a large group of women to accept a new dress fashion or accessory gave me a self-confidence that I needed. In my opinion, these shows made a great contribution to the enhancement of Neiman-Marcus's reputation for fashion leadership. What my father had started so well in his newspaper editorializing I carried one step further by face-to-face commentary.

In a further effort to apply myself to an area not already preempted by someone else in the organization, I decided to try to update the graphic design of our packaging. My father had no objections, so long as I didn't get involved in any large expenditure. This gave me the opportunity to make use of some of the typographic knowledge I had acquired in college. After redesigning some of the garment box labels, I concluded that what we needed was a trademark, like the motor car companies and other national organizations. One day when I was on a buying trip to New York, someone told me about a young French designer who had just come to this country who might be able to come up with a design for very little money. I paid him a visit and told him what I had in mind; he reached over, picked up a letter, quickly watercolored a rough sketch on the back of it, and asked, "How will this do?" I inquired how much he would charge me and he replied, "Would $75 be too much?" I told him I would have to think about it over the weekend, but I'd let him know the following Monday morning. His name was Raymond Loewy. I got approval from my father, and Loewy quickly completed the finished artwork, which became incorporated into our advertising and labeling for a time. I didn't see Mr. Loewy for about twenty-five years, during which time he had risen to fame as one of the great industrial designers of the world. At a cocktail party in California we met again. He looked at me with a smile and said, "We've both come a pretty long way since that day you called on me and gave me my first commission in America. You know, my prices have gone up quite a bit since then."

I was occasionally called in to the morning advertising meeting at which the merchandise for the following day's advertising was selected. After the decisions were made, the articles were sent to our staff artist to be sketched in two hours. One of my first suggestions was that we worked too closely to the deadline, and that we should plan our advertising at least a week in advance. This was rejected by my father on the grounds that "advertising is news and has to be as fresh and topical as the headlines in the paper." The merchandise ultimately selected depended on what had arrived from New York that morning and what departments were in most urgent need of sales support. Throughout his business life, my father took an active interest in the advertising approach of the store and, with his intense desire for perfection, was the advertising department's most constant and vocal critic. Even after he let me plan the advertising with Miss McCauley, our very able advertising manager, it was only with the greatest effort that I was able to get planning established on a regular basis. He had a keen sense of fitness, with a determination never to permit vulgarity of word or concept to creep into a Neiman-Marcus advertisement. He rejected the word "fake"; he forbade the use of the word "stolen" in characterizing a fashion borrowed from a man's topcoat, declaring that Neiman-Marcus had never "stolen" anything in its history and that the use of the word, however descriptive, demeaned the institution. One day he came downtown with his usual collection of overnight notes and said, "The advertisement this morning used a word incorrectly when it referred to the shoe as being a product of one of the leading *cobblers* of the day." I disagreed with him, saying that a cobbler was a man who made shoes by hand. "Look it up in the dictionary," he ordered. I did and found that there was an archaic meaning, which defined a cobbler as "a clumsy workman, a botcher." Needless to say, the word was forever banished from Neiman-Marcus advertising. Some years later, though, when an enterprising young buyer wanted to name a shoe boutique "The Cobbler," I was able to set him right by asking *him* to look up the definition of the word.

The family business life was not always peaceful, for my father and Uncle Al had numerous disputes relating to inventory position, personnel policies, buying decisions, and all the other mass of minutiae that make up the fabric of daily business. Sometimes debates between the two became acrimonious, with Aunt Carrie desperately trying to remain neutral. Frequently Uncle Theo would act as the intermediary and help resolve their problems. Uncle Al spent a large part of his time in New York and usually reflected a "market" point of view; he tended to take the part of the manufacturers; he even had his cronies in the market whom he tended to favor with orders, even when the particular lines didn't justify them; he had the failing of many buyers who liked to write "big" orders rather than cautious ones. He was volatile, egotistical, opinionated, and emotional. My father concentrated the bulk of his time on running the store, planning the new buildings

with the architects and store fixture designers, dictating the advertising, devising ways of enlarging the store's clientele, and appraising
the inadequacies of the stocks as he learned of lost sales. He was
critical, logical, egotistical, and unfortunately sarcastic. No wonder
the two partners collided many times.

In preparation for the designing of the new building, my
father decided to make a tour of some of the more recently built
retail establishments around the country. He took his architect
and me with him to St. Louis, Chicago, and Minneapolis, and
pointed out the features he liked and didn't like. When we
reached Minneapolis we saw the new Young-Quinlan specialty
store, whose Italian-influenced architecture suited my father exactly. Miss Elizabeth Quinlan, its founder, was a market friend of
the family, and she was most generous in permitting our architect
to make sketches of various features which appealed to my father.
The Young-Quinlan business was very similar in quality and
fashion standards to ours, and not being in competitive markets,
the interchange of ideas and market resources was most free. In
1927 there was only a handful of specialty stores in the nation.
Foremost was Bonwit Teller in New York, headed by its founder,
the great merchant Paul Bonwit; Franklin Simon, which operated
on a more modest price level, also located in New York; Blum's
Vogue in Chicago; I. Magnin in San Francisco; Young-Quinlan,
and Neiman-Marcus. Saks Fifth Avenue was founded in 1924,
and Bullock's Wilshire in 1929.

The formal debut of contemporary design at the "Exhibition
des Arts Decoratifs," which I had the good fortune to see on my
trip to Paris in 1925, had made a terrific impression on me, so it
was natural for me to suggest that since we were designing a store
for the twentieth century, we should build it in the style called
"Art Moderne." My father, visionary as he was in many areas,
was at that time an architectural conservative, and vetoed my
proposal in favor of his architect's interpretation of Miss Quinlan's architects' version of the Italian Renaissance. An interior

51

decorator, favored by Aunt Carrie and my father, was chosen to design the interiors, which she proceeded to do in authoritative period style. The Sport Shop was done in French Provincial, the Gown Salon in French Empire, the Coat Department in English Tudor. Her color sense and fabric selection were superior to anything that had hitherto been introduced in a retail store anywhere.

In a preview article the day prior to the formal unveiling of the enlarged store, the *Dallas Times Herald* reported,

The Neiman-Marcus store as it stands today, after twenty years in the life of Dallas, is one of only a dozen such stores in the United States . . . And because it is an experiment in more ways than one in the history of such establishments, leading merchandise men and style magazine representatives from over the United States will be present Monday for the formal opening . . . The outstanding impression of the new Neiman-Marcus store is: This is not a store. It is too spacious and colorful. It is something with beautiful clothing in it. But it is not a store.

The writer was only partially correct, for Herbert Marcus, in planning the enlarged facility, did insist on a quality of spaciousness provided by broad aisles, did inject new concepts of color, and insisted on apparently extravagant details, such as a fountain in the midst of a foyer, but all of this care was directed at building a store, a marketplace, where women of refined tastes would enjoy the act of shopping. He was criticized by some of his peers in retailing for not having merchandised every square inch of space, but this was done with deliberate intent; he understood that "air" was of vital importance in setting the proper background for the presentation of fine merchandise, and that, as a result, the goods being offered would look more expensive than in the jammed quarters of a typical department store. He gave his customers a fresh aesthetic experience, one that even set new standards for the decor in their own homes.

Uncle Al suggested to me that I might be given the assignment

52

of merchandising one of the new departments, the Sport Shop, a merchandising classification then just coming into prominence. This was the opportunity I had been seeking, and I was thrilled by the prospect of the challenge. My buyer and mentor was a distant cousin, Adele Miller, who had served for some years as our blouse buyer and was an experienced market professional. She introduced me around the market, taught me market manners, pointed out the differentials in quality, what and how to buy, which manufacturers to trust and those of whom I should be wary. Neither Aunt Carrie nor my father were ever to be greatly enthusiastic about sportswear, which I think they secretly regarded as a bastard child of the apparel business, and as such, a claimant to a share of the fortunes of better ready-to-wear.

There was a little space left over on the first floor, and my suggestion that we open a stationery department, featuring fine engraved writing papers and invitations, was accepted. We had no one with expertise in this field, so I was commissioned to buy the opening stock until an experienced buyer could be located. My knowledge of papers was limited to printing papers, but I learned fast and expensively. I had never realized that there could be so many sizes of paper, such a multitude of envelope sizes, so large a number of permutations arising from different types of colored linings and stripings. I made the common error most green buyers make — I bought a little of everything instead of concentrating in depth on fewer items. But I learned from this experience a lesson I was able to pass on to subsequent new buyers in other fields. I had to sell what I had bought, and I found, by exposing samples of our stationery to customers who had come in to buy a pair of shoes or a dress, that many of them became interested in our new department and the beautiful writing papers we had to offer. To our out-of-town patrons I sent a letter enclosing a few engraved letterheads, which produced such good results that I became convinced that letters would sell paper just as they had sold books for me in college. Soon thereafter we located a bright young assistant buyer, Charlotte Kramer, at B. Altman's, whom we induced to come to Dallas as our first stationery buyer. Our choice proved to be a happy one, for she combined great flair in buying with a tremendous sales ability and held the job for forty-two years until her retirement. Soon, every socialite in the community was using Neiman-Marcus engraved stationery.

One of my less fortunate purchases had been a fairly large stock of deep lilac paper which no one seemed to want. One day, Miss Kramer noticed a customer on the selling floor who was dressed in a purple outfit. She realized that the lady must like purple, so she approached her in another department, introduced herself, and showed her a sample of our deep lilac overstock, saying, "Since you seem to like purple, I couldn't resist the temptation to show you one of our very lovely papers in a shade which is very difficult to find in most stores." The customer was so genuinely pleased by this attention that she not only bought our entire stock of lilac paper, but ordered more. Which only proves an old retail adage that "there's a customer for everything."

My new responsibilities called for fairly frequent trips to the New York market, which enabled me to pick up my ties with college associates from whom I had been cut off during my first two years in business. Most of my friends were in the East, and I thoroughly enjoyed meeting them at the Harvard-Yale games and in the New York speakeasies. This also gave me the opportunity to visit New York stores to see how they operated the types of departments I was running. For the first time, I understood my father's fascination with store shopping. The first thing he did on arriving in any city, at home or abroad, was to shop the stores in hopes of picking up a merchandise trend or a display idea. He taught me to have an open mind and a healthy curiosity.

In the planning of the enlarged store, one floor was built for future expansion. To use it to produce income without requiring capital investment, which was again stretched pretty thin, it was decided to lease it to a man named Najeeb E. Halaby, an Oriental rug dealer, who proposed to open a deluxe interior decorating department. This would offer an added service to our customers, and if successful, would yield a welcome increment to the profit column. Unfortunately, Mr. Halaby died shortly after the opening, leaving a debt-ridden estate incapable of continuing the department. Years later in Washington I met his son, "Jeeb" Halaby, then head of the Civil Aeronautics Board, who informed me that he was the little boy I used to see in the Decorating Studio at Neiman-Marcus.

The demise of Mr. Halaby and the forced cancellation of his contract made it mandatory to find another use for the space. The idea of continuing with the decorating business appealed to my father, and he decided to find a decorator to head it, and at the same time, to utilize part of the area for a gift shop, featuring china, glass, silver, and antiques, all selected with a specialty store point of view rather than in the traditional manner of the department or jewelry stores. We had great difficulties in locating a decorator who combined the qualities of our standards of taste, a selling ability, and the administrative capacity to supervise and direct the activities of other decorators. This proved to be a continuing problem as long as we operated the decorating department. We did find a brilliant gift buyer, Kay Vedder, who had moved to Texas from the East and had run her own shops in Dallas and Fort Worth, in addition to having bought for A. Harris & Company. She possessed that elusive quality, flair, with an unsurpassed ability to select and present her merchandise in an interesting and dramatic manner. Shortly after her employment, I received a phone call from Leon Harris, the vice-president of A. Harris. He must have been skeptical about the amplification capability of the telephone, for he never talked on the phone, he yelled. "I hear you've engaged Kay Vedder to buy gifts for you," he bellowed. "Well, all I can say, she's the greatest gift buyer in the world, and before you get through with her, you'll have to build a warehouse to take care of her purchases. She buys like a drunken sailor. Good-bye."

Forewarned, we tried to keep her buying under some reasonable control, but we never did succeed in convincing her that it wasn't enough just to buy nice things, in addition, it was necessary to make a net profit. Profit-making was hard for her to understand. She did set a great standard for us and for the entire giftware market, in which she was regarded as one of the giants of all time.

In its greatly enlarged new quarters, the store in 1927 did a little less than three million dollars in volume, showing a modest profit of about $145,000, despite the many unusual expenses attendant to the opening. Tensions between my father and Uncle Al continued to mount, caused no doubt, in part, by my presence in the business. My father was very ambitious for me, and eagerly pushed me into situations which continued to antagonize Uncle Al. He made the mistake of giving me assignments which he should have given to those primarily charged with those responsibilities. This naturally caused resentments among some of the older department heads, who took their cause to Uncle Al, pouring fuel on an already existent bonfire. I was inexperienced in dealing with people, and no doubt I handled many situations inexpertly. Being the first college graduate to enter the Neiman-Marcus executive level, I was surely suspect. My father and mother went to Europe in the summer of 1928, and during those months, alone with Uncle Al, I lived through a reign of terror. He was in sole charge, and I had no one closer than Europe to whom I could go for help or advice. I made a memorandum of the events to present to my father upon his return:

Various accusations have been made against me in the past ten days, so for a matter of record I am writing them down:

Tuesday, July 24
1. Poor judgment on the telephone contract.
2. Poor judgment on revolving door. I merely asked for estimate for consideration.
3. Promised Malloy, McCauley, Edward trips to New York.

4. Undermined Adele Miller.

5. Broke A.L.N.'s promise to Miss Boyce [a buyer]; in N.Y., he denied having made it. Now he denies that I had told him about it. When I had told him in N.Y., he denied having promised her the trip, and said that my action was correct.

6. Overstepping my authority and encroaching on the payroll by advising Davis [the store superintendent] to let off two stock girls.

7. Business going only 40% efficient because of me. Everyone up in the air.

8. I over-ruled buyers in open meetings, causing embarrassment.

9. I stepped on his toes in an advertising decision. Philipson [the sales promotion manager] repeated our conversation to him and distorted it.

10. That Dad was busted in Atlanta till he came back from N.Y. and made some money.

11. That he [A.L.N.] went to N.Y. and borrowed money which saved the business.

12. That the whole family had been unfair to him, including his wife.

13. Inferred that I was not nice to employees — like he was.

14. That I used too much "I" in my letters. Instead of saying, "I would suggest," I should say, "Don't you think?"

15. That the budget was set too high this spring, and that was the reason we were overbought.

16. That people were afraid to make suggestions to Dad or me, because we wouldn't listen to them.

I'm sure that there was an element of truth in some of the charges, but others were devoid of fact, except as they were distorted by a few people who thought they might benefit by playing me against him. In my innocence of the business world, I was almost destroyed by my zealousness, aggressiveness, and my associates.

Upon my father's return, he found a partner unhappy with everything: his business association, his nephew, his marriage. He told my father that he could no longer continue as things were, and made a "buy or sell" proposition. After family mediation proved unsuccessful, they agreed on a price of $250,000, and my father went to the bank and borrowed the money to buy Uncle Al's interest, Aunt Carrie having indicated she would not be party to the dissolution. About this time some gossip came to Aunt Carrie about an affair Uncle Al had been having with one of the buyers, which he admitted. This was the final blow for her; she decided to sue for divorce. Under the purchase contract, Uncle Al agreed not to enter, or be associated with, any retail business in Dallas for a period of ten years. Several months later, he violated the contract by joining Woolf Brothers of Kansas City, which owned Dreyfus and Company, located across the street from our store. My father was forced to go to federal court to enforce the contract, where the judge upheld my father's plea on the grounds that "Mr. Neiman has come into court with dirty hands."

Simultaneously, Herman Philipson, who was the number two man in their employ, left, for he had been inextricably caught up in the machinations of playing one partner off against the other. This left my father with the controlling interest in the business, but with no administrative assistance to help carry the burden — except for me, with only two years of full-time business experience. He could have gone out and found someone with more mature business credentials, but he decided to take a chance on me. He threw me into the water, not positive whether I would sink or swim. Fortunately, I was able to swim.

4

Weathering the Depression

THE COMMUNITY WAS SHOCKED BY THE DIVORCE, and by the dissolution of the long-time business association. Friends and customers alike took sides, but public opinion as a whole swung towards Aunt Carrie and my father. Market relationships had been conducted, in great degree, by Uncle Al, so with his departure it was decided that I should take over the merchandising of the better apparel departments and solidify our vendor connections. In addition, I was supposed to exercise financial control over the two buyers, my Aunt Carrie and Moira Cullen, neither of whom had ever shown much interest in fiscal responsibility. They both loved beautiful things and would never pass a desirable garment, however overbought they might be. Under them I received a post-graduate course in specialty store buying, for they were buyers with courage, taste, fashion awareness, and a noncompromising understanding of quality. Miss Cullen had, in addition, the ability to know not only *what* was wrong with a garment, but *why* it was wrong. Even in 1928, many manufacturers still hadn't mastered the technique of balancing a garment, an attribute essential to perfect fit and comfort. She had "caliper" eyes, and the slightest errant detail would be the subject for a lengthy dissertation and subsequent correction. At first, I often wondered how manufacturers could put up with what seemed to me such "nit-picking." They did, I learned later, because they usually found her to be right and they could improve their product by listening to her. Finally, they listened because we were important buyers, and on Seventh Avenue the power of the pen that writes the orders is all-powerful.

In looking at a line, Aunt Carrie would remark, "That dress has a rayon binding. We must change it to pure silk, for our customers won't accept rayon." It probably cost the maker $1.50 to make the change, but he acceded without undue argument. They would agonize for thirty minutes over the selection of the quality of lace to go into a ball gown, or the best shade of black for a winter coat purchase. Until then, I had always thought that there was just one shade of black, but to my astonishment I learned that since World War I, dyestuffs had been made in the United States instead of in Germany, and that we had not yet mastered the making of a *black* black with any consistency. Too many of the black coatings had either a blue or greenish cast. I learned to look for handmade buttonholes, and to be willing to pay extra for them to improve moderately priced garments. I was taught to look inside a dress to see how cleanly it was finished, and how much under-pressing had been used in the course of making it. Aunt Carrie and Miss Cullen weren't designers and they had no false illusions about it. But they were creators of a *style*, a Neiman-Marcus style, which they accomplished by fabric substitution, "always for the better"; by the replacement of garrish buttons, pins, and belt buckles with simpler ornamentation; by insisting on handsewn linings, deeper hems, and subtle colors.

Herman Seigenfeld, of the firm of Maurice Rentner, and later of Bill Blass, gives Miss Cullen single-handed credit for having forced his firm, and then the entire market, to make the "step-in" dress, with buttons down the front, which permitted a woman to step into her dress instead of having to pull it over her head, thus mussing her coiffure. This was a major contribution to the dress business which this remarkable woman made, and which has been little recognized. As the result of working with these two women

62

over a long period, my eye became attuned to what they saw, my critical faculties became sharpened to the nuances in taste and fashion. When I first started going to showings with them, I was apprehensive of my own judgment — they knew so much and seemed so positive — but in the course of time I found that I could pick styles with confidence and be as right as they were.

We might be in the midst of an important seasonal buy when a special order would come in from Dallas for a garment for a very particular customer, or the very important customer might show up in New York, wanting to be taken around the market to make selections at two or three of the leading designers' show-rooms. Miss Cullen or Aunt Carrie would interrupt their work to take care of the request, inconvenient though it might be, for that's the way the business had been built. "How can you afford to devote so much time and effort to a single customer when you are buying for thousands of customers?" I asked. Aunt Carrie replied, "We can't afford not to. If we don't take care of these unusual requests from women who are depending on us, they might drop in to a competitive store in New York, and then we would lose them for good."

Many of us thought Aunt Carrie's taste was infallible, but she disagreed, saying, "No one's judgment is infallible." Then she taught me a very important lesson when I reminded her of the failure of a particular fashion a few years back. She said, "It's a mistake to base fashion predictions on the past. There are no rules in the fashion business." She almost always wore black, with a strand of pearls around her neck and two handsome gold bracelets on one wrist. She had strong convictions about what she liked and didn't like, but she was probably the most modest woman I have ever known.

Specialty store retailing in particular, I soon learned, consisted of a mass of minutiae, and you made and kept your customers by your ability to remember small details, such as anniversary dates or birthdays; a promise to get a certain evening bag in time for a specific social occasion; an assurance that a purchase wouldn't be billed until the following month; a promise that the dress bought for a girlfriend would be billed to the *Mr.*, not the *Mrs.*, account; the new name of your thrice-married best customer; a stock check to find out why we had missed the sale of a pair of black patent leather pumps; an investigation to discover who in the organization had indiscreetly commented that a certain designer's collection was poor. None of this was trivia; it's what specialty store retailing is all about.

In December 1967, Samuel Feinberg, a columnist for *Women's Wear Daily*, wrote a column about me, which was possible only because I had learned very early in my retail career that nothing in my business was too insignificant to deserve my attention:

FROM WHERE I SIT

BY SAMUEL FEINBERG

"There Are Neiman-Marcuses and There Are Korvettes"

An interesting exchange of letters has resulted from one of my columns carrying this quotation: "In retailing, there are Neiman-Marcuses and Korvettes. In our hotels, we're in the Neiman-Marcus business."

The man who made this statement is James H. Lavenson, senior vice-president and a director of Hotel Corp. of America, 30-unit chain whose flagship is New York's Plaza Hotel. The HCA executive said he is determined to maintain the highest tenets of personal service in the face of "the trend of other hotel market expansion primarily through convenience and price."

Stanley Marcus, president of the Dallas–Fort Worth–Houston chain of specialty stores, wrote Mr. Lavenson:

"We're highly flattered by your reference to our stores, and I'm happy that our standards of quality have inspired you. Just in case you haven't received our Christmas catalog, I'm sending a copy to you under separate cover. I hope that it may assist you in your Christmas shopping. To make things easier, I'm opening a charge account in your name."

In his own pixy style of humor, Jim Lavenson replied:

"You are too good to be true! I felt I was exaggerating about Neiman-Marcus, and particularly you — just to prove my point as to how good I was. Your having picked out my reference to Neiman-Marcus and our hotels in WWD just demonstrates that your commitment to personal attention to your business is actually true — and this creates a tremendous burden for me in the knowledge that I've been telling the truth all these years.

"Since I have acknowledged you as our Svengali, and you have committed to writing your acceptance of this flattery, I must continue to respond to the examples you set for me. Therefore, I am enclosing *our* Christmas catalog of hotels in the hope that it might assist you in your travels — Christmas or any time of the year. I thought I would match your generosity by also enclosing an HCA credit card, but I learned that you already have one."

Mr. Marcus, whose company's volume this year is proceeding at a rate of more than $60 million, must be sore beset to keep up personal attention to which he is dedicated in the conviction that every businessman is a citizen, too.

Like sending out Christmas catalogs and charge-account cards — tasks others in his position might think too menial for them. How many other bigtime retailers personally bother themselves with such "trivialities"?

During 1928, my brother Edward entered the business. He had spent six months at Harvard, having passed the entrance examinations which I had previously failed, but he devoted most of his time to playing bridge, which he mistakenly believed to be a required course of greater importance than English A and other academic subjects. The authorities at Harvard had different ideas and asked him to leave. He then tried the University of Texas, where he demonstrated his Ivy League bridge talents, much to the distress of the local faculty. My father, quite disgusted by this time, told him, "If you won't accept an education at college, then go to work." By "going to work" he didn't mean "go find yourself a job somewhere," he meant "start working at Neiman-Marcus." It was inconceivable to my father that any of his sons might even contemplate any other line of endeavor. By this time, Eddie, somewhat chastened, entered the family business without argument.

Eddie was very bright, as attested by his bridge-playing skill, but he simply wasn't prepared to accept the self-discipline college life required. He had a brilliant mathematical mind which had been demonstrated throughout his high school days; he could solve all types of mathematical puzzles in seconds, while I was trying laboriously to understand them. He was tall and thin, and had a fun-loving charm which endeared him to all of his associates, in and out of the business. He started work, too, in the ladies' shoe department, where Mr. Griffith had his second Marcus boy to prepare for retailing.

I doubt if my father ever gave thought to the problems that he might be creating by forcing all of his sons into the same business, or the conflicts which might eventually surface as the result of differing levels of capabilities, ambitions, or seniority. I think he was such a supreme egotist as far as his sons were concerned that he sincerely believed that since they all had his genes, they would all turn out to be equal in all ways. This was manifestly unfair to all of us, particularly to the three younger brothers who followed me.

I had been given a head start and an unusual opportunity by the precipitate departure of Al Neiman from the business. I had the advantage of being there first, of having had more exposure to the store in my early years, of having a natural aptitude for retailing, and of possessing a driving force which made me determined to accomplish my objectives. I had a lead which in itself cast a shadow on those who were to follow me. Consciously or unconsciously, I was the model by which they were constantly being measured. There were no problems between the brothers in the early years, but later, unhappy tensions did develop, as egos expanded, marriages occurred, and pillow talk exerted itself.

Nineteen twenty-eight was a year of crisis, but it was also a year of innovation. There had been a small space on the ground floor which had been leased out to a tenant who proved to be unsuccessful, so we decided to take it over for a man's shop. Our reputation had been built solely in the women's field and our credibility as menswear merchants had to be proved to a doubting male clientele. We employed the same methods that had brought success in other areas, building customer by customer. We felt that one man would tell another if we could render satisfaction through superior service and merchandise. Most of the top-quality furnishing business was going to New York to Sulka's, simply because no merchant in Dallas brought in the fine French lisle socks, imported shirtings, and English and French neckware; when we proved that we had the same things hitherto available only in New York, Dallas men were only too glad to buy them at home.

That year also marked our invention of personalized gift-wrapping, a service that became one of the distinctive hallmarks of our store. The idea of Christmas-wrapping the thousands of gifts purchased to individual order, instead of putting them in the traditional holly-decorated box, came, I believe, from Zula Mc-Cauley, our advertising manager. The idea caught on well, and our gift-wrapped packages achieved a national reputation. Customers in New York would order a New York–made bottle of toilet water easily available in a half-dozen New York stores, to be gift-wrapped and sent back to New York, just to get the gift-wrapping. Years later we employed full-time professional designers, whose sole job year-round was to design gift wraps for all of the gift occasions of the year. One Christmas Eve, I observed a Christmas "extra" wrapping some of her own presents; they were so original in concept that I asked her to come back to see me the day after Christmas. Her name was Beverly Morgan, and I gave her the job as our designer. After she left us to marry one of our wealthy oilman customers, my attention was called to a young Korean-American girl, Alma Shon, who has turned out to be an outstanding gift-package designer and whose designs have been copied all over the nation.

Years later, a young man came to see me whom I didn't know. He came right to the point by saying, "My name is Ted Strauss. I'm new in Dallas, and I'm going to go into the gift-wrapping business and will sell a line of wraps to other stores. You don't need me, but I need you. You have the best wraps anywhere, and I can do one of two things: I can either copy your packages, or you can join forces with me. Obviously, if I knock off your designs, you won't get a cent, but if you will help style my line and assist me to get into other stores, I'll cut you in for 10% of my profits." Faced with such alternatives, I chose the latter, and we collected several hundreds of thousands of dollars in royalties.

George Feifer in the *Daily Telegraph Magazine of London* recounted an often-told story about our gift-wrapping service:

The story which most satirically illustrates the intimidating potency of the Neiman-Marcus name begins in the wrapping room during the Christmas rush. One hard day there, a harassed employee accidentally wrapped her lunch instead of the luxurious gift intended — and discovered her mistake only after the morning's parcels had been shipped. But no one ever came forward to complain that he, or she, had received a stale ham sandwich and mouldy orange for Christmas. Store officials are convinced that the recipient of the extraordinary gift decided that, coming from Neiman-Marcus, it had to be something wonderfully special.

Another gift-wrap incident became the subject for a column by Paul Crume in his Big D column on the front page of the *Dallas Morning News*:

Everybody knows that Neiman-Marcus is 99.9 per cent perfect. It takes the low mind of a newspaper columnist to find that other .1 per cent, and here it is.

Early in the week Katherine Altermann ordered some bath oils as a present for a friend. At 4 P.M. Tuesday, when the delivery hadn't been made, she checked by telephone. She told the lady in the toiletries department that she had ordered some bath oils and had asked that they be delivered to her office on the 12th floor of the Southland Center. The time was late and the package had not arrived.

Probably it was the holiday season.

"Southland Center?" said the lady in toiletries. "Is that in Dallas?"

"It is," said Mrs. Altermann.

"Then you'll have to check with local delivery," said the lady.

Local Delivery didn't have her package but did find out it had been giftwrapped. "I suggest you try Gift-Wrapping," suggested Local Delivery.

At Gift Wrapping, nobody had seen the bath oils either, but the lady there was undismayed.

"I'm sorry that we have no record of it," she said, "but it is bound to come by here sooner or later. I suggest you just sit and wait for it."

"But I can't wait. It's a gift, and I need it now."

"Then I would suggest that you call the superintendent's office," said the woman pleasantly.

The superintendent's office had never heard of the package.

"Let me suggest," said the spokesman, "that you call adjustments."

At each of these calls, Mrs. Altermann had had to repeat the whole story, and the story, of course, was growing like the verses of Old MacDonald Had a Farm.

"Oh, no," she said. "I'm so tired."

The superintendent's office expressed its regrets but assured her that Adjustments would clear everything up if she would only check it.

When she called Adjustments, she had to wait awhile. It seemed 10 years. Finally, a man's voice was on the phone, and she was telling her story again.

"Look," she had said, "I'm so tired. Would you please just listen to my sad story?"

She told it while he listened politely.

"Let me suggest . . ." he began, and she broke in.

"Oh, no."

He went on to say he wished he could help her but that he couldn't.

"Why not?"

"I'm in stemware," said the man.

"Why did you listen to my story?" wailed Mrs. Altermann.

"You asked me to," said the man, "and the longer I listened the sadder it got. I didn't have the heart to stop you."

Somehow it made everything seem a lot pleasanter.

A few hours later, the whole thing began to get funny.

And next morning the package, which hadn't been anywhere in the Neiman system, showed up at her desk.

Skirts became longer in 1929 and the stock market crashed, not that the two have any demonstrable connection. The Depression was around the corner, but not until the fall of 1930 did we begin to feel the effects of the severe economic dislocation. Declining sales made it necessary to curtail purchases and to institute salary reductions, first for executives, but later for all employees. With prices falling at wholesale, our prices at retail reflected the changes, but at no time did we ever yield to the temptation, as did some other retailers, to lower our quality standards to bring in more sales. My father, burdened with a larger store and a backbreaking personal bank loan, stood firm, and exhorted his buyers not to succumb to the temptation of cheaper inferior goods just to get badly needed sales. He urged them, time and again, to maintain the standards of quality our customers had learned to expect from us.

Painful as the experience of the Depression was, I've always felt a degree of regret that my younger colleagues, especially since World War II, never had to go through the tempering ordeal of the period, and thus to learn some lessons in how to operate in adversity, when every dollar spent was important, when every customer had to be treated as if she were the last one you would see. I'm glad my education covered this span in economic history.

During the Depression, one of our customers inquired if we could give his daughter a job since he was not in a financial position to send her to college as he had planned, and he figured that the next best substitute for a college education was the opportunity to learn about people and goods at Neiman-Marcus. We gave her employment and when she quit to get married, she came to thank me for her three years at the store. I asked what had particularly impressed her during her time with us, to which she replied, "People.

70

I never knew there could be both so many nice and mean people in the world. I've learned to deal with both, something I doubt I would have learned at college." Rarely do people reveal themselves for what they really are as they do to salespeople.

In 1930, when the nation was in the depths of the Depression, the great East Texas discovery well came in. Exploration of the area indicated that the East Texas oil field would be the single greatest reservoir to have been found in the country. Thus, at the very moment when other parts of the United States were faced with declining values of national assets, Texas suddenly found itself with great new sources of wealth. Dirt farmers, florists, anyone who owned a piece of land, were transformed overnight from poverty to riches. Fortuitously, Dallas was located midway between the new oil fields to the east and the oil fields to the west, and Neiman-Marcus was in Dallas. The new rich behaved in a predictable manner; they did exactly the same things the Gold Rushers in California did in 1849 and the successful oil drillers of West Texas in 1918. They came to town to spend their money for some of the things they had dreamt about for so long. Prosperity spread from the new oil landowners to the local lawyers, bankers, accountants, title companies, and others in the community life of Tyler, Longview, Henderson, and other Texas towns.

Not true was the often-repeated story of a barefooted oil queen who supposedly appeared at Neiman-Marcus one day and said, "Dress me up. Give me the works"; but it was true that many plain-looking country families came to us, shyly in some instances, to buy a new church outfit or a winter coat. Perhaps they entered with some trepidation, for Neiman-Marcus, like all stores dealing in expensive merchandise, had unwittingly, from the management's point of view, developed a reputation of hauteur and aloofness, but when they found that they were treated with kindness and under-standing, they went away convinced that Neiman-Marcus was *the* store for them. It doesn't take long for poor people to adjust themselves to newfound riches; most people want to eat well, dress better, own fine automobiles. They accept lower qualities not out of choice, but through necessity. Improve their incomes and they immediately move to higher quality levels within a very brief period. This we experienced with East Texas, and again when the wartime boom gave employment and increased salaries to millions of low-income workers.

Many times I've toyed with the question of whether I could have had the courage, foresight, and general business acumen to have started a business from scratch as my father had done. To this day I don't know the answer, and I never shall. I entered the store when it was firmly rooted, when the early financial tribulations had been overcome, and although we went through some gales and even typhoons, it required completely different talents to stay afloat than to set forth on the lonely journey alone. My contributions to the business took shape in my ability to translate the store's ideals into ideas that a larger number of potential customers could find credible. Somewhere in my education I had picked up a sense of promotion, an understanding of how to do things that would get a maximum amount of desirable publicity, a flair for communicating with people by doing things that commanded attention.

After my first success with weekly fashion shows, I conceived the idea of putting on a definitive bridal fashion show, on the assumption that everyone loves a bride. We showed not only wedding and bridesmaids' gowns, but entire trousseaux geared to several different budgets, along with bridal lingerie and wedding gifts, which the mannequins carried. I invited the editor of a bridal magazine to come down to be a co-commentator and to lend additional authority to our presentation. Such shows are commonplace now, but in the thirties it was something brand-new. It proved to be a huge success, and it enabled us to assume the dominant bridal position in the city.

One day in 1934, Eddie and I were talking about the policies of the national fashion magazines, which limited their editorial credits to the New York stores that advertised with them. If a woman picked up a copy of *Vogue* or *Harper's Bazaar*, she would read "available at Bergdorf Goodman, or Saks Fifth Avenue." We concluded that sooner or later our customers would be thus influenced to shop at one of these New York stores, and that the only way to combat this no-advertiser, no-credit policy was by becoming an advertiser ourselves, thereby earning our own credits. We took the idea to my father, and despite the fact that we were in the throes of the Depression and financial retrenchment, he approved our first national advertising commitment. We reasoned that we would not only get credits, but would also make our local customers very proud of the fact that "their" store was being nationally advertised. We thought that when Mrs. Brown, the wife of the president of the Magnolia Petroleum Company, a Standard Oil subsidiary, went to New York and was entertained by the wife of one of her husband's business associates and was asked, "Where did you get that beautiful fur coat?" she would reply, "Why, at Neiman-Marcus in Dallas, where I buy all my clothes." Having made this declaration, we reasoned that it would be difficult for her to then shop at Bergdorf's. We relied on our understanding of the psychology of small-town residents, who have a certain inferiority complex in relation to people from metropolitan areas, coupled with a consuming desire to own something of recognizable merit. Small-town inhabitants like to boast of a movie star or a writer from "their" town. It gives them a sense of identity. We wanted to give them a label which would provide them with what has come to be known today as a "security blanket." So went our theories.

Our first two advertisements appeared in *Vogue* and *Harper's Bazaar* that fall, and were prepared for us by an advertising man, Abbot Kimball, who had been recommended to us by Dan Palter, one of our leading shoe manufacturers. Upon the publication of our advertisements, we made sure our local customers were made aware of this bit of audacity and even persuaded one of the daily papers to editorialize with pride on the civic contribution that Neiman-Marcus had made in carrying the message of its fashion leadership to the outside world. At that time, Dallas as a city was yearning for national recognition, and Neiman-Marcus was hailed by its leaders for its boldness.

In connection with the insertion of our first advertisement in *Vogue* magazine, I paid a visit to its publisher, Condé Nast, who I think was a little curious to meet his new advertiser. At luncheon with him and *Vogue*'s distinguished editor, Edna Woolman Chase, I explained why we were advertising in *Vogue* and why it was of importance for us, and them as well, to depart from their established "credit" policy. I explained that there were women of wealth and taste living in Dallas, Indianapolis, and Los Angeles who read the magazine, but who would like to know where they could purchase the featured fashions locally. I described some of the social events which took place hundreds of miles from the eastern seaboard and the number of chic women in these remote places whom they were depriving of legitimate information. We were lunching at Voisin's, where Mrs. Chase's blue-gray hair melted into the blue-gray walls of the restaurant, and I can recall Mr. Nast turning to his editor, "See, Edna, that's what I've been telling you for a long time. There *are* things going on outside of New York." Then and there they decided to change their "credit" policy (aided and abetted by the prospect of additional advertising revenue coming in from the hinterlands).

We didn't sell anything from the ads, but we provoked a tremendous amount of talk in New York. We had created a "man bites dog" story overnight. As the first store in Texas to advertise in the fashion publications, we became the object of instant scrutiny by potential customers, designers, and the news media.

The State of Texas celebrated its Centennial with an exposition in Dallas in 1936. Of all the cities in Texas, Dallas had least claim, from a historical point of view, to be named as the Centennial celebration location. But Dallas could provide the exposition grounds of the State Fair of Texas as a base, and it had a group of energetic citizens willing to put up large sums of money to bank-roll it. For the opening, we decided to stage a gala fashion show depicting fashions from 1836 to 1936. We embarked on what was to be one of our first creative merchandising efforts by making a series of clothes and accessories inspired by the colors and motifs of the Southwest. The colors of cactus flowers found expression in dresses designed by Clare Potter; cowboy chaps, cattle brands, saddle leather, barbed wire, and lariats were found adaptable to a wide variety of accessories. Fifteen hundred socialite customers from all over the state came to this first Neiman-Marcus evening fashion show.

I invited Mrs. Chase, the editor of *Vogue*, who had never been farther west than the Hudson River, to come to Texas as our guest for the Centennial fashion show. She accepted on condition that I would accompany her on the train trip, for while she had made scores of trips to Europe, she had no experience with domestic travel. She may have thought that Indians might still be lurking in the Ozark hills. I accompanied her from New York, and on chang-ing trains in St. Louis we had the good fortune to run into Matt Sloan, the president of the MK&T railroad, whose private car was attached to the train we were taking. He invited us to be his guests for dinner, at which he served the famous "Katy Kornettes," a corn-bread specialty of his dining service. I'm sure it was Mrs. Chase's first experience with cornbread in any form, but she adored it, and insisted on getting the recipe.

She was genuinely overwhelmed by the store, and by the warmth of Texas hospitality. Alice Hughes, the Hearst syndicated column-ist, reported: "We overheard her [Mrs. Chase] mention that all of her life she had one dream of a perfect shop for women. On seeing the store, Mrs. Chase believes her dream has come true. She finds in Neiman-Marcus that kind of store and we second her belief heartily." Nineteen thirty-six marked not only Texas's

75

Centennial, but also the year in which the United States discovered Texas, and Dallas. From the date on, Texas became a focal point of the nation, with hordes of writers, photographers, and visitors descending upon the state *and* Neiman-Marcus, its best-known institution. The Depression was lifting, with the economy being given the stimulus of wartime preparations. We had survived the Depression with dignity and reputation. We had suffered minor financial losses in 1931 and 1932, but we ended 1936 with a record volume of sales of $4,500,000, a net profit of a quarter of a million dollars, and an increase of 105% in the number of charge accounts as compared with the number at the beginning of the Depression. We had broadened our market successfully.

In our New Year's message on January 1, 1937, we stated, "Someone said to us recently, 'You keep on building and improving.' Of course we do. This Dallas-owned institution belongs to Dallas, and we shall continue to put back into property and merchandise that which is made possible by a generous patronage. Shortly, we shall announce new plans for enlarging certain shops."

Our first big national publicity break occurred when *Fortune* decided to do a story on us in 1937, an idea which had been stimulated by Dan Palter, who had a friend, Bill Harris, on the staff of the magazine, and whom he was able to interest in the newsworthiness of Neiman-Marcus, deep in the heart of oilland. *Fortune* assigned Louis Kronenberger, one of its editors, to write the piece. We, particularly my father, had some trepidation about exposing ourselves as completely as we knew the magazine would require, for we had never published our operating statistics, and *Fortune* had been known to deal fairly harshly, and at times venomously, with some of its subjects. When Kronenberger arrived, we invited him to dinner so he could meet all the members of the family at one time. I expressed our apprehensions to him, and told him I knew he wanted to do a fair account of Neiman-Marcus. I told him I realized that he couldn't give me the privilege of editing his story, but that I would appreciate it if he would let me read it before publication, with the right to challenge any inaccuracy. To this he readily agreed, and though he was totally unfamiliar with retail operations, he didn't write one thing to which we could take exception. This affirmed an idea about press relations that I had, and that has stood me in good stead for many years: if you level with a reporter and help him honestly, you will be repaid in kind. Only once have I ever been let down, and that was my fault. I talked too freely and indiscreetly to a foreign reporter, giving her off-the-record background information which she promised not to use — and then did. Fortunately for me, her story was published in Australia, and not many Texans read Australian papers.

The title of the *Fortune* article, which appeared in the November 1937 issue, was "Dallas in Wonderland." To the best of my knowledge, it was the first time *Fortune* had recognized a Texas institution, and our customers everywhere shared our pride in this distinction. Kronenberger set the locale, gave a brief résumé of the history, and then commented perceptively:

As for Neiman-Marcus' executives, they too live just one idea: The Store. It's madcap, or inspired, beginning sprang from an enthusiasm — an almost religious enthusiasm — that has never ceased. Herbert Marcus and his sister Carrie Neiman, and his three sons in the business, have sublimated and channeled every ounce of their considerable selves into four floors of beautiful merchandise. The reason is not that they lack other interests: it would be a ghastly mistake to think of Herbert Marcus as one of those pencil-behind-the-ears Babbitts who hum brightly when they think of volume and markup and inventory, and droop and dwindle (and sometimes die) when they are forced to retire; or to think of Carrie Neiman as a hustling, bustling, lynx-eyed, tailor-made fury who should have been a man; or to think of Stanley Marcus as someone who spends his evenings reading trade journals, but never reading for fun. It's the other way around. They are exciting business people because in one sense they aren't business people at all; and they live the store, not by lacking outside interests, but by transferring them all inside. With his mobile Jewish expression, Herbert Marcus quotes Plato or Flaubert at you, displays a Canaletto in his dining room, and dreams of owning a Renoir; but his real creative and artistic self is released on Neiman-Marcus. Similarly his sense of drama is expended there, his sense of prophecy (those hunches that have been worth their business weight in gold), his powers of psychology, his strong moral sense. This moral sense runs through the whole family, uniting them less in a sense of duty toward one another than in a common sense of duty to the store. It exceeds practical necessities: it isn't a matter of being 100% on the job (though all of them always are), but rather of being dedicated to some austere and lofty mission.

But that sense of dedication has its dollars-and-cents value. It makes no detail too trivial for notice, no project too vast for consideration; Herbert Marcus is one of the last of the tribe of "eye" merchants. . . .

Dallas women came to look on Neiman-Marcus, not simply as a place where they bought dresses, but as a place where they were educated about clothes. To this day they lean heavily on Alma Mater, still come by the dozens, saying, "You know better than I do what I need." The store is like a doctor or lawyer that people swear by. And dressing well in Dallas has become more than a personal matter, it has become a civic one. Perfect clothes are as much the cultural expression of Dallas as art is of Toledo.

Collier's magazine sent a reporter, Selma Robinson, to Dallas in 1939 to do a firsthand study of this new phenomenon. She wrote,

At this moment, the eyes and ears of the fashion world are focused not on Paris. Not on New York. Not on Hollywood. But on Dallas. Yes, Dallas, Texas. Here, in a city of 300,000, fashion experts will see what the rest of the nation's women will be wearing next month or the month after. The manufacturer will know with comfortable assurance which fashions to promote and which to forget. Because Dallas is the prognosticator of fashion in America. It shops three to six weeks ahead of the rest of the country. Chic, wealthy, positive, its shopping population comes from all over the Southwest. New York and Paris may create fashions, but Dallas tells them what American women will wear.

What New Haven with its tryouts is to the theatre, Dallas is to the fashion world. It is the proving ground, the court where fashions are tried. And for excellent reasons — economic, geographic, and social. Its per capita purchasing power is second only to Washington. Take its geographic location: It is fashion headquarters for Houston, Fort Worth, San Antonio, and El Paso — indeed for the whole Southwest. Take its climate, varying from freezing to steaming. In January, spring arrives in pastels and prints. In mid-July and August, while the rest of the country is buying its second bathing suits, the women of Dallas buy fur coats and fall dresses (with the thermometer at 100 degrees in the shade) to take out of town with them.

Take one more fashion factor for a complete picture — the Marcus family of Texas: Herbert Marcus, three of his four sons, Stanley, Edward, and Herbert Jr., and his sister Carrie Marcus Neiman. Together they make up Neiman-Marcus, most important specialty shop in the American Southwest and one of the five largest distributors of high style in the United States. . . . In manufacturers' showrooms in New York, to say "Neiman-Marcus ordered this" is almost enough to clinch a sale. A whisper travels along the grapevine: "Marcus is buying bright brown for fall." And from the fabric maker to coat maker the word goes that "bright brown will be good." The salesman, pencil poised, advises confidentially, "Stanley Marcus just reordered on this one." It gets so irritating to other merchants that one of them in self-defense nailed an irate sign on his wall for all salesmen to see. "I don't care how many Neiman-Marcus ordered," it reads belligerently. . . . For here, under one roof, are gathered the designs of Hattie Carnegie and Nettie Rosenstein, of Louise Barnes Gallagher and Clare Potter, of Palter De Liso, and Daché, and John Fredericks, and others like them, a collection representing more great fashion names than any shop even in New York or Chicago can boast. . . . Many of its customers are wealthy, grown rich from the product of mine or field or oil well. Dressing well is not merely a personal affair with them. . . . "Any store can dress a few women beautifully," say the Marcuses. "Our idea is to dress a whole city that way." Today the store is more than an emporium. It is a vital part of the community life. It is a center of style education. Women go to have a look, even when they don't need anything. Office workers drop in on their lunch hours. Men go shopping with their wives. There is always an exhibit to see. Or a fashion show going on.

79

This was just the beginning. Soon after, *Life* did a picture essay, and we became a favorite topic for the columnists around the country. Like a snowball, we picked up size as we rolled. A good part of the stories was related to basic ideas I kept reiterating: "one of the five largest distributors of high fashion merchandise in the United States" and "more fine names under one roof than any other store." If we had been located in Richmond or Cleveland or Indianapolis we wouldn't have received one-tenth of the attention, but the mere fact that we were located in Texas made the difference. Texas combined the lure of the Old West with the discovery of oil, and we suddenly were thrust into the position of being the best-known name in the state every magazine editor wanted to feature.

This pursuit by the press encouraged me to engage a full-time public relations director to handle the growing volume of media requests and to initiate stories based on the numerous human interest events that occur daily in every store. One of the contributing reasons why Neiman-Marcus has received, and continues to receive, so much publicity is that we know what makes news and never hesitate to exploit a bone fide news story. My choice for this job was an unusual young woman, Marihelen McDuff, an ex-newspaper reporter. She was divorced from the normal advertising department connection and reported directly to me, with the charge never to plant a story not based on truth, and never to ask anything unreasonable of the press. This policy has paid great dividends.

When I was in New York on a buying trip, I met the extraordinary Ben Sonnenberg, one of the best-known public relations men in the country. He recognized my latent talents as a publicist, took me under his wing, and imparted much of his sage understanding of human motivation, which is the basis of all good public relations work. He would jokingly comment, "Here's a guy who takes the best out of me, and has never yet paid me a fee." We have been friends for forty years, and I can truthfully say that I have learned more from him than any person except my father.

At the time of my advent into the store, the fur business of Dallas was effectively controlled by Max Goettinger, one of the principals in the firm of Titche-Goettinger, a department store located across the street from us. He held a unique position of authority in furs, and it was very difficult to sell anything in competition with him. I concluded that I couldn't do much while he was still alive, but that I would try to inherit his mantle. I didn't have to wait for his death, for his company was sold to Allied Department Stores and he retired. Thereupon I started working to capture the Dallas fur business, which up to that time had eluded us.

Furs had been a fairly utilitarian business, based in large part on the sale of durable skins that would last the life of the wearer. Any time we sold a fragile fur, it would come back with the complaint of poor service. The first thing I was forced to do was retrain our saleswomen *not* to guarantee any fur, but to explain that the durability of furs, like any fine fabric, was subject to the manner in which the furs were treated. We would guarantee the quality of our skins and workmanship, but we wouldn't guarantee them against wearing out. Next I set out to build younger and more fashionable coats by transforming some of our perkier cloth coats into fur. I used a balmacaan raincoat as a model for the first raglan-sleeved fur coat, a velvet evening cape for an ermine ball wrap, and a Norfolk suit jacket for a kidskin college jacket. I specified fine-quality silk linings and two-inch fur facings, instead of the standard half-inch, which satisfied the rest of the market. I spent $50 apiece for handmade sterling silver buttons by Georg Jensen of Denmark to adorn black broadtail coats retailing for $1,500. I learned that most of my competitors were always trying to knock off a few dollars on every coat they purchased, so I followed the opposite strategy — I offered to pay our manufacturers extra if they could make our garments finer. It paid off,

81

for I took away the temptation to cheat, and as a result the furs in our department were always better than those of the competition, a fact which our sales staff and customers soon realized.

The building of a fine fur collection in the commercial market required great skill, for most manufacturing furriers knew little about making stock-sized garments. Miss Cullen taught them more about balance and fit than they had ever known before, and many of the great furriers of today benefited from the stringent requirements we imposed on them forty years ago. The fur business has always been notorious for "paying off" buyers. They realized that Miss Cullen and I were "untouchable," except for our demands for the best product they could turn out. We dealt with big furriers and small ones, whoever could meet our requirements, but for some reason we had never done business with the biggest producer in the market, a man named J. Weinig. One day he phoned me at my New York office and asked if he could come up to see me. I told him that I would be glad to meet him, and made an appointment for the next day. He was a short, stocky man who spoke with the broken accent of a Russian-born immigrant, although he had come to this country when he was a child. He was known in the market as "The Silver Fox King," in recognition of the fact that he chopped up more silver foxes than any other man in the world. He opened up very directly, "Mr. Marcus, I am a very successful man in my business, and you are going to be very successful in yours from what I've been hearing about you from my son Al with whom you went to camp. We don't do business with each other. I can get along without you, and you can get along without me, but we could both do a lot better by doing business with each other." I was impressed with his blunt frankness and promised to visit his showroom. We liked what he had to offer and gave him our first order. Mink coats were just coming into fashion, and we were having difficulty getting them made the way we wanted. We asked him to make some minks for us, but he declined on the grounds that his experience was solely in long-haired furs. Finally he agreed, and we brought him a bundle of skins with which to experiment. After some abortive trials, he produced the best commercially made mink coat we had seen. He ended up becoming the preeminent mink coat maker of the market, developing new techniques in mink cutting which eventually became the standard for the entire market, and for the world. As a result of his initiative, he became one of our largest dollar resources, and taught me the invaluable lesson that no man is too big to go out and make a sale. He made a $5,000,000 sale by coming to my office.

It was easy to enunciate lofty ideals, it was another thing to enforce them at a foreseeable dollar loss — particularly in the midst of the Depression, when every dollar of profit was vital. My father periodically reviewed the fur stock with me, making suggestions of customers to call about specific garments, giving me a critique on my purchases. One day he called my attention to a beautiful $2,500 broadtail coat which had been carried over from the previous season. He reminded me that we would have to mark it down substantially if it weren't sold within the next few months. About six weeks later he passed through the department and noticed that I was in the process of selling the coat. He called me aside and asked what I was doing. "I'm doing what you told me to do. I'm selling the coat to Mrs. Simon." "You're making a mistake," he said. "She's an insurance saleswoman and she carries a large leather policy portfolio with her at all times. The friction from her bag will wear out a delicate fur like broadtail in no time." "Don't worry," I replied. "I've explained how fragile broadtail is and she thoroughly understands it." "Yes," he said, "she understands it now, but she won't two months from now when the edges are worn thin. I would suggest you sell her another coat instead." As a dutiful son and employee, I proceeded to unsell the broadtail coat and sold her a Hudson seal coat for $695, which had the sturdy wearing qualities a businesswoman should have. She wore it with great satisfaction for seven years. Two weeks later, we held our annual fur clearance and marked down the broadtail to half

83

price, $1,250, and I sold it to a woman who possessed several other fur coats and had a chauffeur-driven car. She wore the coat only a few times a week, and she, too, wore *it* for seven years. My father knew full well that in killing the original sale, we would undoubtedly have to reduce the price of the broadtail coat, but he was willing to take the loss to preserve his principle of selling satisfaction. In addition, he spent $1,250 wisely to give me an object lesson, demonstrating that "no sale is a good sale for Neiman-Marcus, unless it is a good buy for the customer."

I had made it a rule in our fur department that I wanted to be called in on a sale of any importance, so one day a saleswoman called my office to ask me to pass on a mink coat she was in the process of selling. I was introduced to a man and his daughter who was being outfitted preparatory to going east to college. It seemed inappropriate to me for a sixteen-year-old girl to go away to school with a mink coat, for I could foresee the reaction of her classmates. I tried tactfully to switch her interest to a beaver or a muskrat coat, either of which would have been more appropriate. The saleswoman shot black looks in my direction, the girl pouted, and the father got mad. I explained my opinion to him, whereupon he walked out with his tearful daughter. As the result of giving honest advice, I had lost a $2,000 mink coat sale and hadn't made any sale. The next day I was summoned back to the fur department. The father was back and very contrite. He apologized for his reaction the previous day, and explained that when he told his sister what had happened, she said, "Mr. Marcus was right. A sixteen-year-old girl has no business wearing a mink coat. Go back and buy the one he tells you to." So I sold him a muskrat coat for $295 and made a customer of him for life. Six years later, when the daughter got married, I sold him a mink coat for her.

The combined pressures of the Depression and the enlarged store forced us to explore every avenue for broadening our market. We sent out traveling road trips with several top saleswomen and a fitter to West Texas, Shreveport, Louisiana, and Houston to establish contacts with new customers who hadn't yet found their way to Dallas. We elaborated on an idea spawned by another store of having a special Man's Night prior to Christmas, but we went them one better by putting on a sparkling fashion show in which all types of gifts were paraded in front of our male audience. This proved so successful that we finally had to abandon it — the demand for tickets exceeded our seating capacity — and rather than discriminate among our customers, we discontinued the event.

Henry Dreyfuss, the industrial designer and one of my closest personal friends, used to help me out with ideas for our Man's Night shows and its successor, "Christmas Gifts Walking." Henry had started his designing career doing stage sets for the old Strand Theatre in New York, so the challenge of creating costumes out of Christmas gifts was not too great. We used to sit at a table in the Oak Room at the Plaza Hotel in New York for hours talking about our next show, and as I described the merchandise to be featured, Henry would turn out quick, creative sketches, the majority of which were usable. Instinctively he was a merchant; he was interested in finding new ways to sell merchandise. This unpaid fashion show assignment was a relief to him, I always thought, from his normal problems of designing new telephones, farm equipment, bathtubs, and cameras. He was a marvelous human being, generous with his time and friendship.

While they lasted, our Man's Night affairs produced great volume as well as customer good will. We provided an ample supply of drinks, but followed a policy of never permitting a man to buy something expensive if he had obviously imbibed too much. I don't recall a single instance of a cancellation the morning after. Many of the customers bought the long-time standard Christmas gifts: lingerie, perfume, and handkerchiefs, but others challenged our ingenuity to come up with unusual ideas. One man who had shopped the entire store complained that he hadn't found what he was looking for. When I asked him what that might be, he confessed that he didn't know, but would recognize it if he saw it. He gave me a description of his wife's size, color preferences, and her interests. Suddenly I conceived an idea. "Give me ten minutes and I think I can produce what you want." He concurred, and I went to work to assemble a unique gift. I recalled a giant-size brandy-type glass, which had been made for use as a goldfish bowl. I filled it with layers of fine cashmere sweaters in various colors to give the appearance of a pousse-café, finishing with a white angora sweater to suggest whipped cream. I then topped it with a ten-carat ruby ring costing $25,000, to simulate the cherry. I brought it down for him to see, and he exclaimed, "That's exactly what I was looking for! I'll take it!" A sale for $25,350 was made, the customer went out satisfied, telling the story to all of his friends for the next ten years.

On another Man's Night, Dick Andrade, a local independent oilman, was searching for a series of presents for his wife which would surpass his previous Christmas gift efforts. Everything we showed him he rejected, on the basis that he had already given her something like it. Finally, in desperation, I suggested that we go outside and take a look at the show windows, hoping we might get some inspiration. We passed one window filled with a variety of gifts ranging from lingerie to a white ermine evening wrap, handbags to perfumes. He paused and said, "If you could reproduce this window, as it is, in my playroom, I'll take everything in it." I assured him we could, if we could have the room twenty-four hours prior to Christmas Eve. It was a large room, and we were successful in building a replica of our display just as he had seen it, using huge sheets of cellophane in place of the glass windowpane. Inside was a large display card, which read, "Merry Christmas, to Mary from Dick." The press got wind of the story, not through us, for we conscientiously protect our customer transactions, and it was reported in newspapers and magazines the world over for many years. Another story was added to the Neiman-Marcus legend.

One afternoon I received a phone call from a West Texas oil-man, asking me to bring some mink coats over to his hotel room so he could select one to take home to his wife. A salesman and I went over and found him in his underwear, just recovering from the night before. He didn't know his wife's size, but he thought she came just about to his ear, and was approximately his weight. He offered to try the coats on, and after modeling the six garments, made his selection. We sent the coat on to him with a covering letter, assuring him that we would be glad to credit his account if for any reason he had a change of mind upon his return home.

A member of our staff once questioned the ethics involved in selling a man a piece of jewelry for $165,000 while he was on a binge in a hotel suite. He had the habit of going off on periodic drinking bouts, and to get out of the doghouse, it was his custom to buy a peace offering. While I never have liked sales of that type, I'm enough of a pragmatist to know that if we refuse to make the sale on moral grounds, there will be four other jewelers who will snap it up without any such scruples. I told the salesperson that there *was* a matter of ethics involved, but not in *making* the sale. I said, "The ethical consideration is what we do *after* the sale. The customer won't remember anything you tell him now, but send him a letter to his office marked 'personal,' advising him the sale is not binding if he changes his mind. That's more than most of our competitors will do."

My second brother, Herbert Jr., had joined the business in 1932. He was a handsome young man with an engaging personality, an aversion to disciplined study, and a propensity for spending money. He showed no inclination to go to college, so he, too, went to work in the store. I don't believe he served an apprenticeship in selling shoes, but was immediately inducted into the position of assisting our first floor merchandise manager, Marx Baum.

Herb wanted to get there in a hurry, without having to do the basic groundwork so essential to the acquisition of knowledge from which real authority is derived. For some reason, difficult for me to understand even now, my father had a blind spot regarding Herb, and excused or tolerated his demonstrations of authoritarianism, temper, and spendthriftness. I told my father frequently that Herb was in the position of the man who wanted to be able to sit down at the piano and play, without ever taking music lessons. I urged him, without success, to put Herb in a position where, by his own efforts, he could win a deserved promotion. But that he would never do, partly because of Herb's financial requirements, and partly on the grounds that Herb had such good taste, it would be a shame to waste his talents on a menial job. I kept reminding him that good taste was not enough, one had to work, too. Though he agreed with me in principle, Dad and I never agreed about how to handle Herb. He liked to entertain customers and vendors alike, without ever a thought of the costs; he could invariably produce a choice table at restaurants or nightclubs; he always acted like the son of a rich man, a man, I might add, much richer than his father. In retrospect, I think he suffered from a great inferiority complex, for he was following two brothers who had already achieved some business success. He was sweet, personable, had a keen sense of family ties, and an explosively hot temper. I shall always consider my inability to help Herb become a success in the store as one of my major failures. Perhaps my own ego kept getting in the way.

With four active Marcuses, or "Marci" as we were often referred to collectively, staff members started calling us by our first names — "Mr. Herbert," "Mr. Stanley," "Mr. Edward," "Mr. Herbert Junior" — to avoid the confusion arising from the designation of "Mr. Marcus."

Upon my return from a market trip, I discovered that a new Sport Shop manager had been employed by Eddie in my absence. She was blond, charming in manner, graceful, and apparently competent. Her name was Mary Cantrell, though she carried the nickname of "Billie." I started taking her out in the evenings, although this violated a policy which I had established myself — that of not going out with female employees, to avoid store gossip. She was born in St. Louis, had grown up in a small town in southern Illinois, and had moved with her parents to Dallas. Our courtship lasted several months, and after resolving in our own minds the problems which might arise from a mixed marriage — she being a Christian, and I a Jew, though not a practicing one — we decided to get married. Her family accepted the news with good spirit; mine was stunned. My parents had the typical Jewish skepticism of mixed marriages, foreseeing all of the problems which might arise. My father, I am sure, had envisioned my marriage to the daughter of some leading Jewish merchant or banker, and I suspect he felt that I had let him down; my mother rallied very quickly, and embraced her future daughter-in-law with warmth and affection, as did most of the other members of our tightly knit family. Dad soon came around when he recognized that Billie was a person of extraordinary quality and character. No natural daughter could have ever been closer or more loving than she. Aunt Carrie, who knew Billie from her contact with her in the store, received her with enthusiasm, and my Aunt Minnie, who was convinced that no one was really good enough to marry into the Marcus family, finally succumbed. My brothers were delighted at the prospect of getting a sister at long last. I, who had established a record for fickleness, while deeply in love, harbored doubts as to how long it might last. I felt sure that I could make it for at least two, maybe three years, but beyond that duration I didn't want to commit myself. On that basis, with renewal options, Billie took me.

She was keenly interested in her work, with no desire to become a housewife. She stayed with her job as a sportswear buyer until she was pregnant with our first child, four years later. With Billie continuing to work during those first years of our marriage, we shared a wide community of interests, and we both adjusted to

89

married life with a minimum of trauma. She thoroughly enjoyed her sportswear buying job, her social activities, and the close family life into which she was drawn, and to which she made meaningful contributions with her warmth and sincerity. She was a young woman with tremendous integrity, unmarred by the slightest trace of pettiness or vanity. My business success had come pretty fast for me, and undoubtedly I was beginning to show some signs of cockiness, which she observed and proceeded to temper. I might disagree with her, but I could never question her motives.

Our first child, a daughter whom we named Jerrie, was born at the end of summer in 1936. Billie retired from business and devoted herself to being a mother. Two years later we were expecting another child, and to the surprise of both of us and the obstetrician, two arrived, a boy and a girl. We named them Richard and Wendy. We had just moved into our new house, rationally designed for a family of four, so we immediately had to add an extra room. I encouraged Billie to get involved with various civic activities, but she refused because she felt she had a full-time community activity right at home, which she correctly judged to be more important than being on a dozen different committees. The result was three perfectly normal children, well adjusted, and without any hangups. Their mother, endowed with fine standards and great common sense, deserves the bulk of the credit. I was what might be called a "fifteen-minute father." I left at eight-thirty in the morning and I could never get home before seven in the evening. When I did return, I adored them for fifteen minutes; fortunately, it was then time for them to go to bed. I would adore them again in the morning before I departed, for fifteen minutes. But she adored them all day long.

My father was entranced with his first-born grandchild, and later with the twins. He and mother invariably came to see them during eating time until Billie insisted that they come either before or after supper, a regulation which was difficult for them to learn to observe. However engrossed my father might have been with business problems, he would always melt when he saw his grandchildren.

Shortly after our marriage, we started to think about building a house, that is, after renewing our marriage contract on our second anniversary. By this time, I was a confirmed "modernist" in architecture, and had converted my "colonial" wife to my way of thinking. We started our search for an architect in the East, since modern architecture had not been discovered in Dallas up to that time. We interviewed Lescaze in New York, considered Neutra in California, and finally ended up visiting the great Frank Lloyd Wright at Taliesin. We described what we wanted and solicited his advice about which of the modern architects he would recommend. "Son," he said, "Why take the imitation while you can still get the original? I'll do your house." That was the beginning of an interesting episode in our lives, and a rich, though sometimes painful and expensive, education in modern architecture.

My father not only wanted me in the business, he also wanted us to live near him. As we started our search for a building site, he settled it by giving us six and a half acres immediately across from his home. It was a beautiful piece of property, and it helped our financing problems so much that we couldn't afford to turn him down. We had told Mr. Wright that we could only afford to spend $25,000, which was a lot of money in the Depression year of 1934, but which he assured us was quite feasible. We invited him to come to Dallas to see the site and to pick his location for the house. He arrived on January 1, with the temperature at seventy degrees. He concluded that this was typical winter weather for Dallas, and nothing we could tell him about the normal January ice storms could ever convince him that we didn't live in a perpetually balmy climate. When his first preliminary sketches arrived, we noticed that there were no bedrooms, just cubicles in which to sleep when the weather was inclement. Otherwise, ninety percent of the time we would sleep outdoors on the deck. We protested that solution on the grounds that I was subject to colds and sinus trouble. He dismissed this objection in his typical manner, as though brushing a bit of lint from his jacket, by assuring us that I wouldn't get colds if I slept outside. Finally though, with great reluctance, he did enlarge the bedrooms.

He provided little or no closet space, commenting that closets were only useful for accumulating things you didn't need. After explaining the nature of our social life and obligations, which required fairly large wardrobes, he yielded to our request for more commodious storage facilities with some reluctance. Billie and I leaned heavily on my father's judgment, since he had built both stores and two houses, thus generating Mr. Wright's displeasure, since he regarded "Senior," as he termed my father, as having no real understanding of contemporary architecture. My father had warned us about the necessity of staying within our cost commitment, but at each review of the plans, he stretched the size of the rooms and the height of the ceilings. In our innocence, we had started off wanting a modest-sized house, but influenced by my father and stimulated by a growing perception of our needs, the scope of the house expanded — as did the costs.

Mr. Wright was always in need of cash to help support his Taliesin project, making frequent appeals for financial assistance, which I was unable to give him. As a result of his visit to Dallas, seeing the store, and meeting my father, "Senior," I think Mr. Wright made a reappraisal of me and concluded that I wasn't of the modest means that I had represented myself to be and which, in fact, I actually was. Almost every letter contained a request for a contribution of a further advance. In May 1935, he asked for a loan of $750, for which he offered to send us some prints as security, with the provision that if the amount were not repaid in eighteen months, the prints would belong to us.

Financially extended though I was, I couldn't turn down this urgent plea, little knowing the nature of the prints he was planning to send. In due course a large and heavy case arrived containing a complete set of the prints comprising "The Tokaido" by the Japanese master printmaker Hiroshige. Later Mr. Wright explained that at the time he was building the Imperial Hotel in Tokyo, he acquired a set, and that later he either bought or received another set as a gift from Mrs. Spaulding of Boston. Which of the two sets he sent to me, I never knew. He never did redeem it, so it became ours.

With Mr. Wright's concurrence, we engaged a local architect, Roscoe DeWitt, to act as local agent for him and as an interpreter of his plans to us. We had been forewarned that Mr. Wright's buildings were leak-prone, so we had asked Mr. DeWitt to be on guard for inadequate flashing specifications, a precaution Mr. Wright deeply resented. Since we were separated from Mr. Wright by over a thousand miles, our discussions of the plans had to be conducted, for the most part, through the mails.

In response to some questions I had raised, Mr. Wright reassured me he was an authority on the subject of acoustics (as he was on every other topic) and that our living room would be acoustically perfect. Since we had observed sweating walls and glass at Taliesin, we were eager to avoid this condition in our house. He promised us we would not have sweating glass or walls in our house. I'm sure that Mr. Wright thought the majority of our queries and doubts were of a mundane nature and somewhat provincial. We knew firsthand about his leaking roofs and sweating walls and we were determined to safeguard against them if we could, even if he considered such subjects mundane.

We received preliminary estimates of the cost of building the house, ranging from $90,000 to $150,000, three to five times more than our revised figure of $30,000, advanced from the original $25,000. I must have written a letter of doubt and distress to Mr. Wright for I received an answer from him attacking my lack of faith in him and denouncing Roscoe DeWitt. He also wrote angrily to DeWitt, who, despite the verbal lashing Wright gave him, replied in a most restrained manner:

Dear Mr. Wright:

I have received your letter of the 27th, and as you requested I am returning the tracings of the Marcus house to you.

Some of the criticisms contained in your letter are doubtless just, but most of them are not. It was not impressed upon me that we were to receive further data regarding the steel framing or that we were to return the tracings or the prints until a figure had been obtained. I regret very much that I did not understand this.

Your conception of my attitude toward you personally and toward your work is entirely wrong, but your method of expressing it is such that it leaves me no choice but to let the matter rest with a bare statement that you will never have a more ardent admirer than I am.

With high esteem, I am

Yours very truly,

ROSCOE P. DEWITT

The final bids did come in at $150,000, which I relayed to Mr. Wright by phone. He retorted that the contractors didn't understand his plans. When I asked him, "Whose fault is that?" he retorted by saying, "I'll build your damned house myself for $35,000." When I asked if he would put up a performance bond, he hit the ceiling! We were a big disappointment to him because we lacked the fundamental faith necessary for a Frank Lloyd Wright client. We emerged from the experience with a Frank Lloyd Wright education, which proved to be of great help with the house we eventually built. We turned to Roscoe DeWitt, for whom we had great respect, to design our house in the same location. His house bore no resemblance to the Wright original. It was a highly controversial though not a historical piece of architecture; and it proved to be a home which met our living requirements better than the Wright house would have done.

Several years later, DeWitt wrote me:

94

As to the leaks — roofs were never Frank's most endearing quality — certainly not a quality which he cultivated. Perhaps he was a bit fatalistic about the matter — people had been building roofs for five thousand years and all during that time some leaked and some didn't. Who was he to change the course of history, so to speak.

All the greats seem to have had their bêtes noires. Frank, his roofs and Mies his posts. If Mies didn't carry them all the way to the ground, the owner, like Dr. Fransworth, had to buy sheep to keep the weeds down. When he [Mies] did carry them down to the ground, he had troubles of another sort. Walking by his Lake Shore [Chicago] apartments the other evening, I noticed he had attempted to alleviate one condition by the generous use of signs requesting tenants to keep dogs away from the posts!

5

Over the Hump

It WOULD BE NICE TO THINK that all testimonials and public recognitions happen spontaneously, and some do. However, they frequently have to be set in motion by a slight nudge. In 1937, when we were getting ready to celebrate the thirtieth anniversary of the founding of Neiman-Marcus, it occurred to me that it was only fitting that my father be honored on the occasion. I mentioned the idea to two of his banking associates, Fred Florence and Karl Hoblitzelle, and they readily agreed to sponsor a testimonial luncheon in his honor. It made worthy publicity for the store, it paid a well-deserved tribute to one of its founders, and it gave others the chance to say nice things about his contributions to the community, which would have been difficult for us to have voiced. My father was very touched by this honor and expressed great gratitude to both Messrs. Florence and Hoblitzelle for their thoughtfulness, never knowing I had stimulated their action.

From the outset, it had been my father's habit to recognize an anniversary of the store with some pronouncement about the fashions of the season, in order to get the fall business moving. In Texas, September was still a hot month, providing little stimulus for the purchases of fall wardrobes. Sometimes we had to wait until mid-October for a "blue norther" to break the succession of hot days. I studied the advertising of our early years carefully, and one day I came across the phrase "presenting a veritable *exposition* of fashion." This triggered an idea — why not create an event of such importance that we could make it an exposition in fact as well as in words? In discussion with others in the organization, the idea bloomed. We would invite some of our designers to make personal appearances, just as the movie stars did to promote a new picture, we would bring down artisans to perform their work in the store, and we would back all of this up with a great fashion show to dramatize the new fall fashions. There was a movement afoot, begun by Lord & Taylor, to recognize American designers. We decided it was time to bring American *and* European designers out of the anonymity under which their employers had carefully obscured them, so we established, in 1938, The Neiman-Marcus Award for Distinguished Service in the Field of Fashion. For the first year's awards we selected Mr. John, the milliner, Dorothy Liebes, the textile designer, and Germaine Monteil and Nettie Rosenstein, dress designers. They came, and the awards were presented at a gala evening fashion show in the store to a capacity audience of 1,750. The demand for tickets was so great that we were forced to repeat the show four additional nights. Customers came from all parts of the Southwest to see the shows, meet the famous names in fashion, and start their fall wardrobes — even though the weather was ninety-eight degrees. We had created a totally new sales promotion device! The following year we honored Hattie Carnegie, Clare Potter, and Elizabeth Arden. In 1940, Mrs. Chase of *Vogue* returned to Dallas to receive the award, and for the first time we presented the award to a European, Elsa Schiaparelli of Paris. In the years to follow, virtually every well-known and some unknown designers made special trips to Dallas to receive our award, for it came to be recognized as the Oscar of the fashion industry. Obviously it was a great publicity device, and the award presentation stories and pictures were picked up by the press here and abroad.

We were very strict in our selection of awardees, insisting that each must have made some contribution to fashion, either in designing, publicizing, or the wearing of fashion in a way that influenced the public. It was on the basis of the latter criterion that we selected Mrs. Howard (Slim) Hawkes as our first fashion consumer awardee, for in 1946 she epitomized the "typical American" look to the fashionables of the country. Later the award was given to Madame Henri Bonnet, the wife of the French ambassador to Washington, for her chic representation of the fashions of France, and then in 1955 to a rising young motion picture actress, Grace Kelly, soon to become Her Most Serene Highness, Princess Grace of Monaco.

The night before the award presentation, we gave an outdoor party at our home, to which we invited some five hundred guests. When Jacques Fath, the brilliant young French couturier, came to America especially to receive the award, we put on a western party with ranch-style food and square dancing for entertainment. He was so taken with the whole affair that he and his wife Geneviève repeated the party at their new château outside Paris the following year, with ranch-style food prepared by French chefs and square dancers costumed in outfits he designed for the evening. He imported from Texas the same square dance caller we had used, and my wife and I spent several afternoons in his Paris apartment teaching specially selected guests how to square dance, including a very tall young man named Hubert de Givenchy, the famous models Bettina and Sophie, and two fellow-couturiers, Pierre Balmain and Jean Dessès.

Following his introduction of the "New Look" in 1947, we extended an invitation to the new star ascendant Christian Dior, who came to Dallas — his first trip to America. He was very shy, and Edward and his wife Betty met him at the boat in New York and accompanied him to Dallas. When we took him on a drive to see something of Dallas, I started in the direction of the better residential district. Dior interrupted me and asked to be taken to see the slums. "The rich live about the same all over the world; I want to see how your poor people live," he said. At the time of his visit, he was just formulating the idea of creating special collections for the United States twice a year, in addition to launching his perfume and hosiery lines. We warned him about trying to extend himself in too many directions, and into too many different markets. Fortunately, Mr. Boussac, his backer, provided him with one of the ablest business managers I've ever known, Jacques Rouet, who took the burdens of syndication off Dior's shoulders. Designing collections for two markets proved to be more than Dior could handle, and he was forced to delegate the New York assignment to a young protégé. Dior, with Boussac's money and Rouet's help, founded the greatest of the postwar couture houses of Paris, setting standards of taste and quality which have been perpetuated under his two successors, Yves Saint Laurent and Marc Bohan. The burden of the venture was too great for him, and he died of a heart attack just three years after his Dallas visit.

Standards of taste and quality were established in the early years and enunciated repeatedly through newspaper advertisements that my father wrote and by the very merchandise that was bought and sold with such great care. We added a visual demonstration of these standards through our skillful use of the fashion show technique, during which the commentator could editorialize on our fashion point of view. We could say, "Neiman-Marcus has more fine lines of merchandise under one roof than any store in America"; "Neiman-Marcus is one of the five largest distributors of fine merchandise in the country"; "We think that this color should be worn only by those with very fair skins; all others stay away from it"; "We think we made a mistake in putting this hat with this particular costume; it should be worn with an after-five outfit." We were suggesting ideas and fashion philosophies which our customers repeated to their friends everywhere. The increasing renown of Neiman-Marcus gave our patrons a sense of pride in the store they had helped build. It was the showplace to which they took all of their out-of-town guests.

Aunt Carrie rarely attended a fashion show outside the store. She was too busy selling to her customers, and helping saleswomen sell to theirs. Rarely did she find time even to go out for lunch, usually eating a sandwich in one of the fitting rooms. If she saw a customer walking out without having found anything to her liking, she might bring her back to a fitting room and sell her a dozen garments, some of which the customer had previously seen and rejected. She never had or wanted an office, or an assistant. She did promote a star saleswoman, Laura Goldman, to a buying assistantship and later to buyer. From Aunt Carrie and Miss Cullen, Laura learned the nuances of both taste and quality. She was among the last of the buyers of the old school. There will never be buyers again like that trio, for the market of today is so differently organized. Today there are good buyers of a different breed, capable of meeting today's multiple-store problems and buying today's mass-produced products.

It is only fair to note that all visitors did not respond to the fame of Neiman-Marcus in the same manner. A typical Texas rancher came into the store one day, pushed his Stetson back on his head, and started looking around the store. An attentive saleswoman approached and asked if she could help him. "I reckon not," he said, as he shook his head slowly and then decisively. "In all my time I never saw so many things a body kin git along without as I have here."

Many of our customers in those days were slow payers, particularly the most wealthy ones, who followed the cattle country tradition of settling up once a year. This put a considerable strain on our finances, so one day my father took me to meet the partners of E. Naumberg and Sons in Wall Street, who were buyers of commercial paper. They looked at our balance sheet and our audited annual statement, with a list of past-due customer accounts of over $50,000 each. When they observed the total of about

$750,000 in this category, they turned to my father and said, "Mr. Marcus, you're not running a mercantile establishment, you're running a bank." My father suggested that if they would get financial statements on the various individuals so listed, they would find these customers all represented fortunes ranging from $10,000,-000 to $100,000,000, and that he personally would guarantee that each account would be paid up by the end of the year. They accepted my father's word and bought our paper. The next year when we went back, my father showed them the list. All had paid up completely, but were back in debt for about the same amount. The Naumberg partners conceded, "Mr. Marcus, you certainly know your business. We don't." Our credit losses were negligible, even during the Depression when many of our customers were very slow in paying; some might ride us, but few at that time ever cheated us.

On a night flight to New York in June 1940, I was seated next to Charles J. V. Murphy, one of the senior editors of *Fortune*. The following morning, when we stopped in Philadelphia for refueling, newspapers were brought aboard which carried the headlines announcing the fall of Paris to the Germans. The news was not unexpected, of course, but the actuality of it made for a depressing breakfast. In the course of discussing the effects of this event on the United States, I ventured the opinion that the fashion industry would be in for some radical changes, since it had been so dependent on the French textile industry and Parisian couture. Murphy showed great interest in my ideas, and as we disembarked, he asked if I would be interested in writing a piece for *Fortune* on the subject. He told me to get in touch with Richardson Wood, the managing editor, whom he would alert for my call. I met with Wood, who was also intrigued with the idea, and he suggested that I write a story for publication in an early fall issue. He couldn't make a final commitment until he saw my manuscript, but urged me to get started on it at once. When I submitted it to him in August, I received an immediate reply, saying, ". . . I think we have in it the makings of the article you and I discussed here some weeks ago. So strongly do we feel that, that we have definitely scheduled the article for publication in the November issue."

My title was "Paris Falls out of Fashion," which they changed to "America Is in Fashion." I attempted to anatomize the American fashion industry, its dependence on the French couture, and the factors which differentiated our manufacturing process from their custom-made approach. At that time there was a tremendous amount of mythology about how fashions originated, with little understanding of the economic factors which made creativity in Europe easier to accomplish than in the United States. I wrote:

The American garment industry is now in a position to prove whether it can make a silk dress, or whether it will be a sow's ear. For decades our garment industry has depended for inspiration on a handful of French designers . . . the American garment industry is left to its own devices. How will it get along? For not only must it create designers for dresses, but it must find its own inspiration for new materials and then weave them; it must devise its own buckles, invent new buttons, trimmings, and beads, and see them translated into actuality. . . . All arguments about the merits of American fashion designers are virtually futile because American designers have never been put to the test. Even those who claim they never looked to Paris for inspiration may unwittingly have been influenced. It will take several years for the influence of Paris to thin out of the bloodstream of American design. Only then can we properly appraise the true creative ability of our American designers.

The article was received with acclaim from those in the fashion business, with a minimum of dissent. I was paid $500 for it, my first income as a writer. What was even more important, I was given a by-line, the first, to my knowledge, that *Fortune* had ever

105

bestowed on an unknown writer. As a result of the publication of my analysis and prognostication, I was considered an authority on matters relating to fashion, resulting in numerous speaking invitations and interviews.

War preparations brought new industry to Dallas, and new customers to Neiman-Marcus. War workers, like wildcatters, wanted the best as soon as their incomes rose sufficiently to enable them to buy the best. Sensing that restrictions might be placed on new construction, we pressed hard to complete another expansion and redecoration job. This time we went the contemporary route, employing two different interior designers, Robsjohn Gibbings, an Englishman, and Eleanor LeMaire, an American. We were so satisfied with the latter's understanding of store design problems that we continued to use her services for the next thirty years, until her death. We moved and greatly enlarged our Man's Shop; we redecorated two of our major apparel floors. To finance this expenditure, we made our first public stock offering of $700,-000 worth of preferred stock, all sold in Texas.

Again we felt the need to explain Neiman-Marcus, perhaps because of the influx of so many new customers. On September 1, 1941, in an advertisement marking our anniversary, we asked, "What is Neiman-Marcus? Why?" We answered our own question by stating,

It's a crystalization of ideas and ideals. It's high adventure in store keeping, carried forward as public acceptance demanded larger space, new departments. Here's a business founded on the determination . . . to buy and sell not just good merchandise, but the finest! It's the determination to do things with savoir faire — gift wrappings or weddings. It's an eye for what's new and smart and choice, wherever it originates — New York, Staffordshire, England, Cambodia, or Taos, New Mexico.

And then, when we were in the war, our New Year's message on January 1, 1942, read,

And now we come to 1942 — and a world engulfed in war. Doubtless many of you are asking the question, "What about a store like Neiman-Marcus in war time?" We have thought about this question a great deal, too. We believe, that as distributors of fine merchandise, we have a special function to perform — now perhaps more than ever before. It concerns that nebulous important quality called morale. . . . It is only the article of quality that endures. That is why Neiman-Marcus has always said "buy quality," and we say it now, and think it is more important than ever. We have made every effort to prevent runaway prices. And we pledge to you once again, that we shall continue to price our goods on the lowest possible basis consistent with our high standards of quality.

On December 27, twenty days after Pearl Harbor, I received a call from Washington from a man I didn't know, Bob Guthrie of the War Production Board, asking me to join the clothing division of WPB and to head up the women's and children's sections to develop fabric conservation programs to help the war effort. I was thirty-seven, with three children, and beyond the current draft age limit. I discussed the proposal with my wife, father, aunt, and brothers, and we all concluded that I had no choice. I must respond to the call. My brother Herbert was joining the army, my brother Lawrence, just graduated from the Harvard Business School, had an ROTC commission in the army. Eddie, who was thirty-three and single, had received no draft notice, so he stayed in Dallas to help run the business, with the understanding that I would return, if possible, should he get a draft call. I reported for work in Washington on January 5, 1942, for what proved to be one of the most enlightening experiences of my career.

6

The War Years

EVERYTHING ABOUT WASHINGTON WAS NEW TO ME: the city, the highly charged atmosphere of the war drive coupled with a "business as usual" attitude, bureaucratic procedures, and my office associates, some of whom had been on the job for several months. Many of them had been serving on a three-day-week schedule, returning to their businesses and families between times. I came into the organization as a dollar-a-year consultant, with only transportation paid by the government. In the beginning I had the idea that I'd go home weekends until I could estimate how long my assignment would take. With a low airline priority rating, it soon became obvious that weekend trips could not be planned with any certainty. Billie visited me once, and we attempted to find a house, but rentals were both difficult to arrange and expensive. With the threat of a $25,000-a-year income freeze, which was being suggested by the administration, we were loath to commit ourselves to the sizable expenditure such a move would demand. I could get to New York on Friday nights without too much trouble, for there was usually adequate plane service even for low priority holders. My weekly trips home finally dwindled to once-a-month appearances, but on the Saturdays I was in New York, I was able to meet with our buyers who were in town and so keep in touch with what was going on in the store.

111

Fortunately for me, the head of the men's section of the WPB was the vice-president of one of our men's clothing resources, Irving Squires. He gave me guidance, explaining the objectives of the division and the methodology that had been established. With his pseudo-English accent, which had earned him the nickname "Clip," he had established good rapport with the various division heads at WPB, the army and navy representatives, as well as the specialists from Labor and the lawyers from John Lord O'Brian's office, general legal counsel to the WPB. Since many of the activities of the board dealt with matters affecting free competition, Mr. O'Brian was seriously concerned lest we violate any laws. While the war posters adorning the walls of our offices urged Action Now, the legal division held us up with time-consuming delays as they reviewed and revised the wordings of our conservation orders. One of the bromides which developed was, "We might lose the war, but we can be assured it will be perfectly legal."

Several days after I started working, I noticed that none of the section heads dictated any letters; instead they used the telephone, making lengthy long-distance calls twenty and thirty times a day. I voiced some dismay to my friend Clip about this apparent waste of government money during what was supposed to be a period of wartime austerity. He replied, "Don't let that worry you. Our calls won't amount to more than $100,000, and that's a drop in the bucket compared to what they're spending on this war. Besides, one day after the war there's likely to be a congressional investigation of WPB, and what you don't have written in the files can't be used against you."

My assignment was to call together representatives of the various branches of the apparel industry to get their advice about steps which might be taken to conserve textiles, thereby saving not only yardage, but also the labor, which could be diverted to the war effort. Under Mr. O'Brian's mandate, these "Industry Committees" had to be organized in a democratic manner, with representation by geographic areas, by large and small producers, and by differing product price levels. The problems of different segments of the industry varied so greatly that we had to set up committees to represent the producers of dresses, coats and suits, children's wear, lingerie, and corsets. After the lists were approved by counsel, about twenty representatives of the specific industry would meet with me in Washington to listen to my scare talk about the forthcoming shortages and, as industry leaders and patriotic citizens, to suggest what kind of limitation orders would be effective in accomplishing the savings without disrupting either civilian production or the traditional competitive forces within the trade. In mid-January 1942, it was very difficult to convince many of them, who still remembered the Depression, that shortages could *ever* exist in the United States. Most of them, flattered by being called to Washington for meetings and advice, were confident of their own abilities to scrounge for fabrics if things became as tough as I predicted. As a whole, though, they were for doing little or nothing, and at times, it became questionable whether the Battle of Two-Way Stretch and the Retreat of the Nylons were not of greater importance to the industries than the military engagements in the Coral Sea and Tunisia.

Pressure was applied to me to soften the proposed regulations by many of our own manufacturers and even by one retailer. Earl Puckett, then president of Allied Department Stores, asked me to visit him at his corporate office one Saturday morning. "Why are you going through this silly conservation rigamarole? There's not going to be any shortage," he said. I replied that on the basis of the forecasts supplied to us by the Bureau of Labor Statistics and by the Department of Commerce, we could foresee shortages in the months ahead. "I don't believe them," he said. "I have my own statistical sources and there is no indication of shortages. Besides, what you are proposing to do won't hurt my business, but it will kill yours." This was as close to a bribe — an appeal to self-interest — that I received during my tenure at WPB.

The menswear section under Irving Squires's direction had been working on a conservation order prior to my arrival at WPB. Very shortly, they issued orders eliminating vests, cuffs from trousers, two-trouser suits, patch pockets, fancy backs, and pleated trousers, restricting the number of pins to be used in packaging men's shirts, and embodying other minor curtailments. These were met with skeptical criticism from the industry and the trade publications, which questioned the value of the potential savings. This gave me a preview of the techniques in drawing up an order and the methods of disseminating the information afterwards.

Despite my years in ready-to-wear buying and merchandising, I had been dealing with an infinitesimal part of the industry. In my innocence, I had not realized that in 1940, less than 10% of the dollar volume of the dress business was done at wholesale prices over $16.75, and that only 2% of the units made, and yardage consumed, were in the so-called better dress end of the business. I found myself exposed to a mass of technical information about the manufacturing process involving pattern-making, the manner in which garments were cut, and the general tricks of the trade. I recognized my own limitations of knowledge, so I searched for an assistant with experience in the production end of the garment business who could protect me from some of the booby traps I suspected were being set for me by some of our "industry advisers." I had the good fortune to locate a man named Julius Jacobson, vice-president in charge of production at L'Aiglon of Philadelphia, one of the leading manufacturers of housedresses, and he joined my staff for three days a week as a consultant. His contribution was enormous in helping to write the conservation orders in a manner which accomplished our objectives, but which were equitable to the various segments of the industries involved. Nina Randell Smithdeal, a former Neiman-Marcus sportswear buyer who had moved to Washington, became my assistant, and as one of the few female staff members at WPB succeeded in cutting through the bureaucratic red tape better than any male might have done. She smiled, cajoled, argued, and sweet-talked the various department heads to expedite drafts of our orders ahead of others.

In addition to writing regulations which would save fabric, I had two other objectives: to devise orders (1) which would be self-enforcing and (2) which would virtually freeze fashion as it was in 1942, thus forestalling any radical change in fashion making existing clothes obsolete. Both of these points seemed extremely important. Many of the spokesmen from industry favored a yardage control order, saying, "Give us a limit as to the amount of fabric we can use, and then let each of us use it as we see fit." The trouble with this solution was that it would have required an army of enforcement agents to visit every factory in the land to check for compliance, and in wartime the government couldn't afford to tie up precious manpower in that manner. Hence we settled on certain prohibitions, such as lengths, sleeve fullnesses, patch pockets, ensembles, hoods, sweep of skirts, width of belts, and depth of hems. These details would be easy for any patriotic woman to discern and for any competitive manufacturer or store-keeper to check on. We depended on the customer and the competitor to become our major enforcement agents.

The restrictions we put into effect froze the fashion silhouette; it effectively prevented any change of skirt length downward and it blocked any extreme new sleeve or collar development, which might have encouraged women to discard their existing clothes. At that particular moment, I had greater fashion power than any monarch or couturier in the history of the world. I felt this responsibility keenly, and spent many a sleepless night wondering if I had decided wisely, if I was causing industry dislocations which might force any manufacturers to the wall. I was mindful of the statement which was voiced in every industry advisory meeting we held, "This regulation will force us out of business." My counselor, Julius Jacobson, quickly reassured me, "Don't worry, there's no rule we can write that will put a dress manufacturer out of business. They'll find a way to live within the law and prosper." He proved so right! I learned for the first time the remarkable ingenuity of the human being to survive, even when circumscribed by new limitations, new regulations.

The next job was to present our first conservation order, officially titled "General Limitation Order L-85," in a manner that would get maximum support from both the public and the trade. Here my retail promotional experience was of great assistance, for I realized that this was another selling campaign, and if done well should be successful. From the bad experiences the Office of Price Administration had encountered with their promulgation of price control regulations, I was determined not to make the same mistakes. It seemed vital, even in wartime when everyone wanted to cooperate with the war effort, to give them the "why" of any impingement on their normal habits and prerogatives. I was able to persuade my bosses at WPB to permit me to hold a full-fledged press conference to announce and explain L-85. Up to that time, all orders had simply been sent to the press mimeographed, without explanation. In addition to the regular Washington reporters, I invited editors from the leading fashion magazines and newspapers, columnists, reporters for the various fashion newsletters, and anyone else I thought might give us a good send-off. As a result of our precautions we received a wholehearted endorsement from both the industry and the press. *Women's Wear Daily* editorialized, "We predict that the influence of this order will be distinctively beneficial to these [apparel] industries, that it will achieve a new and patriotic cooperation between buyer and manufacturer, between retailer and customer, who are essentially interested in the furthering of all types of conservation, in conserving waste as the Government ordains." Lew Hahn, general manager of the National Retail Dry Goods Association, commented, "There will be no stagnation in fashion designing as a result of these rulings." Philip Mangone, a leading coat manufacturer, said, "It seems to me that the Government has worked very thoughtfully in drafting the new rulings. With great wisdom they have avoided the kind of arbitrary checks that would be a hindrance to creative design."

We had leaked our story to *Women's Wear Daily*'s very able Washington reporters, Alice and Bert Perkins, in advance, and against all WPB rules, so that they might be able to have sketches ready to accompany the publication of the order. The results justified the means, for the explanatory artwork made the restrictions crystal clear to members of the industry. The afternoon following the official announcement, I flew to New York to appear on a national news program to explain the reasons for the regulations and to give assurance, with accompanying sketches, that existing fashions were not being made obsolete and that there was no reason to rush to buy new clothes. In a speech to the Fashion Group in New York two months earlier, I had tried to prepare the fashion press for their responsibility in the war effort. "The job of the fashion magazines, as I see it, is to interpret conservation to the readers in the various social and economic strata to whom they appeal. The magazines have the power to fan a great flame of demand by their endorsement of a given fashion. They can serve best by endorsing both editorially and pictorially those fashions which in their opinion are the best expressions of our conservation program." This appeal bore dividends, for the fashion publications gave full support to L-85, and helped make the restrictions fashionable.

I went around the country talking and explaining L-85 to manufacturers' associations and press groups, with the result that we received the best press and acceptance of any order issued by the WPB. Leon Henderson, director of the Office of Price Administration, asked at dinner one night, "How in the hell do you get such good acceptance for your orders, and I get such lousy response to all of mine?" "Yours is a much tougher subject to sell," I replied, "but if you would only take the time to tell people *why*, you'll have better results." "Come over and work for me as my public relations director," he proposed. Flattering as the invitation was, I declined, for I saw my job was coming to an end, and with the prospect of Eddie's departure for military service, I was needed back in Dallas to help run the store and give my father, who was not in the best of health, needed assistance.

When I first went to Washington, my boss gave me a warning, "The first week down here you'll be bewildered, the second week you will be discouraged, and by the third week you will be excited." His predictions were accurate. I left Washington in June 1942, not only happy that I had made some contribution, but with a feeling of indebtedness to my government for the privilege of having served it. I left with the conviction that if more citizens could serve their government for even six months, we would have both better citizens and better government.

When the war broke out, none of us at Neiman-Marcus had any idea of what the effects were going to be on our business. My father, usually the optimist and the expansionist, was not inclined to take chances on big commitments. "Why take such risks when the government is taking 90% of our profits in taxes?" he asked. My reply was that as long as our doors were kept open to the whole public, we had a responsibility to try to serve all who entered. If, on the other hand, we were willing to let only those come in who were proven Neiman-Marcus customers, we could carry smaller stocks and avoid the risks. I contended that no institution could afford to ignore the demands of the market, and that it was up to us to take the risks to satisfy as many of the new war-affluent as possible as well as our regular customers. "Besides," I added, "if we're wrong, the government will be paying 90% of our losses." Which argument convinced him, I don't know, but he gave us the green light and we began making huge commitments, for a store of our size, for rayon stockings, white shirts, gabardine suits, dresses, and skirts. In order to insure fair distribution of scarce stockings to all of our customers, and to prevent long queues in the department, we created the Neiman-Marcus Hosiery-of-the-Month Club, through which we agreed to mail each member two pairs of stockings a month. Many women opened charge accounts just to become members of the club, and in a short time we had a membership of over 100,000, extending all over the country.

Some one million people found themselves unexpectedly in Texas, and they seemed to know about only two things in the state: the Alamo and Neiman-Marcus. They visited both, but they came back to Neiman-Marcus. A supply of new customers, big stocks, and a marvelously friendly sales staff brought pyramiding volume gains.

Eddie, in the meantime, had received a commission in the Air Transport Command, so my father and I were left alone with a business made even more complex by the uncertainties of supply, the difficulties of travel, and a rapidly expanding sales volume.

With Europe shut off, Mexico became a favorite vacation land for the wealthy and Dallas was a natural stopping-off place. Many were bumped from planes in Dallas by military priorities, forcing them to wait sometimes for several days to continue passage. They all visited Neiman-Marcus, and many were given personal tours of the store by my father or myself. When exposed to the quality of our merchandise, and warmed by our pride in the store and its goods, nearly all of them bought clothes and furs for themselves, or as gifts to take home. Customers from far away were unaccustomed to being taken through a store by its heads and were tremendously impressed by such examples of personalized service. There was barely a day that my father and I couldn't account for an extra $10,000 worth of sales from these escorted tours. Even more important was the large number of new friends we made for the business from these personal contacts.

Bennett Cerf phoned to tell me that the wife of John Steinbeck would be passing through Dallas with her small child. Steinbeck had called him in great anxiety because Mrs. Steinbeck would need a supply of fresh milk for baby, and in view of wartime shortages, asked if he could arrange for a supply to be delivered in Dallas. Bennett assured him that he had a friend there who could supply anything, hence the call to me. We arranged for the milk, improved her hotel accommodations, and put mother and child on the train the following day.

Requests of this type have been commonplace and not only in wartime; thus we have become widely known throughout the country as "the store that can get you anything." Once a man called from New York to see if we could get a pair of ducks delivered to his grandson, who lived in a small town seventy miles from Dallas. I assured him that we would deliver them in time for Easter, quoting a price that I thought would cover both the ducks and the transport. Then I learned that neither Railway Express nor the bus service would deliver livestock, so to keep faith with the customer, I hired a car and chauffeur to make the trip. The costs were triple those I quoted, but I had made a deal and I stuck with it. The customer never knew of my predicament, but we were very careful thereafter in accepting orders for anything alive.

A New York banker wanted a bleached steer skull for decoration over his bar in Westhampton; after the war, years later, a Japanese innkeeper wrote us for a pair of Texas longhorns for his restaurant in remote Fukuoka. (He was so delighted with them that he invited me to be his guest for a week, which I've never had time to accept.) A rancher from the King Ranch country sent us a box of "floating bones" from a lion, a leopard, and a cheetah to be set in eighteen-karat gold as pins for his daughters; he was so pleased that he sent a pair of lion's teeth to be made into cuff links. A man from California ordered a pair of stockings for a wedding present for the then Princess Elizabeth, because he was sure I would know what size she wore. With discretion, we ascertained the correct size. A customer called from Chicago and said, "I need a present for the Duchess of Windsor. I know you can find the right thing — not too personal, and under $500." And we did. Calls for gifts for foreign heads of state are commonplace, though at times our ingenuity is taxed, as it was when a couple of men came in to select a present for the wife of the president of an Asian country. We had never seen a picture of her, but a discreet call to a friend in Washington provided a good clue to the proper gift. It's great fun to be challenged with requests like these almost every day of the year.

7

Waiting for the War to End

Despite his driving energy, or perhaps because of it, my father's health was fragile. He had hypertension, necessitating periods of rest and relaxation which were hard to persuade him to take, so wrapped up was he in the whole fabric of his business. However, upon my return to the store, he felt able to go for vacations to California and Florida, keeping in touch with me daily by phone to tell me about interesting items he had observed in the shops and what the well-dressed women were wearing at the best restaurants. I took advantage of some of his absences to implement new policies or procedures which would have been difficult to effect had he been on hand. He never disagreed with my decisions after the fact.

Aunt Carrie had, from time to time, dabbled in precious jewelry for the store, buying on occasion a ruby-studded bracelet or a sapphire domed ring, always selling them to her personal customers. I was impressed by her success, so I suggested that we open a special department for fine jewelry. The climate seemed right, with a growing affluent public and a minimum of local competition. Aunt Carrie was all for it but my father had a few reservations based on the capital requirements for such an operation and on his knowledge that jewelry was rarely sold at a fixed price. From the beginning of the store, he had been adamant about maintaining

125

prices, assuring his customers and sales staff that "Neiman-Marcus is a one-price store," regardless of the size of the purchase or the name and standing of the customer. After deliberation he told me, "If you can assure me that you won't ever deviate from this policy, then go ahead; but remember, you have a whole store's reputation at stake. You can't cut prices in jewelry without endangering your fur, dress, and coat business." I assured him that I'd live up to the policy faithfully regardless of the temptations. We selected a little island on the first floor near the main entrance for our jewel presentation, and I went to the market to try to locate a jewelry buyer who had the necessary qualities of integrity and taste and a willingness to abide by our one-price policy. Finally I ran across Chapin Marcus (no relation), formerly a partner in the firm of Marcus & Company of Fifth Avenue, who accepted the challenge, although he warned me that we would be the only jewelry store in America which wouldn't break a price under some extenuating circumstance. He said, "The biggest and best jewelers on Fifth Avenue will make a special price if they see they are going to lose the sale to a competitor." I warned him that if he ever felt his resistance weakening to remember our initial conversation, and that if he ever broached the subject to me, he would be automatically fired. During our first year, we let a lot of customers walk out until they finally became convinced that Neiman-Marcus was perfectly willing to lose a $100,000 sale rather than cut one single dollar off the retail price.

Prior to opening the new department, we decided to hold a preview of our collection in New York to get the benefit of the publicity which we could feed back to Dallas. My Texas-born friend Mary Martin had just opened in a new show on Broadway called "One Touch of Venus," so we invited her to be our special guest at a cocktail party at the Hotel Pierre at which we named an unusual necklace "One Touch of Venus" in her honor. Many friends from show business were on hand, as well as numerous New York and Texas socialites. We received wonderful press comments, which were duly incorporated into our opening advertisement in Dallas two days later. The authority of New York acceptance was a valuable ploy at that stage in the development of Texans' self-confidence. It worked then; it wouldn't today, as succeeding generations of Texas customers have become more sophisticated.

A new department and a new buyer, strange to the city, required a great deal of personal effort on my part to introduce them to our best customers. As I chatted with a customer in the gown department, I would casually pull a ruby bracelet from my pocket and start a conversation about our new jewelry shop. If she showed any interest, I would call Chapin Marcus to come up and meet the customer. It wasn't important to make a sale, but it was very necessary to get our jewelry in front of the best clientele of the store.

The day before Christmas that first year of our jewelry experience I received a phone call from our top salesman to come and meet a man who wanted to buy a diamond for his wife's Christmas present. I asked who the customer was, and recognized the name as that of an oilman who had recently moved to Dallas and was reputedly very wealthy. After I was introduced to him, we talked about a number of unrelated subjects for a few minutes and then began reviewing the diamonds he was considering. The salesman indicated the stone the customer had selected and asked me what I thought of it. I looked at it very carefully and said, "I'm sorry, but I don't think this is the right stone for him." With that remark, I got a kick under the table from the salesman, which meant, "Don't crab the sale. This is what he wants." The stone was priced at $7,500. Unintimidated, I picked up another larger and finer stone, priced at $22,500, and said, "This is the stone I would recommend. There is nothing wrong with the other stone, except it's not fine enough for your wife. I don't want to sell you a diamond that won't compare favorably with those of your wife's friends." He looked at it for a few minutes, thought about it, and said, "I think you're right. I'll take it with me." The salesman almost

127

fainted, for not knowing who his customer was he had misjudged his buying capacity. I did know, and what was more important, I made the sale of the stone which *would* be right for his wife. (There is a fine line between making a good and a bad sale, for if you sell a person an article beyond his financial capacity, you've made a bad sale; if you sell him something not as good as he should have, you've also made a bad sale. In both instances, it is likely that the sale won't "stick." It all comes back to selling satisfaction.) But that's not the end of this story. Since the new customer wanted to take the ring with him, he gave us a bank check for the full amount. The question now was whether he was, in fact, the man I thought he was or an imposter. None of us had ever met him, so he couldn't be identified in the store. It was three-thirty on Christmas Eve, all of the banks were closed, and the bankers were off attending Christmas parties. Finally I reached a vice-president of the bank on which the check was drawn and asked him to describe the man to me, but his description was inconclusive. I asked if he had any distinguishing marks or characteristics. "Yes," he replied, "he has a slight cast in one of his eyes." I ran out, talked to him a moment, scrutinized his eyes, saw what I was looking for, returned to the telephone, and said to my banker friend, "Thanks a lot, I'm satisfied it is he." While we were trying to establish identity and stall for time, I suggested to him that it might be a nice idea for him to pick out a mink coat for his wife, too. By this time I had his full confidence, so the coat sale of $7,500 was made very quickly.

Large ticket sales are always exciting, though I'm prepared to spend just as much time helping a customer make a modest purchase as well. One customer from Lubbock, Texas, had been looking at a mink wrap for several years. Each time she came in, I spent an hour or two trying to encourage her to make up her mind but without success. Finally she came back the fourth year and, after another two-hour session, at last found her dream stole. Then she started to bargain with me. I assured her that our price was firm, and no matter how long she wanted to discuss the matter, the answer was going to be the same. Undaunted, she turned to me and said, "Since there has been no salesperson involved, why don't you give me the benefit of the selling commission?" to which I replied, "Mrs. Allen, you have had the benefit of the undivided attention of one of the highest salaried salespersons in Neiman-Marcus, with more knowledge of furs than anyone in the Southwest, for which you have not been charged one extra penny. Neither you nor anyone else can buy this garment for less than the marked price." Very meekly she accepted this final verdict and wrote a check for the full amount.

A few days later I was tested by a man who came into the fur department accompanied by his wife and sister-in-law. The wife very quickly selected two fur coats and her sister found one to her liking. The three garments totaled $9,000. The husband pulled out a roll of hundred-dollar bills and offered me $8,500. I thanked him very much, but told him that we had only one price on our merchandise, whether it was for cash or credit. He counted out another $500, commenting, "Well, it didn't hurt to try."

Several years before, we had eliminated the traditional "August Fur Sale," which most stores ran, on the ground that in most cases the values were not bona fide. Many years back, when there was little or no fur business in August, manufacturers would make special merchandise at some savings, which retailers could advertise to lure in customers during the summer, but as these sales proved successful and as manufacturers found August becoming their peak month, the special values began to disappear. We advertised these changing market conditions and told our customers that if they wanted bargains, they should wait until our January clearances and special purchases, but if they wanted to buy from maximum stocks at fair competitive prices, with the additional advantage of paying over a six-month period of time, they should buy from us in August. We guaranteed that our regularly priced August furs would compete with any other retailer's so-called

August savings, and were able to prove this so often that we built a substantially profitable August business despite competitive sales. It came as no surprise to us that our customers responded to a clear and truthful presentation of the facts.

Normally, any purchases made over and above budgetary limits could be made only after lengthy long-distance telephone discussions with my father. In 1943, encouraged by the booming business trend and the demand for fine merchandise, I took a gamble on my own, which fortunately turned out successfully. In January I was visiting one of our leading fur suppliers, who was so overstocked that he offered me his entire stock — a wholesale value of $225,000 — at a reduction of $33\frac{1}{3}\%$. The collection was of superb quality with a great variety of styles and types of fur. I could visualize a tremendously successful special purchase event, so I made him a counteroffer of a discount of 50%. We argued for about two hours, during which time he grieved about the loss he would be taking at even a third off his regular prices. I had learned enough from my father and Aunt Carrie about buying off-price merchandise to make me stand firm on the proposition that if I couldn't make the buy at the right price to give our customers irresistible bargains, I'd be better off leaving it alone. Finally, at 7:30 P.M., the manufacturer gave in, on the condition that we would send him a check immediately upon receipt of the goods. I went back to my hotel and called my father. "I've just spent $112,500 of our money," I told him how, and then described the various coats included in the buy. He said, "That's a lot of money, but I think you did the right thing." His only regret, I believe, was that he hadn't been present to participate. We offered our customers the finest mink, sable, marten, fox, broadtail, and fisher coats at 50% of their regular prices and within two days had recouped our total investment; within a week we sold 90% of the units purchased. The success of this venture led the way in following years to great January special purchases of the best furs in

130

our manufacturers' stocks, which we passed on to our customers at appropriate savings.

It's one thing to make adjustments promptly and properly. It's another to go out looking for trouble. If a customer comes into the store wearing a Neiman-Marcus suit, the collar of which doesn't fit properly, we call it to his attention tactfully and ask him to bring it back so we can refit it, without charge. This attention to customer's interests *after* the sale has always paid off. One day I saw one of our very good out-of-town customers wearing an expensive mink coat I had sold her the month before. She came over to tell me how much she enjoyed it, and thanked me for the assistance I had given her at the time of its purchase. I asked her to turn around so that I could see the back, and I observed something I didn't like. The guard hairs of the skins in the center back were showing signs of wear, which was most unusual in a fine-quality mink coat. I pointed out this defect to the customer and told her I wanted to either replace the skins, if possible, or make her another coat. She had paid $7,500 for the coat, and was entitled to better wear than she was getting. She might have eventually made this discovery herself, but by anticipating her complaint, I provided her with a topic of conversation among her friends that probably sold another dozen mink coats for us. As it turned out, the skins could not be replaced, and I had to make a completely new coat for her, taking the loss without regret.

Encouraged by my fur buy, I made another purchase later in the year which turned out to be equally successful. I had learned that Parke-Bernet in New York was having an auction of furniture from the estate of J. P. Morgan. I attended the sale and bought, without consultation with my father, about thirty pieces of furniture and porcelain, which we promptly advertised and sold out in a single day. "From the collection of J. P. Morgan" proved to be the magic phrase which brought customers to us from all over the state.

I was an inexperienced auction buyer, but the pieces were good, and the combined labels of J. P. Morgan and Neiman-Marcus gave our customers the provenance they desired.

The subject of expansion was on my father's mind constantly. He was always dreaming how one department or another could be enlarged to improve the quality and scope of our services. He was fascinated with the idea of establishing a branch in a neighboring city, but he could never quite muster the courage to take the final step. Of course there were the problems of financing, but the overriding objection which both he and Aunt Carrie recognized was the problem of maintaining highly personalized buying and selling supervision over remote operations. In 1937 we were offered the opportunity to acquire the Garfinckel store in Washington, D.C., following the death of Mr. Garfinckel. My father was on his way to Europe to visit a health spa and didn't want to cancel the trip to become involved in the negotiations. He told the brokers that if the business was still available when he returned, he would be interested in it, but unfortunately it was sold a month later. It would have been a fine purchase, for Washington was then on the threshold of great growth and we would have been in a position to maintain the fine-quality image which its founder had established.

A few years later we were given the chance to buy a retail business in Houston, so my father and I went there to examine it and to discuss its purchase with the landlord, Jesse Jones, who incidentally owned the most important newspaper, most of the property on Main Street, most of the motion picture theaters, his own electric generating and heating plant, and the two leading hotels. He *was* Mr. Houston! This was long before the days of electronic bugging, but we were forewarned to watch our conversation in our hotel suite, for it was rumored that Mr. Jones could be fully aware of all significant conversations taking place in his hotels. The next day we visited Mr. Jones in his office and told him of our possible interest in subletting the property in question. He was very cordial and expressed his interest in having us as tenants, provided we would agree to run double the advertising lineage in *The Chronicle* (his paper) rather than in the competitive paper, to buy our heating and electricity from his company, and to use his hotels exclusively for our buyers' visits and for entertainment purposes. This generous proposal cooled our interests in downtown Houston, so we shifted our attention to a semisuburban location in a building partially occupied by the Junior League. At the last minute my father shied away from it, because I think subconsciously he was afraid of both the risk factor of another store and the problems of possible dilution of the family's efforts.

In 1945, opportunity knocked on the door again, when the Young-Quinlan Company in Minneapolis was offered to us on the death of Miss Quinlan. This time other factors were involved in a negative decision. The country was at war, my brothers were in the service, we had a distinct manpower shortage, and the very distance between Dallas and Minneapolis militated against the deal. We told the executors of the estate that if the property were still available after the war, we would like to consider it; but it, too, was sold promptly to another retail organization which lacked the understanding of how to operate the delicate mechanism of a deluxe quality women's fashion specialty store. This was unfortunate for both Neiman-Marcus and Minneapolis, because it was an ideal opportunity for us, and we could have preserved the unique character of the business into which Elizabeth Quinlan had poured her life.

During my tenure in Washington, I met a young lawyer from New York City who was a captain in the Chemical Warfare Service branch of the army by the name of Jack Javits. We were both staying at the Hay Adams Hotel and frequently dined together, discussing the effects of the war on our postwar economy. He felt so deeply about the problems he foresaw that he had decided not to go back to the practice of law, but to dedicate himself to some type of public service. He was later elected a United States Senator from New York. He stimulated me to become more sensitive to the forces of social and economic change, and I expressed them some time later in a speech before the Fashion Group in New York on March 17, 1943, in which I forecast:

Surprisingly there are some who still believe that when the war is over, we will go back to the kind of life and business practice we had at the beginning of the war. Those who so believe have failed, in my opinion, to understand the lessons of history. The world is never static and the new problems of the peace and reconstruction will make for a different world than existed in December, 1941.

What kind of retailing we will have will depend on what kind of economy we have after the war. The nature of our economy will depend, in turn, on how long this war lasts and what kind of peace we are intelligent enough to conceive. Two major factors, however, seem apparent to me: First — free enterprise has shown a sufficient belated vitality in arising to the needs of the war effort that it has regained a great amount of prestige that it lost through its hibernation during the depression. Second — the workings of war-time regulations have given many of the critics of the profit system a new respect for the amazing efficiency of the delicate supply and demand mechanism.

Our post-war economy, whether it be on an international or isolationist basis, will necessitate a continuance of governmental influence on industry . . . But a free enterprise system, even subject to governmental regulation of a sound type, is in no way intolerable for retail distribution.

And then, less academically and closer to my own trade, I said:

Democratization of clothes really started with the introduction of rayon. The new fibers and fabrics, the new manufacturing methods of tomorrow should complete the process.

But not only will apparel change, so will *most* of the products we sell. As they change, so will the stores in which we sell them. Mass production may well call for mass distribution on a far greater scale than we have heretofore experienced.

Our customers will change, too — they will have new tastes developed by war incomes, new ambitions as airplanes bring the world

134

to them, new buying patterns instead of the old habits. Perhaps competition will become two-dimensional as customers fly to shop in another city a few hours away, instead of comparing values down the street.

The excess profits tax encouraged extravagant advertising and sales promotion efforts during the war and it helped create loose spending habits, completely antithetical to those we had practiced during the Depression. Since Uncle Sam was paying 90% of the costs, we made our window and interior displays more exciting and dramatic. For special color promotions we brought into the store live magnolia trees, hundreds of blooming rosebushes in a new color, Fashion Rose, seven thousand fresh-cut carnations. At Christmastime, we transformed the store into a fairyland, spotlighting a giant Christmas tree on our first floor, which varied from an ice tree one year to a white ostrich feather tree the next, to a cut-crystal one the following year. All of these efforts were exercises in showmanship seldom seen in retail stores, contributing to the "fabulous" legend which characterized Neiman-Marcus. It encouraged more customers to want to buy from Neiman-Marcus; it also influenced more manufacturers to want to sell to Neiman-Marcus. All of this led the writer George Sessions Perry to declare, "Neiman-Marcus is not a store; it is a state of mind or a state of grace."

My youngest brother, Lawrence, who had been wounded in Africa, was discharged from the army in 1944 and entered the business to start his retail career, despite some earlier consideration of law. He had attended the Harvard Business School following his graduation from Harvard College, and had married shortly thereafter. He spent six months in the store between graduation and his call to the service, but his business experience actually began when he returned.

As an introduction to his retailing career, Lawrence was sent to New York to spend six months under the tutelage of Moira

Cullen. He was serious, analytical, and fashion-sensitive, but stubborn. This latter quality had shown up in his childhood, perhaps as an expression of rebellion against authority, but it persisted through his military and business careers. His reports were thorough and extremely well reasoned, but usually late — another form of rebellion. Being tardy to a meeting or in turning in a requested plan may have been a subconscious way of demonstrating his disregard for constituted authority. On the other hand, he learned the fashion business quickly, piloting our couture business to the most profitable level in its history.

Dealing with designers is no easy job, for designing is a form of exhibitionism just as acting is, and those involved in creativity are necessarily supreme egotists, whose psyches are in perpetual need of massage. They all want to hear nice things about their collections, never the sordid news that their clothes didn't sell well because they were too heavy, too bare, too new, or too old. Some years later, Lawrence had an unhappy experience with one of our top makers, Norman Norell, whose deliveries were always so late that the clothes normally arrived only a week before the seasonal clearances. He went to see Norell one day and told him that the profitability on his line had been seriously affected by the lateness of delivery, showing him selling records with delivery dates noted. Norell flew into a rage, asking Lawrence to leave the showroom and promising to sell someone else in Dallas in preference to Neiman-Marcus, with whom he had been associated since he had started business.

The "someone else" apparently was not too successful selling Norell's late-delivery clothes either, so a couple of seasons later feelers were sent out by Norell or by one of his associates to see if we wouldn't come back. We agreed to talk, but before the meetings could be held, stories had been leaked to *Women's Wear Daily* which reported on the proposed discussions, destroying any possible reconciliation. This was the only time in our history that we lost a line as a result of frankness. The only other time we lost an important line was in the late twenties, when Al Neiman agreed to finance Emmet Joyce, the designer for Hattie Carnegie, to go into business for himself. Miss Carnegie was understandably indignant and closed our account. Several years later, when Joyce had gone bankrupt and Al Neiman was no longer associated with us, I was able to reestablish business relations with Hattie Carnegie. As a result of the Norell episode, we have trained our buyers and merchandise men to handle their more temperamental suppliers with tact and diplomacy, even when we are completely right.

Unfortunately, the better end of the garment industry is the only one which consistently delivers its products with little regard for the consumers' needs or timing requirements. Collections are shown to the store buyers, and in most cases, only after all the orders have been placed are the fabrics ordered. Most of the materials are made abroad; it takes from six to nine weeks to weave them, another week to ship and clear them through customs, and then a month to manufacture them into garments. In years gone by, manufacturers bought their piece goods in advance of the season, so when the buyers came, they could make deliveries in two or three weeks. This system entailed markdowns on unsold fabrics, so the makers decided they would not buy goods until they had orders. Undoubtedly this has helped manufacturers, but at the expense of the retailers' profits and the customers' satisfaction. To overcome this situation, we have sometimes bought the fabrics in advance of the season ourselves, thus relieving the maker of any financial risk.

With the war's end, Edward and Herbert Jr. returned to the store. Availability of merchandise was still a serious problem, so we asked Eddie to move to New York to head our buying office, in the belief that it would augment his experience as a merchant and that he would be able to supplement the efforts of our buyers in getting wanted goods in short supply. He filled that job for several years with distinction before returning to Dallas to relieve me of the general merchandising responsibility. We placed Herbert in the man's store, first as the assistant to the merchandise manager, and

137

then as the buyer of men's furnishings, where he displayed great taste and flair.

With all of my brothers back in the business, I began to guide our publicity stories to emphasize the Neiman-Marcus story as a combined family effort. While the stories usually mentioned all of our names, often they were focused on my father or me. This was embarrassing to me and painful to my brothers, for I'm sure it looked as though I were trying to dominate the show. I complained to Marihelen McDuff, our public relations director, who replied, "The press is almost always interested in a single shot, not a family portrait. If you want your brothers to share in the publicity, get them to go out and do something newsworthy on their own." Heeding her advice, I encouraged them to take speaking assignments as I had done in various nearby towns, where colleges and women's clubs were besieging us constantly for speakers. I turned over fashion show announcing to them, which was a tough assignment, for I had developed a professional technique in entertaining, editorializing, and selling in my commentary. It was not enough to bear the name of Marcus; it was necessary to stand on individual accomplishment.

My father's hypertension began to affect his eyesight to the point that he was unable to read without a magnifying glass. He went to specialists in New York, Baltimore, Boston, and California, but none could retard the continuing deterioration of his sight. We employed a young student to read the morning paper to him and then take him to his office, where one of us took turns talking about business, reading reports, reviewing financial statements, and calling buyers up with samples of merchandise for him to handle. Even when his sight was completely gone, he would run his sensitive hands through a mink coat, saying, "This is the kind I like to *see*." Or, he would handle a pair of shoes, the finish of which he would criticize on the ground that the stitching was too coarse or the sole too rough. He had always been a finicky eater, and his loss of sight must have intensified the discrimination of his taste buds.

He could detect the slightest variation from a recipe, the presence of a mite too much salt or too little pepper, adding greatly to the tribulations of my mother, who was trying in every way possible to keep him happy, while grieving herself about the terrible catastrophe that had overtaken this man whose whole life had been related to what he saw.

One day in the store's restaurant he complained about the ice cream we were serving, insisting that it wasn't like the ice cream we served at home. He objected to the coating it left in his mouth, which I attributed to his imagination. The next month I was in Los Angeles, and one evening about midnight, driving back to the hotel with a friend, we passed a spot on Sunset Strip where a large crowd was lined up on the sidewalk. I asked what kind of attraction could gather a crowd at that time of night and my friend replied that it was a new ice cream parlor called Wil Wright. I decided to try this extraordinary ice cream that could command a midnight crowd, and when I read in the menu the description of it — made from pure cream with no additives, and a 22% butterfat content — and then tasted it, I knew what my father was talking about. Before leaving for Dallas the next day, I called Wil Wright and told him that I wanted to import his ice cream to Texas. He replied that it was impossible. I said, "No, it may be improbable, but it's not impossible. Ship us ten gallons packed in dry ice by air freight, whatever it may cost." When we served the ice cream to my father he was delighted. "That's as fine as we ever made at home. Let's serve it in our restaurant all the time." The trouble was, though, that it cost about twenty dollars a gallon, so we had to develop a method for shipping it by train to reduce the price; later we shipped it by refrigerated trucks when our needs had grown to sufficient size. What my father had noticed in the ice cream and had criticized was the gelatin mix which almost all ice cream producers now use as a substitute for cream. In the interests of economy, we tried to get the ice cream made in Dallas, but as Wil Wright later explained to me, you have to have an old-fashioned ice cream machine to make ice cream with cream; the new machines are geared to gelatin, and cream is simply too thick for them to handle. When I was in his office months later, he had a request for one of his recipes; he reached in his desk drawer, pulled out a printed sheet, and handed it to the customer. I said, "Aren't you crazy to give out your recipes like that?" "No," he replied, "when they find out how expensive it is to make, they don't copy it."

This was one of my father's last quests for the best, and I was happy that I had been able by luck to find the answer for him. We had Wil Wright ice cream exclusively in Texas for twenty years, selling it by the dish in our Zodiac restaurant and by the gallon to party-giving customers all over the state.

During the last year of my father's life, our advertising director, Zula McCauley, retired, and we had to find a replacement for this wonderful woman who had interpreted my father's thoughts so skillfully in our daily advertising messages. We discovered a young woman, Virginia Sisk, in San Francisco, who offered a fresh and more contemporary approach to advertising. We took a chance on her, the art director, Chuck Gruen, she brought with her, and the fashion artist, Betty Brader, he brought with him. The team proposed a radical change in our format and in the style of our fashion illustration. I am frank to admit that if my father had been in good health and had his eyesight, he would never have permitted the changeover. He would have objected violently, but he would have been wrong. The war was over, there was a new mood in the air, and advertising as well as merchandising had to respond to the times. Customers were shocked, but they eventually liked the new look, with the exception of a few of the most conservative ones. We won advertising awards galore, but what was more important, the new advertising sold merchandise *and* the store, and as a result of its success our buyers became enthusiastic about it. We had created the first new trend in advertising since Lord &

140

Taylor developed their unique and successful style under Dorothy Shaver's direction.

Our advertising attained additional heights under the direction of Jane Trahey, a copywriter I had discovered at Carson's in Chicago. She had a complete irreverence for fashion and enjoyed poking fun at it. "Why kick it around?" I asked her one day. "I don't give a damn what you think about fashion personally, but as long as you are in the business of selling it, then you have an obligation to sell as well and as intelligently as you can." She reluctantly admitted to some hangups about the overserious attitude some of her advertising colleagues took on fashion, but recognized that her satirizing approach was not consistent with good selling. She had one of the brightest minds I've ever come in contact with in the retail business, and in a short time she had rationalized the matter to her satisfaction and was turning out some of the most brilliant fashion advertising the country had ever seen. We worked well as a team, for I respected her merchandise judgment and her sharp humor; she in turn took my criticisms of copy approach unbegrudgingly. She has since set up her own advertising agency in New York, where she has developed a small and respected business.

We have contributed presidents to many institutions including Joseph Magnin, Cartier, Germaine Monteil Cosmetics, Bonwit Teller, Swanson's, and others. Some have been successful; some have failed. Part of what they have learned at Neiman-Marcus is transportable, but part is applicable only to our stores. Those who have failed, it has always seemed to me, did not discern properly just what to take with them and what to leave behind. Some Neiman-Marcus techniques work well for the simple reason that our clientele has been educated over a period of time to understand them; some of our own well-tried techniques work in some of our own communities better than in others. No one of our alumni has had any success in transplanting a Neiman-Marcus type operation full blown to another institution. Each store has its own personality, its own heritage, its own problems, all of which require personalized and not ready-made solutions.

I've always felt a reluctance to playing God when any of my associates come to tell me of their decisions to leave us for jobs which apparently offer greater responsibilities, larger salaries, and more glittering titles. Even when I think they are biting off more than they can chew, I hesitate to tell them so, for who knows what heights a person can reach, given the opportunity. My appraisal of their capabilities may be wrong and I don't want to be guilty of slamming the doors of opportunity in the face of an ambitious person. I will review the pros and cons of an offer, but after doing so, I leave it to the individual to reach a decision. Success or failure is often determined not by ability alone, but by timing, economic conditions, internal competition, *and* by luck.

I made one exception to my rule in Paris in 1958, when Art Buchwald, an old friend, asked my advice about getting out of the newspaper business for a possible career in business. "I'm afraid I'll wake up one morning to find out that I've run out of anything funny to write about. Perhaps I should go into retailing or exporting," he said. "No," I replied, "your columns are not based on your own humor but upon the humorous things that happen in the world, and the world will provide you with a constant source of amusement. Stay where you are and continue to do what you are doing." A few months later he wrote his famous spoof interview with Jim Hagerty, President Eisenhower's press secretary. It was so good that the New York edition of the *Herald Tribune* printed it on its front page. That was a turning point in Art's career and he went on from there to become America's best known satirist, with national syndication.

With the return of all his sons to the business, my father established the custom of holding a family meeting shortly before Christmas, at which time he reviewed the accomplishments of

142

the past year and the problems of the ensuing one, his hopes for continued family solidarity and the need for the brothers to be of help to each other in times of individual adversity. "There will be times," he warned, "when one or another of you will be weak, and that is the time when the strong must come to the aid of the one who is in trouble." He then addressed each of us individually, making kind, constructive comments on our performances both in and out of the store. His discourse invariably ended with the directive to maintain at all times the highest standard of ethical conduct in both our personal and business lives. He then passed out his Christmas gifts in the form of equal shares of Neiman-Marcus common stock, with the admonition that we should safeguard this investment, which would become more valuable over the years, and never to let it pass into unfriendly hands. My father had a constant concern about maintaining family control of the business and the discomfort that dissident stockholders could cause. He realized that marriages were not necessarily lifelong contracts, and he did not want the authority of the management of the business ever to be embarrassed by a hostile shareholder. These apprehensions were undoubtedly born from his own experience with Al Neiman and other "outside" stockholders.

His annual message never varied, and any one of us could have predicted his words from memory. Nonetheless, each of us looked forward to the occasion, to the reiteration of his charges and admonitions, and to our mutual pledges of family unity. Mother always attended these meetings, and at her insistence the wives were invited, for although my father was very fond of his daughters-in-law, it took him time to accept them into the familial bloodstream. The meetings in the latter years of my father's life were usually emotionally charged because of his failing eyesight and there wasn't a dry eye in the group.

My father was very devoted to his family and to his business; as a matter of fact, he regarded his business as a member of his family. An old Jewish story might very well pertain to him. It is about a merchant who was very ill, and his four sons gathered at his bedside in filial solicitude. He glanced around at all of them and said, "I appreciate your interest in the state of my health, but who's minding the store?"

Probably the single greatest disappointment in my business career was the failure of my father, on his own initiative, to name me as president prior to my fortieth birthday. Mother had told me that he had mentioned the possibility to her, but he never discussed the matter with me. I am convinced that if I had made an issue of it with him, he would have stepped up to the position of chairman of the board, and made me president, but I was determined not to engineer the move myself. I know that he had full confidence in my ability; his delegation of responsibility and his pride in my accomplishments both within and outside the business were testimony to his regard. He probably never knew how much it would have meant to me to attain this office while I was still in my thirties. I had graduated from high school at sixteen, from college at twenty, and to have made the presidency before forty would, in my opinion, have completed my track record. I was his acknowledged successor; he had obviously thought of the move, yet he was never able to put his idea into action. It was perfectly clear why he was reluctant to make any change in status after his health began to fail, for that would have been a recognition of his own diminishing physical capacity, but why he didn't approach this change at an earlier date will always remain a mystery to me.

In December of 1950, my father had a severe stroke and died a few days later. The Board of Directors elected Carrie Neiman chairman of the board, me, president and chief executive officer, and Edward, executive vice-president.

8

Taking Over the Reins

AFTER THE BOARD MEETING at which I was made president, I gathered my brothers together to reiterate the need for continuing family solidarity and to caution us all that the test of this concept was about to begin. Heretofore, we had been held together by the colossal strength of a great man, our father, who was both the head of the family and the controlling stockholder of the company. "Now," I said, "we stand as four brothers with equal shares in the company, with theoretically equal rights as stockholders. I have been named president and chief executive officer and I shall be forced at some time in the future to make decisions which may be contrary to the judgments of one or the other of you. I shall attempt at all times to be fair and objective, but as long as I am the chief executive officer I shall expect you to accept my decisions, even when you may disagree." All three of them recognized my seniority in both age and experience, and pledged their sincere cooperation without reservation.

Being the boss of three brothers with comparable financial stakes and a closeness in age is somewhat different from being the stock-controlling boss of four sons. No one of us was a shrinking violet, and our egos frequently collided. My father could rule by dictate; I had to administer by persuasion. The situation of four brothers, each separated from the other by only about four years in age, operating within the confines of four walls and under one roof, was not ideal for any of us; yet in some ways we succeeded remarkably well, for a time, at least.

Any successful retail business, in my opinion, must be the reflection of the aims and ideals of the executive director, who sets the basic policies for operation and who vigorously pursues the execution of them. This in no way implies that he does it alone, for he must have the collaboration of scores of able associates, but it does mean that the business cannot function well under a committee management. There must be a head who makes some of the tough final decisions after having heard all the arguments, pro and con, and some of those decisions may prove to be unpopular and even wrong. Nevertheless, he has to make them and make them decisively. My brothers did not always agree, but they did accept my decisions in good spirit. One eventually left the business for personal reasons and I resisted his subsequent attempts to return for business reasons which subjected me to a certain amount of public criticism. This is the type of hard decision which a chief executive must be prepared to make; it is doubly hard when family considerations come into conflict with sound business judgment. The integrity of management is at stake whenever it displays favoritism to a member of the family, and for that reason I have always insisted that members of the Marcus family conduct themselves in a manner as good or better than other persons in our employ. Nepotism is one of the most debilitating of all business diseases.

The wartime bulge in sales did not disappear with the advent of peace; instead, sales continued to rise, further taxing our capacity to serve our customers with dignity and ease. We debated an expansion program in the downtown store and in a suburban area, but were concerned by the rising cost of construction. One night in 1948 I attended a dinner given in honor of the chairman of the board of Sears, General Robert E. Wood, who announced that his company was going to embark on a massive building program, with major emphasis on Texas and the West Coast. After the dinner I asked the general whether he was concerned about building costs. He replied that he thought they were cheaper at that moment than they would ever be again.

This bit of advice encouraged us to reassess our situation and led us to decide to add two floors to our downtown store, to build a suburban store for protection against any outside competition seeking an entry into the Dallas market, and to establish a service center to accommodate our receiving and marking functions, fur storage, and supplies. We concluded to pursue all these expansions simultaneously. The downtown expansion presented us with some vexing problems, part of which involved our internal transportation system and part, the adequate housing of our service facilities. Two extra floors would put a strain on our elevator capacity; the addition of extra elevators would not only be expensive, but would raise havoc with our floor layouts. After careful study, I recognized that escalators were our only solution, but I encountered strong opposition from both my father and Aunt Carrie, who felt that escalators were suited for department stores, but not for a deluxe specialty store. I countered their arguments by saying that specialty stores had never used them because they couldn't afford them, and that department stores had never spent the money to design them as an aesthetic feature, as I felt we could. After months of debate I won, but Aunt Carrie had the last word when she said, "Well, I'll never ride them, nor will any of our good customers." Eleanor LeMaire, our interior designer, did a masterful job of designing them with a hanging garden between them, and thus created a new technique for escalator construction which has been widely copied.

We knew that the downtown store could not handle the operating needs of an additional store, and we didn't want to run two separate receiving and delivery departments, so we were forced into the solution of housing these operations in a new building located halfway between both stores. That's why we had to embark on

149

all three projects at the same time — each move was dependent on the other. My father's sight had gone completely by the time Preston Center, our new suburban store, was completed, so he never got to see it, though it was graphically described to him. He had passed away by the time of the completion of the other two buildings. Aunt Carrie did live long enough to see them, but true to her word, she never did ride the escalators.

In the course of redesigning the downtown store and shifting departments, we encountered some serious space problems, even with the addition of two more floors. Our decorating department gave us particular concern, for it required a tremendous amount of space in order to set up model rooms and to house an adequate display of furniture. It carried a tremendous amount of prestige, but it produced more problems than profits. We were afflicted with customers' changes of mind and decorators' mismeasurements to the point that rejects filled our warehouse space, seriously diminishing our profits. If a good customer decided she wanted pink draperies instead of the yellow she had previously selected, we would try to resist her, but when she said "If you insist that I keep them, I'll cancel the order for the new mink coat I just gave you," we would capitulate. We had debated the subject of whether to close the department many times, but never could reach a conclusion, hating to admit defeat.

The matter settled itself one day after I had been wrestling with space allocations when a customer came to see me about a job we had just completed. "Your decorating department has just finished doing over my apartment and it is perfectly beautiful," she said. I told her how happy I was to hear such pleasant news, and thanked her for taking the time to tell me of her satisfaction. She replied, "There's only one thing wrong, and that's my bill, which is just about twice the amount I had anticipated." "You signed a contract, of course," I commented. "Yes, I did, and here it is, and you will see that my contract is for $24,765, and my statement is for $49,573." "You must have changed your mind at some point during the job," I suggested. "No, I didn't," she said. "I was afraid I might, so I took a trip around the world while the work was going on to keep from being tempted." I immediately called the decorator and asked him to explain the discrepancy between the contract price and the billing. I said, "Did you have any authorization from Mrs. Dunbar to deviate from your original proposal?" "No," he replied, "I just knew she liked nice things and didn't think she would mind." I gave the customer credit for $24,808, fired the decorator on the spot, and decided at that moment to close the department. Costly as the adjustment was, it forced us to make a decision which saved us a great deal of money in future years.

We should never have been in the decorating business in the first place, for we could never exercise complete control over a group of decorators with divergent tastes. We knew what kind of decorating we wanted to stand for, but no member of our top management staff had the technical ability or time to ride herd on ten interior designers, each of whom had individual ideas of what was in good decorative taste. We weren't proud of the jobs on which we made a profit, and we lost money on those which met our standards. We were forced to admit defeat, partly because of our own inability to administer the operation, and partly because most clients who give you big jobs are "psychopaths" at that particular stage in their lives. It was a lesson expensively learned.

Variously I have been described as "the greatest pitchman of them all," "the man who has made more women happy," "the melancholy Plato of retailing," "a maverick," "a left-winger," "a gentleman," "a benevolent dictator of fashion," and "bearded and bald and an inch or two taller than short." Since truth sometimes lies in the eye of the beholder, I presume some of these descriptions of me fit under certain circumstances. I do love to sell, and I make an all-out effort to discover the motivations which make a customer want to say yes. The happiest moments of my day are those involved in devising letters to customers in distant places to inform

151

them of some unusual merchandise offering, or working on a multi-faceted advertising program, or leaving my office in response to a call from the selling floor to close a sale on a sable wrap for $50,000, or helping a man select a $10 sweater for his daughter. We have one inviolable rule in our organization — that the customer comes first — and any staff meeting can be interrupted to meet the call of a customer.

Since whoever described me as "the man who has made more women happy" failed to give full details of what he meant, I must presume that he was referring to the fact that I have tried to create an atmosphere in which women enjoy shopping, that I have brought together the best in fashion and quality from which they can select, and that I have given them honest and candid counsel. That I will admit to. If the writer had anything else in mind, I must take refuge under the fifth amendment!

Women's Wear Daily, with its penchant for pithy labels, hung "the melancholy Plato of retailing" tag on me after a speech I made at the University of Southern California on "The Death of Elegance," in which I made some rather acid comments on the state of fashion and the conditions of manufacturing and marketing. I said,

The death of elegance was forecast over one hundred and ten years ago by Alexis de Tocqueville, when he visited America and wrote *Democracy in America*. Among other prophetic observations, he predicted the inevitable decline of taste in a democratic society. In a stratified society, such as France had at that time, a *fine craftsman has only one set of customers, the aristocracy*. They demand the best and the craftsman strives to give it to them. . . . But those days are gone forever. Elegance was a product to a large extent of hand labor, not mass production; of low labor cost, not $1.60 per hour minimum pay; of an elegant educated aristocracy, not the Great Society.

Despite my great love and devotion to the specialty store retailing field, I don't regard it as the most important activity of

152

mankind, and I don't mind saying so. I take my business seriously and work extremely hard at it, as I would at any other endeavor which attracted my interest, but I can still take a good philosophical look at it and its relative importance to the world scene.

No doubt many of my business friends in the community regard me as a "maverick" or a "left-winger," depending on their own political orientation. It is bromidic to bemoan the use of labels, but that's not going to make people stop using them. I should prefer to describe myself as a "progressive," who believes so strongly in the principles of the free enterprise system that I recognize the necessity for constant reform and improvement to save the system from itself. That, of course, would make me a "maverick" or a "left-winger" in the eyes of those who believe that salvation lies in turning back the hands of the clock to the late nineteenth century. Dallas is a very conservative city and always has been; the majority of our customers are conservative. My support of "liberal" candidates and causes has resulted in some raised eyebrows and has been responsible for some charge accounts being closed in protest. One of the conditions on which I came into the business was that I would always have the right of free expression, and while I have never gone looking for ways to antagonize customers, I have never shirked when I thought I should speak out. People have often asked, "How do you get away with it?" I think the answer lies in the fact that the vast majority of people respect my sincerity, which can hardly be characterized as selfish, and in the fact that I have been financially successful. They may disagree with me, but I think I've earned their respect.

In the early fifties, I was elected president of the Board of Trustees of the Dallas Art Association, which operated the city-owned and partially financed Museum of Fine Arts. The board was split between those who were eager for the museum to buy and show the works of twentieth-century abstract artists and those who believed that creative art had ended with the nineteenth century.

153

When I proposed that we buy a sixty-four inch-high sculpture of the "King and Queen" by Henry Moore for $7,500, I was voted down on the grounds that the work was too controversial and that the community wasn't ready for such radical art. Today that work has a probable value in excess of $300,000. In order to give contemporary art a degree of respectability, I resorted to a device I had learned in the fashion business. People as a whole respect outside authority. New York respects Paris, Philadelphia respects New York, Minneapolis respects Philadelphia; so I encouraged our director to organize an exhibition of avant-garde works from the private collections of some outstanding American business leaders, none of whom even Senator McCarthy could have branded as subversive. The exhibition was called "Some Business Men Collect Contemporary Art," and we borrowed paintings and sculptures from Nelson Rockefeller, Albert Lasker, Burton Tremaine, and a host of other collectors around the country. We then asked each of them to write a letter to a half-dozen friends and acquaintances in Dallas suggesting they drop by the museum to see what he had loaned. I reasoned that if a Dallas doctor or banker or insurance executive became aware that one of his respected peers in another city thought well enough of contemporary art to invest money in it, he might conclude that there must be something to this thing called "Modern Art." The plan worked; the show was a success, and we removed some of the opprobrium from the whole subject.

It must be remembered that this was the time of the McCarthy crusade and the infamous "Dondero List" of writers, artists, and actors who at one time in their lives had been, or were suspected of having been, connected with some organization that Congressman Dondero regarded as having Communist affiliations. Many perfectly innocent persons were ruined by this reckless listing of names without proof and had no recourse for rectification. It was a clear violation of the Bill of Rights, but at that time, the Bill of Rights had not yet been discovered by all the American people.

154

The museum very innocently had booked a traveling exhibition, "Sports in Art," being circulated by *Sports Illustrated*, a publication of that "archradical" Henry Luce to help finance the American Olympic Team's preparation for the Olympic Games to be held in Australia. A few weeks prior to the opening of the show, I received a phone call from the banker Fred Florence, asking me to come over to see him. He inquired about the show, which I explained to him, not understanding the motive for his sudden interest in the affairs of the museum. He said, "I think you're in for some trouble. I've just had a visit from a fellow citizen who is acting as spokesman for the Dallas Patriotic Council, and he has expressed great displeasure about certain paintings represented in this exhibition. I would advise you personally to avoid a controversy and remove the paintings, for the council has threatened to picket both the museum and your store, since you are the president of both organizations." He then gave me the numbers of the objectionable paintings, which had obviously been picked up from a showing in another city since the exhibition had not yet been hung in Dallas. I told him that this was a matter for the board's decision, but that I would strongly recommend against acceding to the request. After I returned to my office and reviewed the catalogue, I found that the artists involved and their subjects were Ben Shahn and his watercolor of a baseball game, Leon Kroll, who was represented by a winter scene with sleighs, William Zorach, who had depicted an elderly man fishing, and Yasuo Kuniyoshi, whose painting was of skaters. Hardly subversive themes!

That was on a Friday afternoon. On Saturday I paid calls on the publishers of the two daily papers at their homes and asked if they believed in the principle of the freedom of the press. Naturally they replied affirmatively. I followed up by saying, "If you believe in the freedom of the press, then you must certainly accord similar rights of freedom of expression to writers, actors, and artists." When they agreed to that proposition, I told them of the

155

efforts being made by a group of superpatriots to impinge on freedom of expression at the museum, and enlisted their editorial support. They couldn't possibly claim freedom of expression for their papers and then deny it to others, so they assented and promised that they would back us on both the editorial and news pages. If the leader of the opposition had got to them first, he might well have presented the matter in a way which would have committed them to the Patriotic Council.

I took the problem to the Board of Trustees, which by majority vote rejected the council's demands in a statement, ". . . the fundamental issue at stake is that of Freedom and Liberty — not just for the Dallas Museum of Fine Arts, but eventually for our school system, our free press, our library, our orchestra, and many other institutions of our society. We believe that democracy cannot survive if subjected to book burning, thought control, condemnation without trial, proclamation of guilt by association — the very techniques of the Communist or Fascist regimes." Neither the museum nor Neiman-Marcus was picketed as threatened. Later, however, the show, which had been scheduled to go on to Australia to be shown at the time of the games, was canceled by the U.S. Information Agency "due to overall budgetary considerations." It might appear that the agency had knuckled under. Twenty years later in neighboring Fort Worth, the new Kimbell Art Museum presented an exhibition of Impressionist painting from the Hermitage and Pushkin museums to over 200,000 persons who came from great distances to see the show — without an iota of protest. Perhaps the stand taken by the Dallas Art Association twenty years earlier had paved the way.

While we won the battle, we certainly weren't winning the war. McCarthy attracted wide support in Dallas from numerous organizations and individuals, to the point that it became almost impossible to conduct an open and free discussion of political subjects at a dinner party or among business associates. I felt there

156

was need for the expression of a more moderate point of view by recognized leaders who were themselves conservatives, and who could not be branded by anyone as "radical." I consulted with Umphrey Lee, the president of Southern Methodist University, who expressed a willingness to host an Institute on American Freedom at the university if I would organize it. I decided that we needed a local sponsoring committee of business leaders, who were not suspected of liberalism in the eyes of the local community. I have found that almost any businessman is reasonable and can recognize a point of equity if you can talk to him in private, but that the same man in a crowd can be swayed to support the most unreasonable proposition. I therefore tackled them individually and had no difficulty in enlisting their support. We invited Paul Hoffman, then chairman of the Studebaker Company, Kenneth Royal, ex-secretary of war, Gerald Johnson, author and journalist, and Henry Wriston, president of Brown University.

In introducing the speakers, I challenged business leadership to speak out on controversial matters, saying, "When businessmen fail to exercise their constitutional privileges because of fear, then they concurrently forfeit all rights to complain. When they yield to pressures, they allow themselves to be transformed into moral eunuchs. One of the most vicious fallacies to which we are victims these days is the notion that the absence of controversy is a sign of unity. If this were true, dictatorship would be established for all time to come." I concluded by warning, "Business leadership is in some places and cases unaware of the attempts to curtail freedom guaranteed to all of us by our Constitution and Bill of Rights. Business leadership should find out what is going on, what are the motives of those who would curtail freedom of speech and inquiry. Business leadership should be ready to come to the defense of freedom in business, education, religion, law, and government, for wherever freedom is stifled by fear, it may next be strangled by hysteria." The speeches were later published in the autumn

157

issue of the *Southwest Review* and in book form by the Southern Methodist University Press. The organization of this event probably contributed to the labeling of me as a "left-winger."

After the usual start-up problems, our new suburban store, Preston Center, caught on rapidly and proved to us that we could operate multilocationally. This prompted us to consider once more the possibility of going to Houston. While we were searching for a site, we were given the opportunity to buy a long-established specialty store, The Fashion, whose owner wanted to retire. We bought it, thinking this would give us a quick entry into the Houston market, certain exclusive merchandise franchises, and a seasoned sales staff. We renamed the store Neiman-Marcus and restocked it with our own merchandise. Unfortunately, we guessed wrong. The Houston public resented the fact that we hadn't come in with a store as large and luxurious as our Dallas stores; the narrow building occupied seven floors of sales area that proved difficult to operate efficiently and economically; the existing sales staff resisted our efforts to retrain it in the Neiman-Marcus standards of service. We limped along with it for about ten years until we approached the expiration of our lease, and then built a handsome suburban store that captured the imagination of the entire community. My brother Lawrence moved to Houston, giving the store the benefit of his fine taste and merchandising ability. He became an active participant in Houston civic and social life and contributed importantly towards making the store an overwhelming success.

Each of the Marcus brothers has his own group of partisans, but there is one Marcus who outstrips us all in popularity and appreciation — our mother. Everybody is in love with mother.

During my father's lifetime, busily occupied with running a household for five males — no small feat in itself — and tending her gardens, she was happy to see the spotlight of public attention concentrated on my father. She must have reveled in his successes, for after all she was the one who had first foreseen his potential and believed in his ambitions. She taught him the discipline of personal financial management; she indulged the idiosyncrasies of his palate and his penchant for home entertaining on a large and constant basis. During the years of his diminishing eyesight, she was his unfailing companion twenty-four hours a day. She felt the ties of family so deeply that it became almost impossible for her to give a party for outsiders — all the seats were already occupied by aunts and uncles, sisters and brothers, first, second, and third cousins.

She had a green thumb, and it was her interest in plants that encouraged my father to bring exotic tropical specimens into the store for their decorative contribution. Mother had a greenhouse on her estate, which was used in part as a reviving station for plants wilted by exposure in a sunless environment. Upon my father's death, mother was elected to the Board of Directors, and was named vice-president in charge of horticulture. We must be the only organization in the country with an officer bearing this title. Shortly after taking office, she was quoted by Frank X. Tolbert of the *Dallas Morning News*, "I thought it was very nice of my sons and the other directors to want me to have a hand in the planting and care of the store's plants. Only I thought it was kind of an honorary position. I've found out it's a lot of hard work — the kind I like, though." At that time there were 1,800 plants in 60 different locations in the two existing stores. She supervised the activities of the gardeners, calling their attention to the plants which needed to be cut back, fertilized, and watered. She was always on the lookout for exciting new specimens which would enhance the stores' display.

As a widow, with all of her sons married, she had the time to devote to numerous civic activities, with particular emphasis on gardening and civic beautification. She was prominent in the building of the Dallas Garden Center, which has permanent displays of unusual plants and is manned by a permanent director who gives aid and advice to all gardening enthusiasts. She stimulated city

officials into beautifying the city with well-planned planting programs, with emphasis on flowering plants. Inspired by her overwhelming civic interest, her four sons and their wives celebrated her
eightieth birthday by making a gift to the city in her name of a
mile of flowering crabapple trees to line a highway leading to the
county hospital.

Once she was observed pulling dead leaves off an *Aurelia
elegantisima* by a customer who wrote, "There's a very nice-looking
woman whom I frequently see in your store picking dead leaves
from your plants. Surely you can find a better position for a person
of such obvious quality." We thanked her, explaining that the only
higher rank she could have would be my job.

She does not restrict her philanthropy to areas of her personal
interests, but tries to support, within her capabilities, causes in
which her friends are involved as well. She visits her grandchildren
and great-grandchildren regularly, imparting the family legends
and homely bits of common-sense advice on work, thrift, and other
virtues, along with a little cash on the side. At the age of ninety-
two, she is in vigorous health, maintaining a daily schedule which
belies her years. She is fiercely independent, and prefers to associate with young people in preference to "old ladies." If there
were a popularity vote in Dallas, I think she would win it hands
down.

9

Running a Store
with a Split Personality

ALTHOUGH WE MAINTAINED a conservative dividend policy, plowing a substantial part of our earnings back into the business, the financial requirements of our growing volume and expansions taxed our resources. Unwilling to dilute our ownership by the sale of common stock, we resorted to open lines of credit at the banks, term loans, and even the sale of preferred stock. Our debt ratio always ran quite high, and finally on the recommendation of Fred Florence, by now a member of our Board of Directors, we decided to ease our problems by the sale of some debenture bonds. At his suggestion, we visited the Prudential Insurance Company in Newark, where we met with Kerby H. Fisk, head of the bond department, and explained why we wanted to sell Prudential $2,-000,000 of debentures. After reviewing the statements and financial history of our business he said, "I question whether we want to get involved with a company selling only 'whipped cream.' I've read about your sensational sales of furs and diamonds, but if a dip in the economy occurs, you are very apt to be without customers." This was the first time our well-planned public relations program had backfired!

We assured him that we were selling much more than "whipped cream"; that in truth we were selling "milk" as well, and that actually, we sold more "milk" than "whipped cream." We suggested that he come to Dallas to go through our stocks with us, and to review our sales by price-line categories to prove the validity of this statement. He accepted our invitation, and was astonished to find that in addition to selling more mink and vicuña coats than any single store in the country, we also sold thousands of garments at $30, $75, and $100. Thus reassured that our business had a very broad base for consumer support, he agreed to the purchase of the bonds.

Curiously, he wasn't the only one to suffer from this misapprehension. Despite the fact that we may advertise a sable coat for $50,000 once in the course of six months, and dresses at $50 twenty times in the same period, a large number of potential buyers will remember only the sable advertisement, and not the ones for $50 dresses. If you were to query these women about what they want to spend for a dress, a large number would reply "$50," and if you were to follow up this question with another, "Do you buy your dresses at Neiman-Marcus?" you would probably get the answer, "No, I can't afford to shop there." They either ignore our advertisements for less expensive merchandise or don't believe them. However, since we sell large quantities of moderately priced articles in all departments of our stores, we obviously have been able to convince a substantial number of customers that we have things to sell at affordable prices.

There is a reverse twist to this reputation for selling high-priced merchandise. There are women who do read both the $50,000 sable coat and the $50 dress advertisements, and who deliberately choose to buy their $50 dresses from the store that sells $50,000 sable coats. A little bit of the luster of the sable rubs off on the label of every $50 dress. What we proved very early in our history was that it was possible to sell both the finest, most expensive merchandise to those who could afford it and simultaneously well-selected, good-quality merchandise at moderate prices to those in other income strata. Obviously there is a thin market for $50,-000 furs, and if we depended on the sale of them for any substantial portion of our volume, we would have a very small business. Stores of our type which failed to recognize this obvious fact went out of business; others, like Bergdorf Goodman, read the signs correctly when they popularized their clientele by adding their Miss Berg-dorf and Bigi shops. It's not enough merely to have less expensive garments for sale; they must be better selected, better made, better displayed, and better styled than similar articles found in the stocks of department stores.

Very frequently I am asked, "Why is Neiman-Marcus so different from other stores? What is the mystique of Neiman-Marcus?" The best answer I can give is that stores are, in a way, similar to newspapers, which all have access to the same news sources. They subscribe to the same domestic and foreign wire services, and while some may have more reporters in various parts of the world than others, they all use approximately the same grade of newsprint and similar types of presses. The quality that makes one paper stand out like the *New York Times* and another like the *New York Daily News* lies in the editing. One paper features its foreign news on the front page, the other buries it in condensed form inside; one plays up violence in its headlines, the other relegates such stories to its local news section. So it goes with stores. Essentially, all of us buy in the same market, but we select differently. One store may buy the most flamboyant costumes from a well-known designer, the other will pick out more subtle clothes. One store may depend completely on the domestic market, others search out the best from all over the world. A customer of ours once described what she discerned as the difference between our store and others when she said, "What I like about your store is what it *doesn't* have. I don't have to wade through dozens of articles to find what I want." She was complimenting our selectivity, another word for editing. This process starts with the head of the store, who must lay down certain guidelines as to standards of taste and quality for which he wants his store to stand. He must express himself clearly and consistently, so that his merchandise men and buyers understand his objectives clearly. He can't take a position for quality one month and a different stand the following month, or he will create confusion. He must judge the results of buying trips with the same yardstick he used when he sent the buyers off to market.

Quality is fairly easy to define, though sometimes difficult to attain. Taste is subjective; it is bound by few mandates but is easily identified when it is good or bad. When we employ buyers we can check their records for integrity, reliability, and operational ability, but in most cases we have to gamble on their taste. Sometimes taste can be improved by exposure and experience if the individual is willing, but taste is so personal and is so wrapped up in the ego that a criticism of taste is likely to be taken as a personal affront. Nonetheless, a buyer's taste at Neiman-Marcus is always up for review, in order to protect our customers against a piece of merchandise which fails to meet our standards. We may be wrong, but someone must make a decision, and it is up to management to decide, not whether the article *will* sell, but whether is *should be* sold.

One day while examining our handbag stock, I came across a polychrome wooden box bag from Italy. I asked the buyer about it, and she said we had sold five hundred of them, with two thousand on reorder. I told her I was sorry she had been so successful with it, for I didn't think it was in good taste. I went on to say that I didn't want to sell any more of them. "But the reorder has already been shipped from Florence; what shall I do with them?" she asked. I recommended that she job them out or burn them, but not to put them in stock. This represented a retail investment of approximately $40,000, and I was perfectly willing to take the loss in preference to perpetuating what I considered a mistake. I didn't think I was being heroic in my action; I think I was simply using good business judgment. The buyer was able to resell them to another retailer who was glad to get them at a discount of $5 a bag. The buyer involved was an experienced one, with as much good

166

taste as any in our employ, and yet she too was susceptible to a momentary lapse.

At the height of the period of civil disorder in the mid-sixties, someone conceived the idea of bandoliers filled with dummy bullets to be worn with sports clothes. A sample order was sent in by a member of our New York office staff, but I exercised my editorial prerogative by rejecting them on the grounds that they were in bad taste for a store of our stature to offer for sale. We had eliminated the sale of cowboy guns for little boys, so why should we sell a fad like this for big girls? Some of my younger colleagues criticized my action, saying that I wasn't "with it," but even though I subscribe to the idea that front-page news influences fashion, I believe our store has a responsibility for maintaining standards of good taste in times of shifting values. Any one of my brothers who had been brought up under the tutelage of our father and Aunt Carrie would have taken the same action.

In 1953, *Business Week* ran a cover story on the store, which it headlined "Running a Store with a Split Personality." The thrust of the article was that our fivefold increase in volume from 1942 to 1953 resulted from the fact that we had found the way of selling to both the "upper crust" and "the less well-to-do, family-budgeted group that might be described as the upper-mass market." It referred to an advertising campaign we had undertaken that year under the heading "Neiman-Marcus does both," in which we showed, in side-by-side ads, a fur-trimmed coat for $695 and another for $115, an Oxxford suit for men at $195 and another for $85. Many years before, when Neiman-Marcus sold just women's wear, my father had said, "Any store can dress a few women beautifully. What we want to do is to dress a whole community that way." This was putting the principle into action. To do both requires a certain skill which does not permit the "upper crust" customer to feel downgraded, nor the "middle range" customer to feel patronized. An airline president commented, after having been taken on a tour of the store, "You have succeeded in selling first-class and coach service a darned sight more gracefully than we have ever done." To be successful, it has to be done skillfully, and it has to start with the first contact the customer has in the store and end when the final delivery is made.

An article in a trade publication, *The Housewares Review,* in December 1954, contained the best summation of the job of a merchant I've ever come across. It led off by saying,

> The business of merchandising is a subtle thing. A merchant need not only be a salesman, but he must be psychologist, sociologist, diplomat, politician, as well as designer, artist, and fashion expert. He has the knack for creating excitement around the most prosaic merchandise. He has the talent to analyze the needs of his employees and answer them. He knows the meaning and above all *practices* the art of good fellowship, both in his business and his community. Most important, he knows that his business reflects the desires of his customers. So he makes sure they get what they want.

Essentially, retailing involves the buying and selling of goods. In order to accomplish these two objectives, all of the other talents mentioned in *The Housewares Review* article are called upon at one time or another. The buying process, or editing as I have described it, is exciting, with its challenges of creativity, entrepreneurship, decisionmaking, and with its opportunities for travel at home and to all parts of the world. It's also laborious, requiring intense concentration in order to make selections and to balance the purchase in the proper proportions of colors, sizes, and types of fabrics. Many a buyer spends her evenings in Paris or Rome writing orders and weighing the relative merits of the many lines of merchandise seen in the course of the day.

Less glamorous, but equally stimulating and more demanding, is the job of selling and sales supervision. Little is accomplished if the sales staff fails to understand the new fashions, if the customers are uninspired, if the merchandise doesn't sell. The buyer must take back voluminous notes, photographs, sketches, and swatches of fabric to be able to transmit her buying enthusiasm to the department managers, who are responsible for passing the information on to the people who do the selling.

I have had the stimulating experience of buying almost every line of merchandise that we sell, from corsets to furs, but I get as much satisfaction from the education and motivation of salespeople as I do from the act of buying. In my opinion, a large share of the success of Neiman-Marcus can be attributed to the superior quality of our sales organization and its warm, friendly attitude to visitors and established customers alike. This hasn't happened by accident, but is the cumulative result of a well-selected staff which has been given good training and constant supervision. We say frankly to sales applicants, "If you don't like people, then don't waste your time or ours trying to sell." We try to create an atmosphere in which members of our organization can be happy; we try to compensate them fairly and treat them with human dignity. In turn, we ask them to bring to their jobs a quality of warmth and sincerity, and a disposition to practice the Golden Rule. We encourage them to get to know enough about the merchandise they are selling to be able to say no to the customer when they feel that a particular piece of merchandise isn't exactly right for the customer's requirements. Any novice can say yes, but it takes a professional to be able to say no to an eager buyer.

We've never liked the word "clerk" at Neiman-Marcus, since it suggests an "order-taker," for which we have no place in our business. In sales meetings I have frequently said that vending machines can take orders for an exact piece of merchandise much better than a salesperson; vending machines don't chew gum or have bad breath, but they can't sell a person a more becoming shade, a better fit, or something so new that it has to be presented with an explanation. That's the function of the professional salesperson, who, armed with authority based on knowledge of the stocks and the individual, can find solutions to the customer's needs.

We face a problem which is shared, I'm sure, with other specialty stores of our type. A peculiar phenomenon seems to happen to perfectly nice people who come to work for us. Somehow, some way, they become overly impressed by their surroundings and the reputation of the institution, and they develop an attitude of hauteur. We observe them "upstaging" customers by little remarks, such as, "You *must* have seen this in *Vogue*" or "I've sold this dress to several of my *best* customers." Left alone, these salespeople will drive customers out of the store in droves, so we are on the constant alert to this danger, and as soon as a selling supervisor detects any signs of an "overimpressed" salesperson, decompression proceedings are started at once.

Meetings of our salespeople are usually held every morning in our fashion departments to exhibit the arrival of new merchandise. About once a month the entire sales organization is gathered together, sometimes with nonselling personnel as well, to hear an address by a senior officer or to participate in an achievement award distribution. I have given so many inspirational messages that sometimes I feel that I've already said everything that needs to be said. I guess preachers share the same experience, but there are certain verities of life and of retailing which need perpetual reiteration. One of the most popular of my "sermons" dealt with my comparison of human beings to brass. I cited a visit to the bridge of a naval vessel where the brass gleamed like gold. I asked the captain how often they had to shine the brass. He replied, "Every day, for the minute you stop polishing it, it starts to tarnish." I correlated this incident to human beings, saying, "None of us is made of gold, we're made of brass, but we can look like gold if we work as hard polishing ourselves as the sailor polishing the brass on the ship. We humans can be better than we really are if we will make the effort." That sounds very trite, but it must have made an impression on many hundreds of people, for almost every week some member of our staff comes up to me and says, "I'm sure polishing my brass."

We expect a lot from our employees — the best of their individual abilities. As a result, I firmly believe we help many people to achieve more in our stores than if they were working elsewhere. We simply won't settle for mediocrity if we believe the person can do better. This all comes back to the quest for perfection started by my father and Aunt Carrie. Of course, we never reach it, but it's exhilarating — and exhausting, I might add — to try. It's contagious, for frequently a salesperson will come to me, complaining about some new procedure, and say, "We can't let this new rule apply to Mrs. X after all she has meant to this store over the years." This type of response delights me, for it is indicative of the type of possessiveness, pride, and responsibility we have been able to develop. This all becomes reflected in our customer service, which in most cases is gracious, friendly, and helpful — not duplicated or excelled in any other store in the world.

A textile salesman taught me a very valuable lesson. His name was Hans Samek, a Czechoslovakian refugee who came to the United States during the war to sell top-quality British fabrics. I had met many good and great salesmen up to that time, but never had I seen a man show his line with such vigor, extol his products with such enthusiasm, sell with such urgency. He approached every sale as if it were the last sale he'd ever make. His spirit was infectious, and before he was through, you wanted to buy as if it were the last chance you'd ever have to purchase such fine cloths. After one such session I turned to him and said, "Mr. Samek, you approach business with such a great sense of urgency. Do you brush your teeth with that same attitude?" "Why, of course," he replied, "I do brush my teeth urgently, as I do anything in life that's worth doing at all." I amended my grandmother's early advice of "Anything worth doing is worth doing well" by substituting the word "urgently" for "well."

This sense of urgency is a quality I search for in executives at all levels, and very infrequently find. The postwar years of continuing prosperity have made commercial life so relatively easy that few people have felt the necessity for an urgent approach to the solution of their business problems. When I discover a weakness in any of our stocks, I want to correct it today, not tomorrow, for in most cases the customer won't wait. When I learn of a dissatisfied customer, I try to establish personal contact immediately, having learned that the best adjustment is the quickest one. I'll telephone or pay a personal visit to straighten out a misunderstanding. If an employee has a grievance, I try to see the person before the store closes to prevent further aggravation overnight.

A few days before Christmas a couple of years ago, the manager of our precious jewelry department called in great distress and told me our credit department had offended a very good customer by its refusal to extend credit on a $150,000 purchase for two years without interest. He suggested that I phone the customer. I told him I'd prefer to talk to him face to face, and if he would be willing to see me on the following day, which was Christmas Eve, I would fly over. The customer said we had nothing to talk about, but he would be glad to see me. We took the jewelry he had returned and flew over to see him. I started out by saying that I had made the four-hundred-mile trip not to save the sale, but to discuss the principles on which we ran our business. I told him that we had a single-price policy on all of our merchandise, whether it be jewels, furs, or dresses; that our prices contained a fair profit margin, but not one so big that we could afford to carry a sale on our books for two years without interest on our investment. I asked him how much he was paying for borrowed funds at the bank. "Seven and a half percent," he replied. I told him we were borrowing at 7% and that was all I intended to charge him. He told me that other jewelers were willing to carry him without any interest and he didn't understand why we couldn't do the same. I said, "We could, if we had quoted this jewelry at $165,000 instead of our marked price of $150,000, but that's not our policy. I don't give a damn whether I make this sale or not, but I do want you to understand how and why we do business this way. I think you are a good enough businessman to recognize

172

that you pay for what you get, and if you want to fool yourself by believing that somebody else is going to give you value equal to ours interest-free for two years, that's your business." With that I started to pack up our jewels. He interrupted by saying, "Wait a minute. I appreciate the time you've taken to come to see me on Christmas Eve. I believe you. You can just leave these things here." We had won because we had treated the matter urgently, and because we had told a true story convincingly. We caught a late plane, and I got back home in time to tell our Christmas Eve dinner guests good-bye.

Another urgency story also had a Christmas Eve setting. I received a phone call from a customer who lived in a little town two hundred miles away. She said she had purchased twenty-four gifts at $5 each, to be gift-wrapped, to serve as table decorations and place cards. The gifts had arrived, but they were not gift-wrapped as specified, and as a result her whole Christmas dinner table decor was ruined. It was then two-thirty, and her party was to start at six-thirty. I told her not to worry, for I would charter a plane and send a gift-wrapper to her home. Our specialist was there by five o'clock, wrapped the presents, placed them on the table, and went out the back door as the guests started coming in for dinner. We spent two hundred dollars to rectify our error on a purchase of $120. We didn't pat ourselves on the back for our urgency, but our customer did.

The next most difficult quality to find in retail buyers and merchandise men, or customers, for that matter, is flair. It's a quality of great rarity, and in our business it's worth its weight in gold. I think merchandising can be taught, taste can be improved, but flair, if not native to the individual, is difficult to acquire. Flair in fashion involves the ability to recognize a new fashion at the moment of its birth, to invent new ways of wearing a scarf, to put garments or colors together in unexpected and novel ways. The buyer with flair will evaluate a new fashion before it is proved and will back her judgment with capital in-

173

vestment while her competitors are still pondering the idea. If she is successful more than she is wrong, then she *has* flair. No buyer is expected to be right in her judgments all the time, but if her failures outweigh her successes, she *doesn't* have flair. The ability to perceive the new in color and line, the courage to lead rather than follow, to translate the abstract concept of an idea into reality, is not an act of rationality, but rather one of keen perception and emotion.

We search for individuals with flair, but seldom find them — we usually stumble upon them by accident, and often right within our own organization. Having found them, the next major problem is to preserve them from annihilation by their own colleagues. Like most virtuosos, they tend to be egotistical, and since they can rarely verbalize the reasons for their decisions, they are apt to become as suspect as witches were in earlier days. However, if once they establish a success record, they attract a following among customers as well as business associates.

I have referred to the necessity for management to set forth clear standards of quality and taste. Too often, though, buyers are apt to judge quality by price alone and taste by their own personal preferences.

In 1948, I wrote an article, "Fashion Is My Business" for *The Atlantic*, in which I commented,

> The taste of the general public isn't as good as that of the sophisticated minority, but it isn't as bad as most manufacturers and retailers believe it to be. The public will buy bad taste in merchandise if it has no choice, but it will usually respond to any product in good taste if that product is presented at the right time with authority. Public taste can be led astray by bad example; it can be elevated by consistent education and by the presence of a recognized set of standards.

> To maintain a standard of taste in any field is difficult. It is even more difficult in a retail establishment which is dealing with large and diverse groups of people. A *couturier* restricts his clientele to those who like his particular type of designing. He may even limit entree to his

establishment to those whose social background he approves. A retail establishment is open to anyone who wants to enter the portals. Its buying is not done by a single person but by a staff of buyers whose tastes vary. Its selling is done by an even larger staff. The management, in the form of one or several persons, must undertake to establish a standard of taste by which it is content to be judged. It requires courage and a certain amount of presumptuousness to be willing to say, "This is good, that is bad." Such a decision implies a readiness to let some portion of business potential go elsewhere, for not all customers will be satisfied with what the retailer believes to be good.

It thus becomes vastly more difficult to maintain a standard of taste in a large store than it is in a smaller one, with a narrower point of view. History and experience are valuable guides for buyers, but if religiously adhered to can be most destructive, for fashion and taste do change. An article that is chic today may be tacky tomorrow, and vice versa. At one time, needlework was for old ladies, now it is an "in" fashion for young women. Macramé for years was considered dowdy, now the best decorators use it. In the ever-changing fashion business, the best advice I can give to young and old buyers is: "Don't let your feet or your heads get set in concrete! Stay flexible in your willingness to consider new ideas; remember the past, but don't worship it."

The development of my own personal taste has been a laborious process, the result of years of looking and seeing, comparing and analyzing, wearing out shoe leather in museums and on the shopping streets of every city I visit. I have learned to look through the clutter of an antique shop to be able to see the articles suspended from the ceilings or tucked under tables on the floor. The eye can be educated, it can be taught to be selective. An individual can afford the luxury of being self-satisfied with his own taste; a merchant must put his taste up to the acid test of market acceptability. No matter what I may think about my taste, it is the discriminating customer who makes the final and critical decision. As a result of public acceptance of my taste and that of my associates, we have exercised a powerful influence in the establishment of taste stand-ards for our city and the entire region.

We normally set up price ranges for the merchandise in our various departments, based on the quality available in the markets at a given time, but here I would make a plea for inconsistency. A buyer should not be so wedded to a price-line concept that she becomes muscle-bound and incapable of recognizing a worthy article of merchandise at a price far below her regular range. If she is buying gifts which retail for from $20 to $50, there is nothing wrong with buying a gift of good quality and taste which retails for $5. She will attract new customers and delight estab-lished ones by offering something new and exciting at a price lower than usual; but if one item is successful it doesn't follow that she should add twenty, for then she simply lowers the average sale of her department; instead of having one "jewel" of a gift at $5, she has a wide assortment of average gifts at $5. This mer-chandising technique is difficult to teach, because it is hard for most buyers to understand the subtle value of being inconsistent on occasion. Running a store with a "split personality" requires the ability to carry water on both shoulders in order to stay balanced. Even though we stock the most expensive merchandise in the world, we never permit our buyers to forget that we must carry assortments of equal size and variety at the other price levels, within the spending capability of our less affluent customers.

Specialty store retailing is not for the timid, the slow, or the myopic. The pace is fast, requiring quick decisions involving large sums of money. Rarely in a business like Neiman-Marcus can the results of judgment be proved in a short period, for most of our buying commitments are made from three to six months ahead of delivery. Thus a good merchant or buyer must have the ability to anticipate fashion movements and customer demand. The Chinese have a saying, "Forecasting is a very difficult business, especially when it has to deal with the future," to which our buyers can testify every time they place an order.

176

Selecting merchandise so well that the majority of it can be sold at a profit is the objective of every buyer; the success of a buyer is judged not only by gains in sales volume, but by the percentage of reductions, or "markdowns," required to move the remainder of a stock at the season's end. Thus a buyer is constantly faced with the conflict of being courageous and being cautious, taking a gamble and relying on a safe bet. Buying is not an easy job.

We encourage our buyers to innovate, to develop merchandise that does not already exist, in addition to buying the best of the various markets. A merchandise manager conceived an idea for fancy bedsheets and he asked one of our largest suppliers to make striped ones for us. The mill had never sold anything but white and pastel-colored sheets, but encouraged by such a large order they made them for us. We had such a fashion scoop that we advertised them in the *New York Times* as well as in our local papers. They were a huge success and led the way to a series of novel sheets including one imprinted with a flock of sheep to help those who counted sheep at night. Our veteran bag buyer has shown great ingenuity in making handbags from both old Kashmir shawls and embroidered panels taken from eighteenth-century Chinese skirts. When she saw the colorful molas made by the Cuna Indians from the island of San Blas, she quickly had them made into tote bags for women. We buy up old Bedouin robes, remove the beautiful hand-embroidered panels, dry clean them, and mount them on new wool hostess robes. We pick up rolls of pure silk kimono cloth in Japan and cart them to Hong Kong, where tailors are willing to make the fifteen-inch-wide fabric into Chinese bankers' robes.

We developed a smock for our fashion show mannequins to wear between showings. It was a simple wraparound with a sash tie, neatly monogrammed with the N-M insignia. One day, one of our wealthiest customers asked if she could buy one, so we decided to market it under the name "The Neiman-Marcus Model's Smock" and advertised it nationally. The response was overwhelming, with orders pouring in from actresses, socialites, and business women all over the country. When Mary Martin wore hers in her dressing room while applying makeup for her *South Pacific* role, every actress in the cast had to have one. How C. R. Smith, then president of American Airlines, happened to see one, I don't know, but he did, and ordered three thousand for his stewardesses to wear during in-flight food service.

On my first visit to India, I came across some handbags made in Agra of a gold lamé fabric studded with effective, but not top quality, precious stones. The bags were so poorly made I couldn't buy them, but I gave them a bag pattern and asked them to embroider the cloth so we could make the bags to our standards in the United States. I picked seven different colors of stones, and when the bags were completed, I had them encased in individual lucite boxes to retail as a set for $2,250. The buyer contended that no one would want seven bags all alike, even though they were differently colored. "Wait and see," I said, and refused to permit them to be sold separately. Shortly afterwards, a wealthy oilman from Houston came up to do his Christmas shopping. I showed him the set of bags and asked, "Have you ever had to wait for your wife in the evening while she was trying to find a handbag to match her evening gown? Here's the answer — she will always have the right color." He was delighted with the idea and bought them. We sold four more sets that year before we decided to let them be sold separately.

Sometimes creative efforts backfire. Our costume jewelry buyer was searching for an idea for a novelty wristwatch just about the time that trade restrictions on China were lifted. She concocted the idea of having the hour numerals replaced with Chinese characters which would spell out a Chinese adage or legend. She commissioned Kenneth J. Lane, one of our leading suppliers, to execute the idea. We advertised the watch and its success was instantaneous. When customers wrote back asking for the translation, we supplied them with the explanation that the characters represented the twelve conditions that an ancient emperor was given by his wise men to regain the lost love of his wife and daughter.

Everyone was satisfied until one day we received a complaint from a Chinese student, who claimed that the translation was grossly incorrect. She contended that in essence it meant "We shall take over America by force." Horrified, we searched for other Chinese authorities, some of whom confirmed our critic's translation. We immediately withdrew the watches from sale, returning them to the manufacturer with the request that he replace the dials with a guaranteed nonpolitical message. I asked Lane, who I knew was personally innocent, to explain how the selection of the original dial was made in the first place. He replied that when the order came in, he turned it over to one of his minor assistants, who cut out Chinese characters at random from a Chinese newspaper and pasted them on the dial. Since Chinese characters express ideas rather than exact words, many differing interpretations can be made of them. Whether the message was actually a propaganda message or not, or whether it was purposeful or accidental, we are still not certain.

A few years before, we had another amusing experience with a jewelry item carrying Chinese characters. We had gold cuff links engraved with the phrase in Chinese meaning "It's later than you think." They sold so well that one of our executives suggested we add another set for our Jewish customers which would say in Hebrew "Shalom Aleichem," or "Peace unto you." One day a customer came into the department and told the salesman, "I've heard about those Chinese cuff links you have. I want a pair to send to a prominent Chinese general in Taiwan." He paid cash for them, and it was only after he left that we discovered he had been given cuff links with the Hebrew inscription instead of the Chinese.

179

He had paid cash, so there was no record of his name. We could only wait until the recipient filed a complaint to make the replacement. That was fifteen years ago and we are still waiting.

Not only buyers and merchants get bitten by the creative bug at Neiman-Marcus, others do as well. In 1947, Jane Trahey and Marihelen McDuff, our advertising and public relations directors respectively, proposed the idea of compiling a Neiman-Marcus cookbook, based on the recipes of our Texas customers plus those of a few celebrities who had passed through and visited the store. We thought it was a great idea, so they sent out letters soliciting contributions. It was only after the recipes started pouring in that we realized we had a responsibility to test the recipes to be sure they worked. None of us had foreseen this mundane requirement. Among the "outlanders" solicited was Paul Gallico, who, tongue in cheek, replied,

Dear Mr. Marcus,

Your letter requesting that I send you a recipe for the book you contemplate publishing, with a story attached, humorous or otherwise pertaining to its origin, received, and it delighted me.

By an odd coincidence, one of my editors who has just paid me $1,500 for exactly such an article was asking me the other day why I did not start a store instead of beating my brains out at a typewriter. I wrote a few people and asked them what they thought of the idea and they replied — great, particularly if I could get the merchandise contributed gratis.

My store is now beginning to take some form. I hope to have it open by summer. I would like very much to have one of your favorite or most successful pieces of merchandise. I would prefer it to be one with a receipted bill of sale and guarantee attached.

Particularly I am interested in a fur evening wrap for my wife, solid gold cuff links, a fine rod and reel for deep sea fishing, a pair of diamond and sapphire clips, with ear-rings to match, a hunting rifle with telescopic sights, a 16 mm. moving picture sound projector, a set of Paris negligees, lingerie and nightgowns, a television set with large screen, a fine silver service, a fitted alligator travelling bag

180

(woman's) and a complete set of Sèvres or Copeland china to serve twelve.

To meet my opening date, it is essential that I have this merchandise at the earliest possible date, and I am looking forward to receiving one or several of your most interesting items.

Cordially yours,

PAUL W. GALLICO

Needless to say, we had to forgo Mr. Gallico's offer, but other VIPs did respond, and the book *A Taste of Texas* was published by Random House and is still selling.

When we enlarged the store in 1950, we installed a large restaurant, the Zodiac Room, to attract more people to the downtown area and as a service to those customers from out of town who were spending the day in the store. Our first few restaurant directors were unsuccessful in establishing a standard of food service compatible with our ambition to make this the best restaurant in the region. We served good food, but not good enough to attract a full-house clientele and we lost a lot of money on the operation. In the search for a more competent food director, I was told about Helen Corbitt, who had run restaurants in Houston and Austin with great success. I wooed her for several years before she called me one day and said she was tired of the hotel food business and was willing to talk to me.

She joined us in 1955, and in a short time the Zodiac was packed to capacity. True, we were still losing as much money as before, but at least we were losing it by serving customers. Under her direction our restaurant gained international attention, for this "Balenciaga of Food," as I once introduced her, had the ability to produce new taste sensations and to satisfy the eye as well as the palate by her dramatic food presentation. I called her affectionately "my wild Irish genius" in recognition of her uncontrollability, her genuine Irish temperament, and her sheer genius in the field of food. When I complained about the heavy losses, she replied,

181

"You didn't mention money when you employed me. You simply said that you wanted the best food in the country. I've given you that."

I had been forewarned that I might have difficulty holding on to her, for she had a record of getting bored with her jobs. Very quickly I discerned that beneath her façade of self-assurance and belligerence, she had a basic need for appreciation. She responded very quickly to praise, so I made it my business to visit her several times a week to compliment her on some dish she had served or a meal she had planned. We kept her busy with a variety of projects, and she never did leave us from boredom as predicted. During her tenure she wrote *Helen Corbitt's Cook Book*, which has earned praise from readers all over the world, and of which we alone have sold over 80,000 copies. She retired after fourteen years, but still serves us as a consultant. She has continued to lecture on food and parties, conduct cooking schools, and even write another book, *Helen Corbitt Cooks for Company*.

A very stimulating suggestion came to us from a couple of young women in our customer relations department. They wanted us to set up a spa, patterned in part on Elizabeth Arden's Maine Chance. We gave them approval to experiment with the idea and it finally evolved into The Greenhouse, located in Arlington, midway between Dallas and Fort Worth, as a venture of the Great Southwest Corporation in cooperation with Neiman-Marcus and Charles of the Ritz. Our interest was in the operation of a facility so superior in luxury and results that thirty-five socialites from all over the nation would come to Dallas every week of the year and eventually become regular Neiman-Marcus customers. Charles of the Ritz was looking for a prestige showplace for its beauty products, and Great Southwest had property it wanted to develop. Helen Corbitt served as food director, designing 500-calorie daily diets that look like banquets. The business started slowly, but within a few years it had become so popular that it was necessary to book reservations months in advance. Not only does The Greenhouse draw distinguished guests from all over the United States, but now its patrons come from Canada, Mexico, France, and Italy as well.

The retail business, like others, has its ups and downs. When business is good, buyers are inclined to take credit for their superior buying skill. When business is bad, management usually blames the buyers for poor buying. It's been my experience, though, that when business is good, no buyer is actually as good as she thinks she is, and conversely, when business is bad, no buyer is as bad as management thinks she is. That thesis is generally known in our store as Marcus's Law! Although sales rise and fall with general business conditions, improved performance above the average can be achieved by exceptionally aggressive effort and the "rightness" of stocks.

I hope our buyers develop self-confidence without smugness, assurance without cockiness. They have to read a lot to keep up with the fashion industry: *Women's Wear Daily, Vogue, Harper's Bazaar, Town and Country, Mademoiselle,* French and Italian fashion journals, and the *New York Times.* Not one but all of these are must reading for anyone in the fashion business. In addition, they should be doing enough general reading to be kept aware of what is going on outside the world of fashion, for fashion itself is influenced by the arts and social and political movements. Eventually, after several years of experience, our buyers develop a certain style, a word which was brilliantly described by Kenneth Tynan some years ago in *The New Yorker* when he wrote, "Style is the hammer that drives in the nail without bruising the wood, the arrow that transfixes the target without seeming to have been aimed. It makes difficult things . . . look simple. When a strenuous feat has been performed without strain, it has been performed with style."

We have always believed that if we can please the 5% of our customers who are the most discriminating, we will never have any difficulty in satisfying the other 95% who are less critical. The latter know the difference between *good* and *bad,* but the former recognize the difference between *better* and *best*. Thus, if you please the 5% the balance will willingly accept their standards. This select 5% are not necessarily our wealthiest or even our best customers, but they are our most exacting ones. They know how a garment should fit, they know that a bias-cut nightgown belt will stay tied better than one cut on the straight, they know the difference between a silk scarf made of twelve-momme weight and one made of sixteen-momme, they can discern a sixteenth of an inch difference in the width of the right and left shoulders. They are often troublesome to please, but once you have satisfied them, you have customers no competitor can take away. And what's more, you learn from them. One of our most exasperating customers taught me lessons in quality which she had learned over a period of years when she had all her clothes custom-made in the heyday of the Paris couture. She demanded the same details in ready-made clothes, and she got them — and so did the balance of our customers.

A visiting manufacturer once remarked that the difference between a department store and a specialty store is the telephone. By that he meant that the specialty store sales staff had both the time and the training to communicate with customers over the phone, to tell them about new arrivals of merchandise which would meet their particular needs. Our salespeople are provided with what we call a "clientele book," in which they are required to record all the purchases of each customer, birthdays, anniversaries, and any other information that might be useful in making contact by phone or letter. By the proper utilization of the customer's purchasing history, it is easy to relate new merchandise to that already in the customer's wardrobe. If a woman bought a purple coat a year ago, then a call about a lilac wool dress to wear under that coat becomes a service to the customer which is usually deeply appreciated. The customer may respond by saying, "I already have a lilac wool dress, but what I really want is an off-white knit." The salesperson has a lead, and can call back when she has one in the customer's size and price range. No one ever objects to a Happy Birthday call, and many salespeople create great customer goodwill by the simple device of remembering the important dates in their customers' lives. One of our jewelry salesmen makes sales about forty percent of the time to the men he calls to wish them a Happy Anniversary.

As obvious and simple as the clientele book system is, its use doesn't come easily. It requires constant supervision and reminding to persuade new salespeople to learn its value. A fine-quality clientele takes time to build, but once it is built it remains loyal. It has to be built like the pyramids, one stone at a time. One satisfied customer tells another about an exceptional salesperson, so the task is one of selling satisfaction, just as the founders announced in the opening day's advertisement. An ambitious salesperson will say to a new customer, "If you have been pleased by the manner in which I have served you, perhaps you would like to give me the names of a few of your friends whom I might call." Invariably, the customer will reply positively, provided she was sufficiently impressed by the knowledge and skill of the salesperson.

We've had a standing offer of $20,000 for the past twenty years for any salesperson who can qualify as a "mind reader" and can infallibly judge the buying potential of a stranger coming onto the selling floor. Obviously, no one has ever claimed the prize, for no one, however skilled they may be, can ever tell what a known customer will buy on any given day. I learned that lesson early in my career when I staged an exhibition of etchings and lithographs priced from $100 to $5,000. Late one afternoon, a little old lady in shabby clothes, carrying a paper sack instead of a handbag, came in and looked around. She didn't look like a potential buyer, but having nothing else to do, I explained the various media represented in the show and told her a little about the artists who had made the prints. After I was through, she glanced about and said, "I'll take that one," pointing to a Rem-

185

brandt etching. While my mouth was still open, she reached into her sack and pulled out a roll of bills, peeled off fifty $100 notes, and handed them to me. From then on, I knew I wasn't a mind reader and I was convinced that appearances were not infallible bits of evidence of a person's capacity or willingness to buy anything. I preach constantly to our salespeople, "As long as the customer is alive, you have a prospect." Many of the customers who come into our store are able and willing to buy much more than they actually do. They are susceptible to something new, something beautiful, and they are grateful when they are given the opportunity to see things they've never dreamed about. I have an antipathy towards "hard selling" and always discourage its practice, but I firmly believe in "intensive showing," so that the customer becomes aware of the great variety of things we have to offer.

There are countless tales of ingenious selling in the Neiman-Marcus stores, but one that stands out in my mind involved a newly appointed fur buyer, David Wolfe, who has the ability to "smell" a potential sale. One day, in our Fort Worth store, a saleswoman passed him carrying two Galanos dresses over her arm to show a customer in a fitting room. "I figured that any woman who could afford a Galanos was a good prospect for a fur coat, so I asked the saleswoman to introduce me to her. She was from Connecticut and a guest at The Greenhouse. When she learned that I was from the fur department, she quickly told me that she had more furs than we did and was not interested in even looking. I told her I wanted to show her only one garment, and when I brought it in she said, 'How did you know that that's the only thing I don't have? I like it but I don't need it. Are you a sporting man?' I replied that I was, not actually knowing what she was driving at. 'Well, I'll tell you what I'll do. Flip a coin and if it comes up heads, I'll take the coat. It it doesn't, then promise to get out of here and leave me alone.' I got down on my knees and prepared to flip the coin. 'What are you kneeling for?' she asked.

I told her I was a praying man as well as a sporting one. I flipped the coin, and heads it was. She took the coat."

Dudley Ramsden, vice-president in charge of our precious jewelry operation, is one of the finest salesmen I've ever known, for he embodies all the qualities necessary for sales achievement; he has knowledge and is able to answer any question his customer may pose, he is completely honest and frank, he has the ability to understand the implications of his client's social position and its relation to the stone under consideration, he knows how to bring the customer to the point of decision, and finally, he has the courage to ask for cash or a planned method of payment. Most good jewelry salesmen like to let the credit department take care of the payment details, and in the course of doing so they often lose the sale. Dudley's sales are so flawlessly executed, his appraisal of his customer's buying potential so keen, his credibility so strong, that he rarely misses sales or has returns.

One of his salesmen had lost a sale on a diamond necklace which Dudley knew was an exceptional value. Not satisfied with the salesman's explanation, he decided to fly down to the customer's ranch in South Texas to talk to the man himself. It was a cold, windy day just before Christmas and the only way he could get there was by chartering a plane and landing on a deserted airstrip on the ranch. He found the customer talking with the vet about his herd, and not disposed to interrupt his conversation to reopen the subject of the necklace. "I've flown three hundred miles to keep you from making a mistake. You've got to give me fifteen minutes of your time," Dudley said. "I want you to look at my necklace and the one you've selected, side by side, and if the difference in quality and value isn't obvious to you, I'll get back on my plane. You've employed an expert vet to advise you on your cattle. I'm an expert in my field, and you owe it to yourself and your wife to get the best advice available." The man reluctantly agreed to give him fifteen minutes, pulled out the other necklace from the pocket of his ranch coat, and laid it on the tailgate of his pickup truck.

187

Dudley put our necklace next to it and said, "Mr. Seeligson, I'm not going to say a word. My necklace speaks for itself." The price of the two was the same, but our necklace was so obviously superior that Mr. Seeligson said, "Son, you've done me a great favor. I appreciate all the trouble you've gone to in saving me from making a mistake." Subsequently I received a warm letter from Mrs. Seeligson extolling Mr. Ramsden's persistence and his efforts. Again, knowledge, enthusiasm, and courage proved to be the difference between making and losing a sale.

My brother Edward had a very good customer in Buffalo whose Christmas shopping he took care of every December by telephone. After getting approval on the suggestions for the man's hundred-name list, Eddie said, "I guess that just about takes care of your problems." The man replied, "Yes, except for Leonard." "Your son?" Eddie asked. "No, my new pet lion." Up to that point, we had never been faced with the question of what to recommend for a lion, so Eddie was a bit nonplussed. "What about a Steuben feeding bowl?" he suggested. That wouldn't do, for there was no Steuben bowl large enough for a lion. Finally Eddie asked, "It's cold in Buffalo, isn't it?" "Very cold," he replied. "Then what about an electric blanket?" That suggestion was accepted, so we made our first sale for a lion's Christmas present. A few years later, though, we had another leonine request. One of our very good customers had a collection of mounted animals, but unfortunately, moths had got into the lion's mane, leaving him completely bald. The customer had noticed our advertisement of a visiting wigmaker, and requested that we send her out to make a toupee for her lion. After our hairdresser recovered from the shock, and upon being assured that the lion was mounted and not alive, she did go out and make the hairpiece — the largest sale of her three-day visit with us.

The Neiman-Marcus charge card is a convenience we extend to all our charge customers, who find it useful, not only to expedite their purchases in the Neiman-Marcus stores, but as a never-failing identification in other cities or countries. One of our Oklahoma patrons found himself in jail one night after a Texas-Oklahoma football game on a charge of drunkenness and disorderly conduct. The judge, after setting bail at $250, asked if he had any friends in Dallas. "None," he replied, "except at Neiman-Marcus." He pulled out his Neiman-Marcus charge card and the judge gave him permission to use the phone to try to reach some official at the store. After several calls he succeeded in locating one of our vice-presidents, who posted the bail and charged it to the customer's account. Needless to say, we don't encourage this particular kind of credit-card usage.

Jack Massey, a prominent citizen of Nashville, had a happy experience with a Neiman-Marcus card when he and his fiancée decided to get married in Dallas by a justice of the peace. When the bride-to-be was asked for some piece of local identification, she confessed that she had none. "In that case, I can't marry you," said the justice of the peace. She looked through her purse again and triumphantly came up with a Neiman-Marcus charge card, which she presented to the justice. "Well, if your credit is good with them, it's good with me," he said, and proceeded to marry them. They never fail to remind me whenever I see them that without Neiman-Marcus they wouldn't have been married that day.

It's axiomatic in the retail business that sales follow inventory. If you have a large stock of well-selected, wanted merchandise, larger sales will ensue. Retailers follow this rule in low and moderate price ranges, but few have the courage to extend the principle to luxury items. The risk is greater, and most stores don't have the patience to wait until they develop a clientele for expensive merchandise. Back in the '30s, our mink business was small, as was our stock. We believed then that the mink coat would become the most popular fur wrap in history, so we decided to

189

enlarge our stock in anticipation of larger sales. When we carried four mink coats, we would sell ten in the course of a season. When we expanded our inventory to a hundred, our sales jumped to three hundred. We had a better size range, style assortment, and greater variety in price.

Then we applied this same reasoning to vicuña coats, which were in great demand after the war. The fabric was very expensive, ranging from $200 to $300 a yard, making it a risky investment for an undercapitalized coat manufacturer. So we bought the piece goods ourselves and farmed the cloth out to various makers, who charged us for making and lining the coats. We built our stocks to three hundred garments at one time, and captured the fine vicuña coat business of the country for both men and women.

Other fine stores carried two or three coats, but no one had the nerve to stock them in the depth we did. One day I received a phone call from New York from a man who introduced himself as Mr. Salvatore from Alexandria, Egypt. He said, "I'm calling you from Tripler's in New York. I'm looking for matching vicuña coats for my wife, my daughters, my son, and myself. They have a coat for me here, but not one for my wife. I've been to Saks and Bonwit's, and they can provide a coat for my wife and daughters, but not for me and my boy. They all tell me the only place in the country where I might find coats for all of us is at Neiman-Marcus. I asked what street Neiman-Marcus was on and was told you were in Dallas. Can you solve our requirements?" I assured him that we could, so they took the afternoon plane to Dallas, bought five matching vicuña coats, and returned to New York.

When the engagement of Grace Kelly to Prince Rainier was announced, I immediately asked if we might be privileged to provide her wedding gown and bridesmaids' dresses. Miss Kelly had been in Dallas six months before to receive the Neiman-Marcus award and had been greatly impressed with the store. The motion picture studio had already arranged to have the wedding gown made by one of the company's designers, but she gave us the assignment to design the outfits for her attendants. This was a great coup, which brought a tremendous amount of international press coverage, adding further prestige to our already famous bridal department. In addition, we sold her a large part of her wedding trousseau. Billie and I received an invitation to attend the wedding ceremony in Monaco. This was one wedding where the bride was as beautiful as she is supposed to be and rarely is. We left our hotel, La Reserve at Beaulieu, at 7:30 A.M. to drive to the cathedral some five miles away, in order to take our places by 8:45 for the 10 A.M. ceremony. It was white tie and tails for the men and short afternoon dresses for the ladies, and while I have come home in tails at 7:30 A.M., this was my first experience going out in them at that time of day. Billie wore a beautiful multilayered, midcalf chiffon dress, which Galanos had made especially for her, and was the most chic of all the guests. As we passed through the receiving line, Princess Grace presented us to Prince Rainier and said, "I'm so glad you came. I want to tell you that I love everything you have done for me — and didn't the girls look beautiful?" And they did.

A dozen or so years later, we did the trousseau and wedding gown for Luci Baines Johnson, the younger daughter of the President. She had selected a design created for her by our leading wedding gown designer, Priscilla of Boston. This was the first White House wedding in years, so the demand from the press for news about the wedding gown and bridesmaids' dresses was intense. We had sworn the designer to secrecy, and I kept the original sketches locked in my desk drawer. Members of our staff were subjected to all types of pressure for information, from cajolery to bribery, but no one leaked the slightest detail to the reporters. One morning, a few weeks before the wedding, I awakened with the horrible realization that the wedding gown was being made in a nonunion shop, and that the disclosure of this information would be tremendously embarrassing to the President, since David Dubinsky, head of the International Ladies' Garment Workers' Union, had been one of his most loyal supporters. I immediately got Priscilla on the phone, explained the situation, and asked if she would permit some other manufacturer with a union shop to make the garment. She understood the predicament and graciously agreed to turn over her design and patterns, although she had already completed the gown. At any rate, the dress Luci wore as she walked down the aisle of the cathedral bore a union label. The day was saved! We had protected our customer from possible picketing and what could have become a public controversy.

There is never an adequate excuse for rudeness or discourtesy in a Neiman-Marcus store. No complaint is too minor to be investigated and we go to great lengths to discover how errors occur. When an organization understands that management won't settle for anything but the best, then each and every member of the staff begins to recognize the significance of individual contributions to maintaining the corporate image.

Some customers are easy and some are difficult — and I'm not referring to the discriminating 5%; they must all be satisfied if humanly possible. We have a fabulous mail-order customer who has never visited one of our stores, but who has, in the past ten years, spent over half a million dollars with us without a single complaint. Then we have some customers who spend $200 a year, return half their purchases for credit, and complain about the $100 worth they keep. That's the nature of the retail business.

Madame Callas, the famous opera star, was appearing in Dallas with the Dallas Civic Opera Company. She needed a special costume for a performance and asked us to custom make it for her in four days. We don't have a custom workroom, but as an accommodation to her, and to the opera company, we agreed to do it, despite the fact that our alteration rooms were loaded with work on evening gowns that had been sold for that very occasion. I told her we would do it if she came to the store punctually for the several fittings required. She demurred, saying it was more convenient for her to be fitted at her hotel suite. We explained that we were doing her a favor, and that the only way we could do it was on the basis we had proposed. She came, she was prompt, and we delivered her costume on schedule.

On the night of her performance, I received a frantic call from the manager of the company at 7:30. "The tenor is having trouble with his zipper. He can't get his trousers on. Do you have a zipper specialist you can send out to help him?" In five minutes I located our expert, who was whisked out to the auditorium with a police escort, and he solved the problem. The curtain went up one minute late. No charge was made for this bit of community service.

A phenomenon of our kind of business is the compulsive buyers. One I recall, whom I shall name "Mrs. X" since she is still living, was the daughter of a wealthy rancher and the wife of a young oilman who had struck it rich in East Texas. She adored clothes, and would come to the store once a month at five o'clock to shop. Since the store closed at five-thirty, this meant that we had to hold a staff of thirty people to serve her in the various departments she might choose to visit. Nothing we could do could persuade her to start her shopping at an earlier hour, and she was such a fabulous customer that we had no choice but to accept her hours. When she bought dresses, she insisted on having hats, shoes, girdles and bras made of matching fabric; when she bought furs, she would buy a stock — eight or ten coats at a time. If she liked a particular dress, she might order it in a dozen colors. Her account ran close to $200,000 a year, all with the knowledge and approval of her adoring husband.

The straw that broke the camel's back was their purchase of an old mansion, which they asked us to decorate. She would review several color schemes, select the one she preferred, and we would proceed to order upholstery and drapery materials. When the room was installed as ordered, she would take a look at it and say, "No, I don't like yellow after all. Change it to pink." We would proceed to do the room over and when completed, she would take another look and say, "No, I really don't like pink. Do it in the green scheme." We protested at each change of mind, but to no avail. This was an expensive way to decorate a house, and even a wealthy oil millionaire couldn't tolerate such waste. He called a halt to the redecoration, paid us, and shortly thereafter they were divorced.

Another compulsive buyer story has a much happier ending. Her expenditures were not for herself but for others. One year, her husband asked what she would like for Christmas. "The only thing I want is an unlimited charge account at Neiman-Marcus, so I can buy presents for all the members of the family, and for all the people who have been nice to us this past year." Her husband gave his approval and she did exactly what she said she would do. She didn't forget anyone. She gave presents to the painter who had repainted her living room, to her manicurist and her children, to the telephone man who installed a new extension, to the garbage collector and his family, to every salesperson who waited on her, and naturally to all the members of her family and their in-laws. Mrs. Fred Lege, Jr., was her name; she bought relatively little for herself, but she brought joy and happiness to the hundreds of people who had crossed her path.

"Silver Dollar" Jim West was a wealthy oilman who liked to pay with silver dollars. Often he would arrive at the store accompanied by several companions lugging canvas bags filled with them. At times he would toss dollars at the salesperson writing up his bill. He bought presents for everybody he knew, and his acquaintanceship was wide — both male and female.

A few days before Christmas one year, he announced that he needed a special present for his bourbon-drinking attorney. He wanted a decanter that would hold a whole case of whiskey. I doubt if any store had ever stocked one with such a capacity, but it so happened that we had bought a gigantic decanter from Steuben a few years before because we thought it was a good display piece for our Steuben shop. It had been placed in storage, so

194

no one had thought of it as a solution for Jim's problem until I was called in to pacify him. Suddenly I remembered it and said, "Jim, I think I have just what you want. Wait fifteen minutes." We unpacked it, brought it in, and he bellowed, "That won't hold twelve quarts." I wasn't sure myself, but the only way to handle him was to bellow back, "Ten bucks, it will." "You're on," was his retort, and he turned to one of his companions with an order to start opening the bottles he had brought with him. Sure enough, it held exactly three gallons. He paid me the $10 and said, "Deliver it," not asking the price of the decanter. I told him that the Steuben decanter would cost him $2,500, but that it was illegal for us to make a delivery of whiskey, and he would have to arrange the transport himself. He was out of silver by that time so he paid in $100 bills.

Not all oilmen are compulsive buyers; many are very conservative in their expenditures; a few are wary buyers. I came into the fur department one afternoon in the pre-Christmas period and saw a saleswoman showing fur stoles to a man reputed to have a great oil fortune. I greeted him and ventured the opinion that one of the three stoles he was considering was a little better in color and quality than the others, although they were identical in price. I pointed to the one on the left. He studied them for a minute and said, "I'll take that one," indicating a stole on the right. He was so suspicious by nature that he couldn't believe that I was giving him honest advice. I never tried to sell to him again.

Mrs. Ernest Medders may not have been a compulsive buyer, but she was the most *willing* buyer we have ever encountered. She and her husband moved to Muenster, Texas, from Tennessee and soon thereafter opened a charge account, giving a large Memphis bank as reference. When we checked with the bank, the official laughed and said, "Don't worry about Mr. and Mrs. Medders. They can buy and sell Neiman-Marcus." They started shopping in a modest way, buying about $1,000 a month for a year, paying their bill promptly on the first of the following month. Then the account rose to about $5,000 a month, and again it was paid promptly.

She bought everything — clothes for herself, her children, and husband, furs, jewelry, fine china, silver — just about all we had to offer. Very quickly she became a favorite of the sales-people, who went out of their way to show her the newest and the best. She never said no. By this time, the payments began to come in more slowly, but, acting on the recommendation of the Memphis bank, our credit department wasn't concerned. One day, however, I ran into a local banker who casually asked me, "What do you really know about the source of the Medders money?" That ques-tion worried me, for neither we nor anyone else in Dallas knew anything more than what the Memphis banker had told us and the fast-paying record they had established. I immediately called our credit manager and asked him to go to Memphis to find out everything he could about the basis of the Medders fortune.

On his return, he reported that Mr. Medders was waging a legal battle to establish his claim as an heir to one Pelham Humphries, whose reputed oil holdings, valued at $500,000,000, were sup-posed to be in the famous Spindletop field. Mrs. Medders, who had worked in a hospital in Memphis, so impressed the Poor Sisters of St. Francis Seraph of the Perpetual Adoration, under whose auspices the hospital was operated, with her intent to benefice the order with a gift of $10,000,000 when their fortune came in, that they had eventually advanced large sums of money to help pay for the litigation costs. Mrs. Medders recounts all of this in her book, *The Medders Story, or How to Borrow $3,000,000 with No Collateral.*

They had used this money to establish themselves in Texas, buying a farm in Muenster that they converted into a showplace ranch, clothes and jewels from us, and Cadillacs from the local dealers. They entertained lavishly and generously for civic and charitable causes. They established early credit by the prompt manner in which they handled their obligations, but they had no

196

income. They went into bankruptcy in 1967. We were able to retrieve a $75,000 Black Willow mink coat made to order for Mrs. Medders but not yet delivered and a diamond necklace that had been sent on approval but not yet charged. Despite these fortunate retrievals, we were stuck for about $150,000 on open account, the largest credit loss we have ever experienced. We realized, as did all the other creditors, including some large banks, that we had made a fundamental mistake in judgment — extending credit on hearsay rather than on hard fact. To this day, we still haven't been able to determine whether we were victimized by cold, calculated intent or by the persuasive dream of a pair of innocents who really believed it was all going to come true. Poorer we are, but wiser.

Our biggest and most consistent buyer, though by no means a compulsive one, is Filene's Basement in Boston, to whom we sell twice a year the remainders of our fashion clearances after our regular store customers have had first choice. Filene's takes the leftovers of broken sizes and colors, good and bad sellers, and offers them at a fraction of the original prices. They act as a clearinghouse for surplus stocks of many fine stores, but the Neiman-Marcus sales generally command the largest turnout of bargain hunters.

10

Europe and the Fortnights

SOME PEOPLE BECOME STAGESTRUCK at an early age and never recover. From the time of my initial trip to Europe in 1925 I was "Europe-struck." And although I shall never duplicate the thrill of my first visit to Paris or London, forty-nine years and fifty trips later my pulse quickens when the plane touches down at Orly or Heathrow. The Faubourg St.-Honoré, Bond Street, and the Via Condotti are as familiar to me as Main Street in Dallas, but despite their familiarity, they never fail to yield a bit more information and inspiration on each successive trip. During the war years, I kept up as best I could with the sparse news of the European fashion industries and wrote regularly to our prewar suppliers, promising we would return to the European markets to do business as soon as transatlantic travel was possible.

Immediately upon the cessation of hostilities in the European theater, visitors from France and Britain began to come to the United States to reorient themselves in the American market and to encourage the return of American buyers. Those were the days when the U.S. dollar reigned supreme! The French couturier Lucien Lelong came to New York with other representatives of the French dressmaking industry, and subsequently visited us in Dallas at our invitation. He was the first member of the French haute couture to come to Dallas and the first live, notable Frenchman to have been in Dallas since 1939, so a commemorative bronze plaque, with his name and the date of his visit, was placed in our couture salon.

Simultaneously we began to receive a new publication from Britain, *The Ambassador*, which informed us how the famous English and Scottish textile mills were regearing themselves to consumer goods production. This magazine, more than any other publication from any other country, supplied us with useful information and kindled our desire to get back to Europe to buy. I doubt if the British government ever realized what this remarkable magazine and its publisher, Hans Juda, contributed to the economic recovery of its textile and garment industries.

In the spring of 1946, I was among the first American buyers to return to the European markets. With the merchandise manager of our men's division, Lillard Wallace, I embarked on the *Queen Mary* on one of its first postwar voyages carrying civilians. There was such great demand for space that Cunard had not been able to spare the time to transform the ship from a troop carrier to a passenger vessel; single cabins still had eight bunks in them; submarine warnings were still in evidence. We landed at Southampton, laden with food packages to take to English friends and with Scotch whiskey bought in New York, which we were advised would be in short supply in the land that produced it.

My first day in London I had luncheon with Gordon Yates, sales manager of Elizabeth Arden's European division, and he inquired if there was anything he could do to help me. I told him there was one man in England I wanted to meet, the publisher of *The Ambassador*, Hans Juda. He replied, "Well, that's very easy. My wife and I are dining with him tonight. Come and join us." This was a great piece of luck, for although I could have called on him at his office, I was able to meet him and his wife Elsbeth socially and immediately. The three of us established a rapport at once, and they became our closest and dearest friends. We have vacationed together in France, Italy, England, Ireland, Switzerland,

Austria, and Germany almost every year since we met. They had come from Germany to London in 1932; after a few years he entered the publishing business and she became a very accomplished fashion photographer, working under the pseudonym Jay. They guided me to the best mills, introduced me to the leading figures in British fashion, and related a blow-by-blow account of what it was like to live in London through the war years. We shared an interest in contemporary art, so they gave me a liberal education in what was going on in the field of painting and sculpture in postwar London.

British industry was perplexed about what to make for American buyers, so it simply made what it was making before the war; France and Italy had no doubts, so they started making the new things they had dreamt about during the war. We saw and bought enough to make us realize that the European markets would make a vast contribution to the quality and fashion levels of the store. Of necessity, during the war we bought piece goods and gave them to our makers to manufacture for us. This helped us to provide wanted merchandise for our customers, and it also gave us fabrics that in many cases were different from the regular selections on the market. Armed with this experience, we didn't hesitate to buy fine qualities of still "short in supply" British cashmeres, worsteds, and silks of better quality than our domestic manufacturers could either find or afford. At that time, many of our makers were willing to accept what is called in the trade "cut, make, and trim" orders, wherein they performed the manufacturing service to retailers who supplied the fabrics.

Mr. Wallace took care of the menswear purchases, but I had to buy French corsets, gloves, Swiss handkerchiefs, handbags, sweaters, stationery, costume jewelry, giftwear, and everything else. Buying was relatively easy, my big job was "selling" my purchases to the individual buyers, who guard their buying prerogatives jealously and are apt to resent anyone, including the boss, attempting to buy for them. I therefore made special efforts to excite them about the purchases I had made for their departments and to persuade them that if they sold the merchandise, they would be going to Europe themselves in subsequent years. Most of them accepted my merchandise commitments with good grace, and the following year a number of them made their own trips. Today some fifty Neiman-Marcus buyers make from one to three trips to Europe, India, the Far East, and South America, in pursuit of the best merchandise available. At one time a "Made in France" or a "Made in Italy" label added cachet to an article and helped to sell the merchandise. Today, however, the snobbery of such labels has worn off, and merchandise sells on its merits of fit, quality, originality, and value. We go where the best product is made, be it Indiana or India, Berlin, New Hampshire, or Berlin, Germany.

My wife did not accompany me on the first postwar trip, but when I was planning my second trip in 1948, I told my father that five weeks was too long for me to be away without Billie, to which he readily agreed, adding the suggestion that we take our three children, aged ten and twelve. "I think it's time they got a broader look at the world. A trip to Europe will greatly contribute to their education at this time," he said. We followed his advice and set forth on a great family adventure in June. I told the children they would see many famous and historic places on the trip, but there was one thing above all that I wanted them to observe, and that was the way people in other countries did the same things differently than we did, whether it was the method of holding a fork and knife or folding a napkin, and still be right. It was quite a game for them, and it wasn't long before Dick discovered that they stacked hay differently in Belgium than they did in France or the USA, and his sisters found that schoolchildren all wore uniforms and carried their schoolbooks in satchels or briefcases. This exercise really opened their eyes to pluralism. Their mother, after tucking them into bed, would stay up late into the night reading about the history of the various places she was taking them to the following day. They resisted museums, as most children do, so she developed a stratagem of limiting the time of their visits to the Louvre and making them beg to go back to see what they had missed on their previous visits. She succeeded.

On my first trip, all of the merchandise that I saw was new to me, but on the next trip I was disappointed to find so little that I hadn't seen before. It took a little time before I realized what I had seen the first time was simply an assortment of traditional merchandise that they had sold for years and would continue to make for years, as long as the commodity was in fashion, and that they actually produced relatively few fresh ideas on an annual basis. This made us realize that we had to encourage the European manufacturers to increase their new product development, to feed the voracious American appetite for something new. We explained that the American market was a fast one, and that what was new today was old tomorrow. I made speeches to British and French and Italian manufacturing groups, trying to tell them how the American and European markets differed, and urging them to visit the United States so they might better understand the variations of demand in a country with as many different climatic requirements as we have. I said, "You don't *have* to sell to the United States of America, but if you *want* to sell us, you have to understand us, our central heating and air conditioning, why a Neiman-Marcus is different from a Macy's." For this and other leadership work I did for French industry, the French government honored me by giving me the Medal of the Legion of Honor.

They took my advice — the same given to them by other retailers — and they did visit our country and learn from first-hand observation much more than I could tell them. The speech I gave them was almost identical to the one I made in China some twenty-four years later to the deputy director of the Corporation of Light Industries, for the problems of the Chinese are virtually the same that Europe faced, having been cut off from western commercial intercourse for so many years.

In 1956 I made my first visit to Scandinavia, and while in Stockholm I saw something which gave birth to a merchandising idea that has had a great effect on our business and on the many other retail enterprises that have copied us. The Nordiska store was having a promotion of French goods, with their windows filled with French merchandise and the tricolor decorating their escalator well. They had a French fashion show and had imported a French chef for their restaurant. I learned from the management of the store that they had received assistance from the French government, through its Comité des Foires. On my return to Paris, I met with the officials of the agency and told them I wanted to do something similar, but on a much larger scale. I envisioned making this into a great community event, in which we would bring over not only the best of French merchandise to sell, but the best examples of France's cultural achievements as well. I promised them the support of our art museum, orchestra, theater, and our library, if they could provide notable and worthy attractions. I wanted them to arrange for outstanding leaders who could speak on subjects as varied as the state of the French economy, trends in French education, and the New School of painting in Paris. I gave assurance that our various luncheon clubs would extend invitations to such authorities to speak to their memberships. I told them I wanted to do a dramatic decorating job which would transform our store into a veritable synthesis of France, and that we would create a façade for our building which would reproduce the Faubourg St.-Honoré. This would benefit not only French industry, but French tourism as well.

For all of this, we would need some financial assistance and a great deal of help in arranging the cultural ties. They bought my idea, so I then called a press conference to make a formal announcement. When I explained to the French press our plan to bring the Faubourg St.-Honoré to our store, I met with some skepticism, for they knew little about Texas and even less about Neiman-Marcus. One of the reporters said, "Mr. Marcus, that is impossible. You would require a building thirty stories tall." I assured them that it could and would be done within the limitations of our building, which I don't think they really believed until they came to Dallas and saw the results for themselves. They did give us very good press, which helped in the publicizing of the program to the fashion industries and to the vast number of private collectors and antiquarians who deluged me with offers to sell us all sorts of esoteric articles. It was at this time that the first rumors arose that I had been considered for the post of ambassador to France by President Eisenhower, prior to his appointment of Amory Houghton to that position. This was a rumor that was to come alive subsequently when President Kennedy was elected, and still again at the time of President Johnson's accession to the presidency. If I was ever considered, I had no knowledge of it, although I did receive a call one day from Chester Bowles, during the Kennedy administration, asking if I would be willing to take a post in South America. I told him I would not, since my entire orientation was European. I never heard anything more about the subject, which pleased me greatly, for neither my wife nor I had any real taste for the diplomatic life and its incessant demands for attendance at cocktail parties and dinners. I was willing to give my life to my country, but not my stomach.

When I returned to Dallas I had to get the cooperation of the community, which I had so blithely promised. We gave a luncheon in the store to which we invited the presidents of all the luncheon clubs; the directors of the museums, the orchestra, the theater; the heads of the schools; the mayor; and everybody else who might conceivably participate. In addressing them I said, "We are going to do something no other retailer has ever done. We are going to disclose our fall promotional program six months beforehand." Normally retailers keep tight security on their future plans to prevent competition from scooping them, but we had planned so long and thoroughly that we didn't think anyone could catch up to us. I explained that the mood of our government was towards the encouragement of foreign trade — in fact, the current Washington slogan was "trade not aid" — and that our proposed French Fortnight could become a valuable instrument towards this end. I gave them the details of the event and cited the numerous cultural tie-ins that were possible and available to any civic organization that wanted to be a participant. The announcement met with an enthusiastic reception; almost to a person, the question was raised, "What do you want us to do for you?" I replied, "We don't want you to do anything for us. Just tell us what would be of interest to you, and we will use our best efforts to help you, without expense to you."

The Museum of Fine Arts wanted an exhibition, so we arranged for a collection of Toulouse-Lautrec paintings, never before shown in America, from the Musée d'Albi. The Municipal Auditorium wanted to be included, and we were able to provide the largest exhibition of French tapestries, from the sixteenth to the twentieth century, ever shown in the United States. French speakers were provided for a half-dozen luncheon clubs, with the exception of the Rotary Club, which requested that we provide them with a capsule showing of French fashions. The hotel night-clubs booked French entertainers, and the *Dallas Times Herald* published an issue set in the typographical style of a French newspaper on the day preceding our official opening. Never had a store anywhere enlisted the resources of an entire community to back its promotional effort.

Two ideas germinated after my first meeting with the French officials. The first was a plan to get a large and distinguished group of French men and women to fly to Dallas for the opening on an Air France plane. We extended invitations to a select group of artists, writers, government leaders, couturiers, and manu-

18

Cordially Invite You to Attend the Formal Opening of the New and Exclusive Shopping Place for Fashionable Women, Devoted to the Selling of Ready-to-Wear Apparel

Opening Day, Tuesday, September Tenth, from 10 A. M. to 10 P. M. A Fashion Show Pre-eminent—Artistic Souvenirs

Tuesday, September Tenth, marks the advent of a new shopping place in Dallas—a store of Quality, a Specialty store—the only store in the City whose stocks are strictly confined to Ladies' Outer-Garments and Millinery, and presenting wider varieties and more exclusive styles in these lines than any other store in the South.

All are cordially invited to attend the Opening, to view the initial presentment of the most advanced and authoritative styles in Ready-to-Wear Apparel for Fall and Winter, to accept one of the handsome Souvenirs which will be distributed in honor of the occasion.

Our Store

In extending you an invitation to be present at the opening of the new store on Tuesday, September Tenth, we present herewith some of our claims to your valuable patronage.

Our decision to conduct a store in Dallas was not reached on impulse. We studied the field thoroughly and saw that there was a real necessity for such a shopping place as ours.

Our preparations have not been hasty. We have spent months in planning the interior, which is without an equal in the South.

We Will Improve Ready-to-Wear Merchandising

A store can be bettered by specialized attention.

Knowledge applied to one thing insures best results.

We began our intended innovation at the very foundation; that is to say, with the builders of Women's Garments.

We have secured exclusive lines which have never been shown in Texas before, garments that stand in a class alone as to character and fit.

Buying Facilities

Backed by the best sort of buying connections in every market, stocked by a corps of skilled buyers, managed by an experienced and expert store management, we are confident of our value-giving supremacy, and no store in the country where qualities and styles equal to ours are sold can offer lower prices.

Our Styles

All the pages of all the fashion journals, American and Foreign, can suggest no more than the open book of realism now here, composed of Suits, Dresses and Wraps of every favored style.

For the most important occasion of Formal Dress.

For the Informal afternoon call.

For Shopping or Business wear.

The selection will meet every taste, every occasion and every price.

Our Qualities and Values

As well as the Store of Fashions we will be known as the Store of Quality and Superior Values.

We shall be hypercritical in our selections. Only the finest productions of the best garment makers are good enough for us. Every article of apparel shown will bear evidence, in its touches of exclusiveness, in its chic and grace and splendid finish, to the cleverest designing and the most skilful and thorough workmanship.

Opening Souvenirs

As a memento of the occasion we will present a handsome Souvenir to visitors on opening day. These Souvenirs will be worthy of the offerings of the new store.

Carrie Neiman, 1903, age twenty

Herbert Marcus, Sr., 1905,
age twenty-seven

Mrs. Herbert Marcus, Sr., in 1910
with Edward, age one, and
Stanley, age five

Stanley Marcus, 1910, age five

Stanley Marcus, age ten,
Edward, age six, and
Herbert Jr., age two, in 1915

VOORHEE'S, DALLAS

*The original Neiman-Marcus store at the corner of Elm and Murphy
streets in 1913 after the fire*

Neiman-Marcus Co
The Store of Individual Shops

Neiman-Marcus Clothes in Society

Will Always Be Found in the Set Where Style and Personal Charm Radiate From the Most Modestly Priced as Well as the Most Expensive of Garments.

—If Fairy Godmothers were in vogue today as they were in the days of Cinderella they could accomplish no greater wonders in the transformation of dress than may be achieved every day in the Exclusive Neiman-Marcus Shops. The magic of the world's couturiers is assembled in these Individual Shops season after season. Throughout the width and breadth of the hemispheres the Neiman-Marcus Shops are without a peer. Traveled women have so conceded. Brides have found it to be the case. Dallas women know it is so. From the tiniest detail of the costume the Neiman-Marcus clothes achieve the Fairy Godmother magic to such an emphasized degree that even the most retiring woman will marvel at the transformation.

To begin with perhaps the most favored garment of a woman's wardrobe—the N.-M. Tailleur Suits.

—Each model, no matter how simple, with the magical touch that only the finest couturier in the world is able to achieve.

—of hard-finished Trycotyne .... —At $35 Upward.

—of soft haired chamois finish as evidenced in the exquisite Silver tones.

—Uniting on the slim silhouette, the narrow skirt, the predominating coat types, different in the individual models. —Priced $49.50 Upward.

—The velvet workmanship and exquisite material of Balbe is given chosen by the mattese and luncheon wear.

—The silk duvetyne, the imported velours, the velvets, the incomparable satin are chosen for afternoon teas and afternoon Country Club wear. —$75 Upward.

New lines and beauty of shade are shown in the N.-M. Coats seen in society.

The Velour Coats for Service.

—of decided military tendency.

—fur trimmed or self-trimmed collars.

—of velour or of rough English tweed. —$39.50 Upward.

The Velvet Wraps With Fur for Evening

—of exquisite twilight and sunset shades.

—of rippling fullness and clever drapery.

—of imposing stateliness. —$95 Upward.

From the ateliers of Stein & Blaine come the Exclusive Furs that wend their admired way in every society.

New Designs in Coats, Wraps and Sets of Separate Furs

—Russian or Hudson Bay Sable. —Kolinsky.
—Dark Eastern Mink. —Nutria.
—Silver Fox. —Gray Squirrel.
—Ermine. —and other fashionable furs.

N.-M. Frocks in society are as decided in their types as are the functions for which they were intended.

The N.-M. Trotteur Frocks for Daytime Needs

—Developed of the velour in the rich shades of green, brown and navy, with the side drapes, the huge white rimmed buttons down the back and on the sleeve. —$29.50

Or the Serge Bustle Frocks

—effecting the return of demure gray under the rolled collar, the perfectly plain, tight fitting sleeve, the graceful back bustle.

The Satin Frock for Afternoon Bridge or Knitting Afternoons.

—in the one-toned color harmonies principally we have an idea to contrast more effectively with the wonderful knitting bags.

—of blue navy, of dove or wood brown, with the simple rolled white satin collar.

Formality, however, demands Velvet—and Fashion adds Fur.

—Hence these clever frocks of cloth, with wide bands of Kolinsky, lux or squirrel.

—Never so far as we remember have more formal effects been accomplished. In one model the cloth is of the azure of the Venetian skies—the fur the richest of notria. —$135

—An evening frock of deepest black velvet, enriched with mother-of-pearl, shaded sequins feature the wide band of fur at the hem.

—Well used to advantage is seen in the fur "cache sex" collar of a simple brown velvet frock, with black bustle drapery.

The magic of contrast takes devious methods for expression in these Afternoon Frocks and Formal Dinner Gowns.

—One flimsy model of Belgian Blue Georgette has gathered note its finance a wonderful design of Terra Cotta embroidery, shot at random with the Indian reds of the Aztec pottery.

—Tunics that combine the bustle in the back and winged in the front are another of the unique modes that need the colorful embroidery to mark the exact termination of the tunic and how gracefully the bustle falls.

—and in one model the designer was so clever about the fastenings that you wonder if the fairy godmother's wand wasn't used after all when one slips the frock on.

—The suit illustrated speaks for its own unique place in a society set. Fashioned of trycotyne with striped collar and cuffs, striped band at hem, a superior silhouette due to superior design.

—Priced $49.50

Neiman-Marcus Co

The N.-M. Blouse is welcome in society.

—"A blouse," so bernard tells us, "should be a simple thing when occasion demands, but should be a decorative thing as well, when conspicuous.

But it takes the wizardry of the N.-M. Blouse Shop to achieve both of these requisites at once.

For Morning Wear Under the Simplest Tailleur Suit

—Georgette Blouses are seen, dipped in the self-same deep color notes of the suit, effectively simple, but dominant enough in style to be conspicuous "when occasion demands." —$10.50

Gifted Lace-Makers Are Responsible for the N.-M. First-Trimmed Blouses

—Developed in White Georgette.

—Simply and decoratively finished with the lace. —$8.50 Upward to $35

Mayer's Artistic Creations for Formal Affairs

—Portrayals of his Blouse mastercraftsmanship.

—Graceful models of Georgette or Chiffon.

—Frosty things of Satin and Lace.

—Exclusive, individual models of Georgette and hand touches. —$25 Upward to $45

THE BOYS' SHOP

Unloose "New" Junior Norfolk Suits for the Small Boys

—of blue serge.
—shepherd's plaids.
—green, gray or brown mixtures. —$6 to $10

Children's Rompers

—chambray or gingham.
—contrasting collars and cuffs. —75c to $2.50

Children's Hats

—white, black and brown velours.
—white, black and brown plushes. —$1 to $5

Neiman-Marcus Shoes in Society

"Without proper Footwear no ensemble can be complete."
—Sailes.

—The wonderful Footwear that has been assembled in the Shoe Shop for the season of 1917 is an attainment in itself that establishes beyond dispute the superiority of the Neiman-Marcus Individual Shops.

For Tailleur Wear

—The illustration to the far right is an example of the wonderful shoe craftsmanship that built it.

—In Beet-Root Brown.

—Tapering heel, arch and vamp. —$16.50

For Evening Functions

—The artistic Evening Slipper beside it.

—Of Silver Cloth, with the iridescence of the moon in the beaded buckle. —$12.50

For Afternoon Affairs

—The American adaptation of the French Spat.
—Vamp of a Wood Brown.
—Chamois top of glowing ochre. —$17.50

—Note the new style of the fastening below.

For Service

—The laced Boot to the left.
—Of Penna Tan vamp, attractive covert top. —$11.50

For Boudoir Ease

—This attractive Novelty Mule.
—In any shade to match the Silken Negligee.
—Of Tufted Satin.
—With garlands of French hand-made flowers for ornamentation. —$3.50

—Mail orders are filled from this Exclusive Emporia to all parts of the United States.

Liberty Bonds.

—Will be accepted at this store on payment of merchandise or monthly bills at par.

—We are entering whole-heartedly in this great and patriotic American movement, and this is our immediate way of serving our Government.

—Not only will we subscribe, but we will accept in payment of accounts or merchandise either the first issue or the second issue of Liberty Bonds.

—We believe in their sacred security—we believe it is everyone's obligation and willing duty to buy as many Liberty Bonds as they are able.

For the Society Woman the Corset Is of Equal Importance as the Gown.

—If a Corset is not perfectly fitted, if it binds and forbids the svelte lines of the slim silhouette it had best not be worn.

—N.-M. Corsets add to the natural grace of the figure—every type of Corset is here ready to create that expensive, inimitable grace. —$5.00 upward to $25.00.

—Or if the Corset is meant for outdoor sports the new Gotham Girdles will accomplish the swing graceful lines of the true athletic woman.

The N.-M. Hats Have Social Distinction for Everyone

—Foremost among the clever new models just received is the illustrated Velvet conception of rich brown with self-colored satin ribbon that tosses its proud ends skyward. —$29.50

Adding height to fashionable women is the role undertaken by many of the N.-M. Tailleur Hats.

—One clever method employs the high bows of self material; another method used forces the brims to unwonted height; still another increases the height by adding a flared crown above a turban. —$10, $15, $25

Picturesque Hats for formal wear are numerous

—Gainsboroughs trimmed in novel flowers and burnt goose conceits are effective.

—Soft contours shading the face are often preferred.

—In black, beetroot, taupe and the glowing shades of the autumn sun may be chosen. —$10, $15, $25

—Imported models are being daily unpacked, a few at a time. Ask to see them.

Neiman-Marcus Co

Neiman Marcus Co.
Individual Shops for Gentlewomen

The Red Cross Roll Call begins this week. Respond surely!

Madame or Mademoiselle, whatever her type, will find in the Neiman-Marcus collections this week exactly the right thing for every occasion. The Greater Store enters its third week of greater activities with the most noteworthy and by far the largest collections of smart fashions in all its brilliant history of fashion selling. The needs of the individual have been carefully considered; one has only to choose.

EVERY IMPORTANT FASHION OF THE SEASON

ACCESSORY RIGHTNESS

Neiman-Marcus Company sponsors the costume built of little things upon the harmony and appropriateness of which lies the chic of the whole.

A knitting bag of Revolutionary days inspired a French bag maker to create a charming bag of crepe goat in mulberry rose, silver moon, or blue with matching kid trim, pictured ... 22.50

New kid gloves from France were picked smartly in three smart shades, pictured ... 3.95

Distinctively modern is this bracelet of beaten metal alternating with multi-colored enamel, pictured ... 22.50

Paris combines in new necklets of rope, pearls, plaques of carnelian, jade or lapis, carved in the ancient Chinese manner and studded with rhinestones, pictured ... 17.50

FIRST FLOOR SHOPS

Rich Furs Tell the Coat Story

79.50 upward to 195.00

Three Smart Modes
for Madame

Left: A jacket frock after Beer in which French jersey in Vassar rose employs irregularities of silk crepe in the same color to accent its chic ... Center: Hattie Carnegie has cut the sleeves of this black satin frock to form an ingenious cape effect which ties in a bow ... Right: An unusual supper frock which dares the short sleeve. It combines a bodice of gleaming gold, green and rose metal lamé with transparent velvet skirt in gold brown. After Cheruit.

These three smart gowns point a fashion truth in fabrics ... jersey, satin, velvet and metal lamé ... and they emphasize the ultimate exquisite chic of the Neiman-Marcus dress collections. The smart woman will find in just-opened arrivals daytime dresses for every occasion at prices she wants to pay.

29.50 upward to 195.00

FOOTWEAR RIGHTNESS

depends upon distinction of materials as well as smart design, and upon fine workmanship as well as appropriateness. Neiman-Marcus combines these essentials of shoe rightness in wide collections of ultimate chic for every occasion ... presented in two smart new shoe shops at

10.00 upward to 32.50

White Is Smart for Evening

Neiman-Marcus sponsors the Paris evening gown of white which doubles its fashion importance by its uneven hemline.

68.50 upward to 250.00

RIDING HABITS

AT NEIMAN-MARCUS

In 1937, seated left to right: Edward Marcus, Herbert Sr., Herbert Jr., Stanley. Standing is Lawrence Marcus

There's a *Trend*

toward magnificence ... but with a mood: Fabrics and furs are fabulous, but the motif is restraint. Ornamentation is rich, but the silhouette is simple. To be beautifully dressed requires a master hand at detail, the fine art of stopping short at the desired effect. Mecca of all the fashionable women in the Southwest is Neiman-Marcus.

Greetings mingle with exclamations over the glory and sweep of the new fashions .. Our 31st year finds us serving the largest clientele in our history ... finds women buying finer and more beautiful clothes than ever

There's a Trend

PATCHES OF SUE . . . used ruthlessly, for accent. For right, seen in honest bands on richly colored latex. An evening gown with its own jacket. Junior Deb salon. **$295**

UNEXPECTED SUEDE . . . deep-toned in bands looking Persian lamb in a jacket over a Babbie Rosenstein's alternate wool dress. *center above,* **$595**

CAPE ENSEMBLE . . . where the lingerie cape swings over a dress as straight and slim as a reed, and wears two flaming red bows to accent the green wool. Hattie Carnegie's. *above.* **$295**

SLIM AS A PIPESTEM . . . again and again. Forming the basis of the perfect black dress, picked up by jewelry-buttons and silver kid belt, right. **$9.75**

BOSOM EMPHASIS . . . usually with cut and seaming or with shirring. Germaine Monteil achieves it by a sapphire blue jersey midriff contrasting against black wool, far right. **$9.75**

SLIGHTLY CONCAVE DIAPHRAGM . . . with high, rounded bustline, and rounded hips correctly gained without the slightest strain. French imports and the ever "power-net" girdles work wonders toward sculpturing your figure . . . Corset Shop

DOG COLLAR NECKLACES . . . hugging a high, neckline Best liked gold, multicolor, and pearl versions in wide choices . . . Jewelry Shop

NEIMAN-MARCUS

Moira Cullen, 1944

Stanley Marcus with his father, 1945

Fashion rodeo at the Flying L Ranch, 1947. From left to right:
Mike Romanoff, pseudo-prince from Oklahoma, Neiman-Marcus vice-president
Nick Parker, Stanley Marcus, Ed Crowley of the Los Angeles Town House,
and tennis player Jack Kramer

Dallas Museum of Fine Arts Publishes Work by Medellin

OCTAVIO MEDELLIN: XTOL, DANCE OF THE ANCIENT MAYAN PEOPLE. Murals from The Temple of the Tigers at Chichen Itza, Yucatan, Mexico. Linoleum Block Prints by Octavio Medellin. Dallas Museum of Fine Arts, 1947. $10.

In "Xtol," the Dallas Museum of Fine Arts has made a model, becoming toward publishing the works of Southwestern artists and is to be highly commended for the result as well as for taking the

$1,500,000 loan

The glittering opening of the State Fair of Texas
also heralds the opening of the much-awaited exhibition of
"old master" paintings secured by the State Fair
from the Metropolitan Museum of Art. More than $1,500,000
worth of art masterpieces are now on display
in the Dallas Museum of Fine Arts at Fair Park. This is a
very exciting showing, for it is the most valuable
single loan ever made by the Metropolitan. The exhibit is now
open to the public from 10 a.m. to 6 p.m. daily.
Shown here: three from one impressive collection of
new looking coats for an exciting fall season in Dallas.

FAMOUS SECOND FLOOR SHOPS

Mr. and Mrs. Herbert Marcus, Sr., 1948

Carrie Neiman, 1948

Billie and Stanley Marcus in Woodstock, New York, 1951

Billie Marcus, Coco Chanel, and Stanley Marcus at Edward Marcus's BlackMark Ranch, 1957

"Miz Jones, we're a little limited on dress materials. We promised Neiman-Marcus we'd go easy on fabrics if they'd quit sellin' chicken feed!"

"It's wonderful, Harry! How late does Neiman-Marcus stay open?"

The Neiman-Marcus façade on Ervay Street during the French Fortnight, 1957

Neiman-Marcus

THE EXPOSITION

This famed event is multi-faceted and even more significant this year in view of our 50th anniversary. To the fashion industry it is the presentation of the most meaningful of all awards. To the southwest, a singular social event. And, to all the world, the very essence of N-M, compressed into one fabulous week. It begins with the fashion show and grand ball tomorrow evening at the Statler Hilton, followed by the fashion show and luncheon on Tuesday — both performances are already sold out, with proceeds going to the Dallas Women's Council charities.

ROLLS-ROYCE

In presenting this year's Exposition, we are joined by the world's most aristocratic name in motor cars. Like Neiman-Marcus, Rolls-Royce is celebrating its 50th anniversary in America, and for the occasion, the largest shipment of the fine automobiles ever to enter the United States has now arrived in Dallas. You can see both the motor cars and some most interesting automotive exhibits on view now in our store and the Statler Hilton lobby.

CHANEL

Our 1957 guest of honor is a single, and most singular designer — Mademoiselle Gabrielle (Coco) Chanel. In one lifetime, she has been a greater and more lasting influence on fashion than perhaps any two others in the designing world. We are most deeply honored to have her as our guest. (This tweed suit, an original from her Paris salon.)

OUR 50TH ANNIVERSARY

Months in planning and preparation, it promises to reveal one of the most exciting periods of celebration the southwest has ever seen. The Fashion Exposition, held in concert with Rolls-Royce is the dramatic "first" in a season of unprecedented excitement to come.

THE GOLDEN AGE EXPOSITION

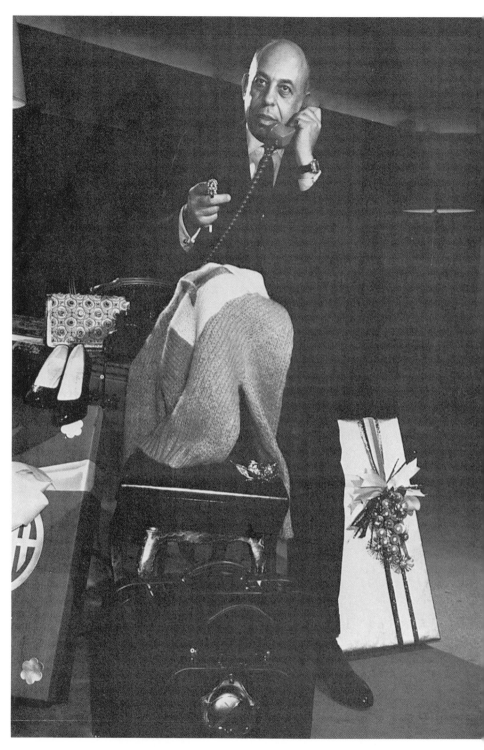

Stanley Marcus amid a selection of Neiman-Marcus Christmas gifts,
1958

*Stanley Marcus with Marc Bohan during his visit to Dallas for the
second French Fortnight, 1966*

Stanley Marcus writing in his black book during an inspection tour of main Dallas store, 1967

Stanley and Billie Marcus, 1971

This is the plate we gave you in 1907.

Neiman-Marcus

We've reached our 60th anniversary! To celebrate we went to Italy and famous ceramist Piero Fornasetti for this 1967 design. This one is a tongue-in-cheek meeting of the years on white porcelain. The first one was fine and described in our opening day advertisement as a "memento of the occasion" ... "worthy of the offering of the new store". So is this one. Bring us one of the 1907 plates and we'll trade even. The 1967 plate is 10.00, in our Gift Galleries, fourth floor, Downtown. Also NorthPark and Fort Worth.

This is the plate we'll give you tomorrow if you bring in the 1907 plate.

Stanley Marcus with President Johnson at the White House for the swearing in of the board of directors of the Urban Institute, April 1968. Whitney Young, then head of the Urban League, is in the background

The opening of the new Houston store, January 1969. From left to right: Stanley and Lawrence Marcus, Mrs. Herbert Marcus, Sr., and Edward Marcus

Stanley Marcus with Perle Mesta at the Neiman-Marcus East Meets West Fortnight Dinner in Dallas, 1969

Jerrie Marcus Smith, 1973

Wendy Marcus Raymont, 1973

Left to right: Richard Marcus, Tom Alexander, a senior vice-president of Neiman-Marcus, and Stanley Marcus, 1973

Stanley Marcus with Mayor Richard Daley in Chicago, 1973

Stanley and Richard Marcus, 1973

Halston
and the Caftan

*Simplicity is his forte. This
seven-ounces of pongee silk…
shell pink or ripe peach… proves
how endlessly beautiful pure line
can be. How wise Halston's
decision to pare down and
down to the almost nothing
that is everything in lyric
movement between a woman
and a caftan. 340.00 in our
Halston collection, Couture Shop,
Downtown, NorthPark and Fort Worth.*

Neiman-Marcus

TO STANLEY MARCUS, WITH THANKS + BEST WISHES,
FROM Tom K. Ryan

facturers. We had to secure landing permission for the plane, since Air France did not have Dallas landing rights. With the assistance of Senator Lyndon B. Johnson this was accomplished. The second idea was to publish a special section in the October 15 issue of *Vogue*, celebrating the Fortnight. We felt this was necessary to give a national dimension to the event. We titled this "The Best of France, from A to Z." Only the top French companies were asked to advertise, and I personally went back to France to explain what the Fortnight was all about, and why they couldn't afford not to be represented in the *Vogue* section. I had to see each manufacturer individually, repeating the same story eighty times, to the point that I found myself dreaming at night about my sales pitch. Some forty-five designers, perfumers, textile manufacturers, and transportation organizations finally completed the alphabet (several letters had more than one trade name listed).

We arranged with the Chambre Syndicale de la Couture to present a joint fashion show from all of the leading designers and to send on the special plane a group of the most famous French mannequins. The fashion show was presented at a gala ball honoring His Excellency Hervé Alphand, ambassador from France, the Saturday evening preceding the formal opening of the Fortnight. A local charity was the beneficiary of the ball, at $100 per person, and we had a capacity audience of the leading socialites of the entire Southwest.

I've often been asked to name the most exciting experiences of my life, and surely the arrival of that Air France plane must head the list. As I saw the aircraft break through the fog and taxi up to the gate, a thrill of accomplishment went through me. For six months I had planned, dreamed, and thought about almost nothing but the Fortnight. Now it was a reality. Aboard the plane were Chanoine Kir, the eighty-two-year-old former Resistance fighter and a current member of the French Chamber of Deputies;

Bernard Buffet, the painter; Pierre Daninos, the writer; Raoul Mayer, managing director of the Galeries Lafayette; Louise de Vilmorin, poet, novelist and playwright; manufacturers; and mannequins.

When our guests assembled for the ribbon-cutting on Monday morning and saw the façade of our building, which had been transformed to resemble the boutiques of the Faubourg St.-Honoré, when they saw our first floor decorated with huge photo-murals depicting the Place de la Concorde and white Renaults in the aisles, when they saw a series of famous Impressionist paintings reproduced in French textiles, they cheered. Of even greater importance, our customers were overwhelmed; not to the extent, however, that it interfered with their desire to buy the choice articles of French manufacture that were on display. It was, as one of the visitors commented, "an artistic triumph and a commercial success." No nicer words could be said about the opening of a play on Broadway, or a Fortnight in Dallas.

The fundamental purpose of the Fortnight concept was to help us overcome a historical business lag, which always occurred in mid-October. Other retailers in the country had this same business slowdown between the end of the fall season and the beginning of Christmas business. They had met the problem of running anniversary or birthday sales, for which they bought special purchases of lower-priced merchandise, thus stimulating extra volume. By staging a theatrical production and by buying large quantities of fine merchandise, we accomplished our objective of enlarging business during a period of passive customer interest. We turned October into a month of peak traffic, even surpassing Christmas; we attracted thousands of new customers to the store, some of whom only looked; we enhanced our national and international reputation; we satisfied the nostalgia of those who had visited France, and we stimulated those who had never been there to want to go; we netted the largest sales increase for that month in our entire history.

If we had any doubts about the Fortnight idea, they were quickly dispelled. Actually, we had a lion by the tail, and if we had wanted to let it loose with this one Fortnight, our customers wouldn't have let us. Before it was over, they were already asking us, "What country are you going to feature next year?" The city-wide cultural attractions helped sell merchandise by creating a greater appreciation of France and its heritage; our merchandise presentation helped bring forth record crowds for all of the various cultural activities.

Britain had sent down an observer to see the French show. They were so impressed that they quickly signed up as the sponsor for the 1958 Fortnight. We brought over the Old Vic Company, and when we were unable to find an impresario to book it for a one-week run, we took over that role ourselves, ending up, much to our surprise, with a net profit. We flew in a London bobby, who created great publicity assisting the Dallas police in directing traffic outside our store. Scottish bagpipers piped the ambassador into the gala ball in his honor; Wedgwood craftsmen demonstrated the technique of making their famous Jasperware; a men's fashion show modeled by some of our leading citizens demonstrated the leadership of Britain in quality fabrics and fashions for men.

The second Fortnight brought hosts of fellow retailers to Dallas to investigate how we were staging the event and what merchandise we were buying. We tried to be helpful by providing them with a list of resources, an extra service which we felt would be beneficial to our co-sponsors. Like all successful endeavors, the Fortnights were copied. The following year there were a dozen foreign fairs staged in as many cities over the nation. Even Europe followed us, and to this day such events are produced annually in Düsseldorf, Geneva, Paris, Amsterdam, and London. Few if any of our imitators were willing to put in as much time or money as we did, and none utilized the total community cooperation that we were able to achieve.

In 1959 we explored South America, bringing back a great deal

211

of inspiration but very little merchandise. We had to "synthesize" the merchandise story, by producing in this country clothes and accessories based on South American colorings and native Indian designs. We had a good show, which maintained the customer satisfaction we had established, but financially it was our least successful effort. We were able to put together, with the assistance of John Wise, the preeminent archeological gold dealer, one of the finest collections of pre-Columbian gold ever shown in this country. Nelson Rockefeller, Paul Tishman, and Robert Woods Bliss were generous in their willingness to lend fine examples from their collections. The Rockefeller pieces alone had a value in excess of $1,000,000, and since they were very fragile, I carried them on my lap on the flight to Dallas. Despite our impressive guest list, which included the entire South American diplomatic corps from Washington, Perle Mesta, and other notables from the various countries, the guest who made the headlines was a live llama from Peru. Her name was Llinda Lee and she had perfect household manners. She appeared on every floor of the store and on television, attracting great crowds of delighted children and adults, who had never before seen a real, live llama. In order to get hotel accommodations for her at the Statler-Hilton, we had to persuade the hotel's board of directors to convene an emergency meeting to lift its ban on the housing of livestock in its hotel.

The following year we turned to Italy, which more than made up for our South American adventure. In addition to providing us with an abundance of merchandise for all departments of the store, Italy offered a wealth of ideas to incorporate into the decoration of the store and a plenitude of cultural attractions. We brought over a group of twenty Sicilian singers and folk dancers, who performed at the Ambassador's Ball. We had housed them at one of our better hotels, two to a room, only to learn an hour before they were due on stage that they were very unhappy and about to strike. We sent in an Italian-speaking intermediary to

212

ascertain their grievances, and discovered that they were dissatisfied with their accommodations. They didn't like being separated, and wanted one large room for the whole troupe. Disaster was avoided when we were able to locate, in one of the lesser hotels, a large reception room, with plumbing facilities conveniently located one flight up. This suited them to perfection.

We imported the sets and costumes for the opera *The Daughter of the Regiment* from the Teatro Massimo Opera Company in Palermo, which were used by the Dallas Civic Opera Company in a distinguished performance. In my research for the Fortnight, I visited every part of Italy and fell in love with it all. Sicily interested me particularly, an island barely emerging from the past into the present, while Venice was a city of the past with no intention of joining the twentieth century. We drove through the whole country, from the Amalfi Drive up through Naples to Rome, and then through the hill towns to Arezzo and Assisi en route to Florence and Milan. Everywhere we found merchandise of interest and met warm, charming people who wanted to do something new for us and to be a part of our Due Settimane, as they translated our Fortnight.

These annual Fortnight shopping trips exposed me to the fine art as well as the folk art of the various countries. I made it my business to educate myself on what was going on in the contemporary art of a country before I arrived. I usually knew what galleries carried the works of the artists I most liked, and then local friends would expand my knowledge of both artists and galleries. We started our collecting activities too late to be able to afford the works of the nineteenth-century Impressionists and even the twentieth-century painters of the prewar years, so we bought what we liked and what we could afford, learning as we went along. Financial appreciation never concerned us, nor was the artist's public recognition of too much importance. The excitement was, and still is, in pitting our judgment against the market,

213

speculating on the future pleasure from a given work of art. Perhaps my experience as a professional retailer had prepared me for this approach to art collecting. We made our mistakes in judgment, but we also had our successes. During this trip to Italy we bought a still life by Morandi at a price of $750, a sculpture by Marini for $1,000, paintings by Cagli for $400, as well as works by other lesser-known artists for considerably less money.

In Sicily I was greatly impressed by the traditional puppet shows performed with puppets four feet tall. The plots of the plays were based on the historic events of the Crusades, filled with the drama of the courageous Christian knights in combat with the Moorish infidels, in which the knights always emerged victorious, slicing off the heads of their foes, which rolled noisily across the stage. I dubbed them "Sicilian Westerns." I found a complete set of the puppets, some forty, which I bought and then loaned to the store for use in the decor for the Fortnight, where they were suspended rather dramatically in the escalator wells. I held on to them for several years and subsequently gave them to the Drama Department of the University of Texas, where they are used for study and occasional performances.

Our Italian fashion show introduced many new designers' names to the Southwest; the ticket sale for it benefited Boys Town of Italy, located outside of Rome. One of our most distinguished Italian guests was the beautiful Giuliana Camerino, a Venetian gentlewoman, who had been forced by the war to go into business making handbags. One day I had spotted a very good-looking girl in our store, carrying a most unusual handbag, so I approached her to find out where she had bought it. It turned out she was an Italian mannequin making a cross-country tour in behalf of the Italian *Alta Moda,* and that she had bought the bag from Roberta in Venice. I made up my mind to make Roberta my first quest when I went to Venice, several months later. It turned out that Roberta was Giuliana Camerino, and we became her first important American customer, and eventually her largest one, establishing

214

a record for selling more of her bags, at prices ranging from $150 to $350, than any other store in the United States.

The day after we met Giuliana, we were taken by an American friend, Bill Weintraub, co-founder of *Esquire* magazine, to a very old textile mill which produced superb-quality velvet and brocaded fabrics on hand looms. The prime customer of this mill was the Vatican, to which it supplied cloths for vestments and upholstery for the papal quarters. We saw a beautiful piece of velvet on the looms in the reds, blues, and greens of a medieval stained-glass window. I bought a few yards and took it over to my new friend Giuliana, asking her to make a handbag out of it for my wife. She too responded to its beauty and quality, and inquired where I had found it, expressing some apprehension about making a bag out of velvet upholstery cloth. She finally agreed, and when the bag was finished two days later she was as thrilled as we were. "Just to think that I have lived all my life in Venice, and was completely unaware of the existence of this weaver who works just two canals away from me," she said. Thus the fashion of the velvet handbag was born, a fashion which became the greatest vogue in handbags after the war. She worked with the mill in developing *trompe l'oeil* designs, which are still one of the great hallmarks of her collections.

She must go down in my opinion as one of the most creative designers in my experience, for she has demonstrated the ability to come up with a constant flow of new ideas in materials, frames, and shapes year after year. Some designers of clothes and ac-cessories make one or two great collections and expend all of their ideas. Then they go on repeating themselves, season after season. Not so Giuliana, who has a never-ending source of in-spiration. This is the characteristic that makes the difference between the great and the not-so-great designers and artists in general. This was true of Picasso, and Dior, and Claire McCardell, and it is true of Galanos, and Yves Saint Laurent. Great art and great fashion design are progressive, not static.

215

Our Italian Fortnight was so successful that we yielded to the requests of our customers to extend it for another two weeks, thus making it a "double Fortnight." This proved a mistake, for it was impossible to prolong the excitement. We learned the hard way something the theatrical profession discovered many years ago — leave them wanting more. By now we had established some records of import purchases which were most impressive; we could show that our first two events had not only resulted in greatly increased purchases from the countries featured, but that our business continued to grow after the Fortnight in the following years. Other countries, impressed with the thoroughness of our presentation and by our attention to the cultural tie-ins, wanted to participate. We, in turn, had learned enough about this new theatrical form of retailing to realize that the success depended upon four factors: first, intensive market research done in the country by a large staff of our own buyers, who not only bought the best merchandise available, but who also helped create new products; second, the store decoration, which had to be exciting and dramatic from the first through the sixth floor; third, advertising, which was concentrated exclusively on the merchandise of the honored country for a two-week period; and fourth, special events, consisting of the various cultural events outside the store, artisans working in the store, and above all, the presence of well-known people from the country involved, for in the long run, it is people who make news, not merchandise.

We had learned also that this package cost $100,000 (now, with inflation, $250,000) to produce. We were willing to put up half the dollars in cash ourselves, if the country, or its trade expansion agency and/or its industry would put up the other half. We did not figure into these cost estimates any allowance for the time and efforts of our staff, for if we had ever done this I think we would have abandoned the whole idea. We categorically refused to guarantee any fixed amount of purchases, saying that it was to our interests to buy as much as we thought that we could sell at a profit, and to the country's interests for the promotion to be so profitable that we would want to come back for more, and not to have huge residues left which would tarnish the merchandise reputation of the country. We turned down countries which were willing to pay the entire cost for the tourism value of the Fortnight; unfortunately they did not produce enough merchandise in our quality levels to justify any sizable investments on our part. Switzerland, Austria, Denmark, and the Far East (twice) each became our partners, and then Italy repeated, and France and Britain each came back for two more Fortnights. In between, we ran a Fortnight USA, featuring the best of American production. It was a good show, but it was difficult to generate the same excitement in decoration and merchandise; they both suffered from over-familiarity; the New York skyline and Coca-Cola are commonplace — Venice and Mouton-Rothschild are not.

An unsolicited testimonial to the pulling powers of our Fortnights came from a Swiss knit manufacturer following our Swiss Fortnight, who said, "As a result of my participation in your event, I opened an important new account." I told him that I was happy to learn of it but not surprised. "Was it a large store in New York?" I asked. "No," he replied. "It was a retailer in Düsseldorf whom I had never been able to lure into my showroom. After he saw that my merchandise was being featured in your store, he came in and told me that if my goods were good enough for Neiman-Marcus, they were good enough for him."

Those responsible for the planning and organization of these affairs get enough experience dealing with foreign governments and their officials to qualify for positions in the State Department. Negotiations are apt to be laborious and frustrating, tact and diplomacy must be employed constantly, and protocol must be meticulously observed. Only in one case have we been left holding the bag, in 1970, when Australia backed away from its commitment, forcing us into a last-minute substitution. For some years we had been pressed by a succession of Australian representatives

217

to produce an Australian Fortnight. We had been quite negative, because we doubted the country's productive capacity to meet our merchandise requirements. They came to us again, and persuaded us to send a member of our staff to survey the potential of their markets. He came back somewhat skeptical, but thought we might be able to pull it off. The Australians then stipulated that if I would go out personally with competent buyers to help explain our needs to the Australian manufacturers, they would accept our standard proposal of sharing the costs on a fifty-fifty basis. I decided to make the trip with two of the most creative members of our organization.

After a few days in Sydney, we realized that it would be a Herculean effort on our part, but that it could be done in a manner which would be mutually creditable. We developed many new lines of merchandise, selected colors and design motifs from their aboriginal art, and promised to send more buyers back to finish the job. It happened that there was some turmoil in their government at the time we were there, and shortly after our departure, the head of their Department of Trade was replaced. Faced by budgetary problems, the new man wanted no part of the deal set up by his predecessor, and wrote us canceling the agreement. We tried to reopen the matter through the former United States ambassador to Australia, Ed Clark of Texas, but without success. It was too late at this point to interest any other government in a Fortnight to be produced in five months, so we were in a quandary, to put it mildly.

An amusing anecdote did come out of our Australian adventure which was recounted to me not long ago by the ex-wife of our former ambassador to New Zealand Kenneth Franzheim. She said her husband had claimed that one of the advantages the ambassadorial appointment carried was that, for at least three years, Neiman-Marcus wouldn't be a habitual way of life for her and that he would be freed the monthly bills from our store. She commented that this did not turn out to be as true as he had anticipated, for the airmail service was quite good.

After they had been in their new post for a few months, the Australian minister of external territories invited them to take a trip to New Guinea, where he promised to take them to the wildest and most exciting parts, rarely visited by Americans. They flew to Papua and were taken up the Sepik River by jet-powered boats past little villages until they came to the one which was the seat of the local chieftain. They tied up at a native-style dock, disembarked, and pushed their way in the rain through the undergrowth until they arrived at the chieftain's hut. While awaiting his appearance, the natives and the New Guinea officials assured them they would find many native handcrafts of rarity and great value and of a type not made for the tourist market. The chieftain arrived and was presented by the interpreter with a full explanation of both the importance of the ambassadorial status of Mr. Franzheim and of the great State of Texas, where cattle with long horns roamed the land. The interpreter indicated with gesticulations the approximate size of Texas, explaining the significance of the state and the power it represented. The chieftain listened attentively and smiled, saying, "Ah yes, Neiman-Marcus." Mrs. Franzheim concluded by saying, "Finally my husband realized that the long arm of Neiman-Marcus reached everywhere in search of unusual merchandise and touched vendors in the remotest parts of the world."

And now a word of explanation about what had happened to set the stage for this coincidence. When we were in Australia, Kay Kerr, our very able vice-president in charge of fashion direction, thought that as long as she was in the vicinity of New Guinea, she would fly there in the hope of finding authentic old native crafts for sale and decoration. She flew to Port Moresby, chartered a bush plane to take her to the back country, and made some purchases at the very village the Franzheims would later visit. The Franzheims were right — Neiman-Marcus does get around.

Shortly after getting the news of the Australian cancellation, I was having lunch with an out-of-town advertising man, who inquired what country we were going to feature that fall. I told him the sad story about Australia and commented that we had just about run out of countries. He said, "Perhaps you'll have to invent one." "You're right," I replied. "You have a great idea. We'll have a Ruritanian Fortnight this fall." At the moment I made the statement I had no idea of the origin of the Ruritania, that it stemmed from the novel *Prisoner of Zenda* by Anthony Hope. It just had an operetta connotation to me. After luncheon, I went up to see Tom Alexander, our senior vice-president in charge of sales promotion, who also had been struggling for a solution. I tried out the idea on him and asked him to sleep on it. The next day he came in and said, "You know, I've always wanted to start a country from scratch, to create its history, write its national anthem, design its currency and postage stamps. Yes, I think the idea will wash." Without further consultation, we announced to our merchandising colleagues, who had been impatiently awaiting a decision, to schedule buyers' trips to Ruritania. First they thought we were stark raving mad, but as we explained that this spoof gave us free license to buy anything, since Ruritania was a free port country, they got into the spirit of the thing, and accepted Ruritania as a fact and not as a fancy.

We had great fun establishing the genealogy of the monarchy, commissioning a national anthem, designing the postage stamps, and creating the coin of the realm, which was made in chocolate for us in Holland, since King Rudolph, the reigning monarch, oddly preferred chocolate to silver. We even wrote an addendum to the *World Almanac,* giving a thumbnail sketch of the history and sights of the country. For the gala ball, we invited Victor Borge to play the part of the prime minister and Gloria Vanderbilt Cooper and her husband Wyatt to appear as the Queen and King.

Our public entered into the spirit of the make-believe country and enjoyed it fully, although it was reported that some customers were finding it difficult to locate Ruritania in their atlas and that others admitted to having visited it on a recent trip to Europe.

Although Ruritania didn't set any sales records, we didn't fare too badly, and we felt encouraged to try another variation of the Fortnight theme the following year by staging a great flower show, which we entitled a Fête des Fleurs. We invited Prince Rainier and Princess Grace to be our guests of honor, and they accepted. Democratic America loves royalty, and the public turned out en masse to catch a glimpse of this storybook romance couple. We created a miniature cactus garden in recognition of Prince Rainier's great collection of cacti in Monaco; the store was decorated from top to bottom with flowers, and merchandise was developed with flower themes and colors.

While Princess Grace was visiting The Greenhouse prior to the opening of our show, I took Prince Rainier to the King Ranch, which fascinated him, as it does all visitors. The only time he was nonplussed was at lunch at the chuckwagon on the range, when one of the cowboys casually commented that the barbecued beef we were eating came from some steers we had seen being herded together just a few hours earlier. As a memento of his visit to Texas, we presented him with a pair of Texas wildcats for his world-famous zoo in Monaco, and cowboy boots and ten-gallon hats for the two children.

Our Fortnights, seventeen years after their inception, still show evidence of great vitality and give every indication of continued longevity. Despite the fact that a large number of our customers have now traveled to the places we portray, interest is undiminished. Much of the Fortnights' success can be attributed to the superb and authentic atmospheric translations created by our designer Alvin Colt, who is a master at bringing the quality of the theater into a retail store. When Gerald van der Kemp, director of the museum at Versailles, first came into the store during our

221

last French Fortnight and saw our reproduction of the Hall of Mirrors of Versailles with mirrored columns, parquet floors, and painted ceilings, tears came to his eyes. He embraced Mr. Colt and said, "You have done this with the soul of a Frenchman!"

Many customers have asked why we don't take the show on the road by moving it on to our other stores. The Fortnights would be great hits in any of the cities in which we operate, but the costs of installation and the impossibility of tying up the cast of VIPs make this idea impractical. All of our stores get a ruboff value from the Fortnights, though our downtown Dallas store reaps the major benefits. They have served the great and useful purpose for which they were designed; they have become one of the outstanding merchandising devices of the postwar era; and they should continue until we run out of either countries or ingenuity.

Although the Fortnights were not conceived in any sense of altruism, I get great satisfaction from the fact that through them we have greatly enriched the cultural life of the entire community. When I see schoolchildren and adults alike enjoying the decorations and displays and artisans' demonstrations, I get a satisfaction of equal importance to the profits derived from the events. Obviously we could not continue to produce them if they weren't profitable, for it is the profits that make them possible. Many older people make their one and only trip to town during the year just to see the Fortnight. Many of them don't buy a thing, but simply enjoy themselves. Many have seen their first Picasso or Toulouse-Lautrec at Neiman-Marcus; many get their first insights into a foreign country they will never visit at a Neiman-Marcus Fortnight and return home knowing more than when they left.

I was quoted by David Hawkins in the *Dallas Morning News* as saying, "Saturday, I stood looking at the biggest crowd ever to visit Neiman-Marcus. It gave me a special feeling — not just because of the business, which, thank you, is fine, but because perhaps ninety percent of these people had just come to look. The Fortnights always push business to a new plateau, but they push cultural interest and appreciation up, too. Some of that, I like to feel, is what we put back into the community."

My grandmother's soup was always superb. I asked her for her secret, and she replied, "I always use a soup bone. First you put good in, then you take good out." This simple rule for soupmaking applies to Fortnights, too.

11

The Christmas Catalogue

For years before our store expansion program was initiated, my good friend and mentor Ben Sonnenberg kept pressing me to capitalize on our extraordinary national reputation. He felt that we had tremendous leverage which we were neglecting by failing to expand into other cities or by franchising our name. The latter suggestion was repugnant, for we realized that we would simply be watering down our reputation, losing all control of our quality standards. Multiplication we did go into, but at a much slower pace than Ben envisioned.

Shortly after we made our first public offering of common stock, October 1959, I went to San Francisco with our treasurer, Bill Bramley, to meet with some stock analysts, and the same question was posed to us by a large brokerage house which had placed a lot of our stock with California investors. The principal of the company, Ted Birr, expressed the opinion that with our unusual national image, we could sell things through the mail if we made the effort. On the plane back to Dallas, Bramley and I talked seriously about expanding our modest mail order program, deciding it was worth a trial to see if this device would give us the chance of cashing in on our reputation. We discussed the matter the following day with my brother Edward, who was then merchandise manager of the store, and agreed to amplify our direct mail exposure — which at that point consisted mainly of our Christmas catalogue — by issuing two additional seasonal mailings. We adopted a loose-leaf format, borrowed from Bergdorf Goodman, featuring a single item per page with an order blank on the reverse side.

At first we mailed only to our regular charge account customers, but as Eddie became more sophisticated in mail-order techniques we bought outside lists, and gradually built a national clientele of mail-order customers, most of whom had never visited a Neiman-Marcus store but had heard enough about our reputation to want to buy from us. Simultaneously, certain changes we made in our Christmas book gave us worldwide publicity and greatly enhanced the pulling power of all our direct mail.

We had been publishing Christmas catalogues for a number of years, directing them essentially to our regular customers and to well-known people in other areas who we thought would like the quality of our merchandise and gift-wrapped packages. We illustrated the best merchandise the market had to offer, plus some things we had the ingenuity to originate, and the booklets pulled fairly well, both in store response and through the mails. About a week before Christmas every year, I would receive phone calls from Ed Murrow and Walter Cronkite, who were doing "wrap-up" stories on the nature of the Christmas trade, asking about unusual purchases made by some of our affluent, free-spending, oil customers. They lived in constant hope that someone had topped the customer who had bought the entire show window a few years back. Usually there was no big story to give them, or if there was, I couldn't tell them without breaking faith with the customer involved, so I would answer them by saying, "Well, this has been a fine year for alligator handbags" or "We've had a great run on nylon stockings," to which they would reply in disgust, "Hell, that's not news. Give us something better than that."

In my efforts to meet their demands, I would find myself

concocting a way-out imaginary tale about a man who had bought seven mink coats for his wife and six daughters, and a sable coat for his mistress. This, of course, delighted them, and they would put the story on the air. One year it occurred to me that if we created one or more exotic gifts and put them in the catalogue, we would pick up coverage, not only from radio and TV, but from newspapers and magazines as well. I threw out this idea to our merchandising and advertising staffs and asked them to come up with some newsworthy proposals for the following year. At our catalogue planning session, one of our merchandise managers, Dave Hughes, proposed that we show "His and Her" airplanes in a double spread. We invited Beechcraft to participate, and the idea, which seemed so preposterous, was reported worldwide by all the media. When network friends called that Christmas, they asked, "Did you sell any planes?" to which I could answer, "Yes, a Her plane," which they duly reported. Thus we picked up hundreds of newspaper stories in this country and abroad and still held on to our TV coverage. Honesty always pays!

The success of the idea was so obvious that we followed it up the next Christmas with a two-person "His and Her" miniature submarine, "the ultimate in togetherness," and the succeeding year with a parachutelike device, "His and Her" parasails, "for those who want to get away from it all." We improved on our technique by adding a second, and sometimes third "improbable" gift, on the theory that we should provide an adequate amount of material for columnists in rival newspapers to draw upon. Writers began to speculate in advance of the release date on what might be forthcoming in the next Neiman-Marcus Christmas Book, but we have guarded our secrets so well that there has been only one leak over many years. All of the publicity which emanated from these "stunt" pages increased the demand for copies of not only the catalogue, but for the other mailers as well. Our list of proven mail-order customers swelled and so did our mail-order volume.

229

Eddie took charge of organizing the whole mail-order business, eventually giving up his other responsibilities to concentrate his efforts on this new field of retail distribution. He developed an expertise, unique in the specialty store field, in building prime lists, forecasting demand, working out the logistics of procurement, and in selecting items to be catalogued. Subsequently other specialty stores got into the mail-order business, with the assistance of former members of our staff trained under Eddie. Despite the efforts to imitate us, though, none of them has achieved the attention or financial success we've had.

The Christmas "idea" pages evolved for the most part into my area of responsibility, for I seemed to have a better understanding than most of my associates about which ideas could be depended upon to produce favorable news coverage and which could not. I have always tried to select concepts which have a degree of credibility (however faint), are not hackneyed, and will evoke the question, "I wonder if they really sell any?" A rolling roast beef cart with semirevolving cover, as used at Simpson's in London, gave rise to the idea of advertising it in the catalogue along with a Black Angus steer, which we offered to deliver either on the hoof or cut into steaks and roasts. We had two orders for live steers, one from Sacramento, which we delivered at noon on Christmas Day, and the other from Johannesburg, South Africa. We accepted that order without realizing that South African laws require a quarantine period of six months for livestock, so we had to board and feed the animal in the quarantine station in South Africa a whole year before we could make delivery the following Christmas. Fortunately for us, our buyer was willing to wait.

A customer from Minnesota was responsible for a page, "How to Spend $1,000,000 at Neiman-Marcus," which we spelled out in great detail, from sables to an eighteen-karat-gold needle. Another year, when we were in the midst of a recession and gloom and pessimism were all about, I was flying to California, wracking my brain, trying to visualize something suitable to feature for people to give under such conditions, and I came up with an idea for the pessimist — a Noah's Ark. Certainly nothing could be more pessimistic than that. Then, it seemed, we should have a facing page with a gift suggestion for the optimist, so I thought that the height of optimism would be to sell acorns, which grow into mighty oaks. I related this to my associate, Tom Alexander, and he improved on the idea when he said quite wisely, "No one is that optimistic. Let's sell oak seedlings."

We offered the ark, to be made to order, complete with a staff consisting of a French chef, a Swedish masseur, a German hair stylist, an English valet, a French maid, an Italian couturier, an English curator/librarian, a Park Avenue physician, a Texas A & M veterinarian, and a working crew of four. Included also, in pairs by species, were 92 mammals, 10 reptiles, 26 birds, 14 freshwater fish, and 38 insects, priced in toto at $588,247, FOB Mount Ararat. The seedlings were priced at $10. Curiously, we received fifteen hundred orders for the seedlings and not a single one for the ark. Which all goes to prove that there are more optimists in the world than pessimists!

One year we featured "His and Her" robes made of shahtoosh, the rarest and most costly fabric in the world, which I had come across on my first trip to India. The fiber comes from the neck of the ibex goat, which has as its habitat the upper slopes of the Himalayas, descending to about 12,000 feet in the springtime to forage on the tender leaves of the low-growing trees. In the process, he leaves a lot of his neck hairs on the branches, which the natives of Kashmir retrieve and spin into a yarn, from which the cloth is woven into shawls for wealthy Indian women to wear over their silk saris. It is, in fact, the Indian woman's mink coat. It is so fine and luxurious that it almost makes the other luxury cloths of vicuña and cashmere feel coarse in comparison. I was so taken with it that I bought up the total available supply for the season,

231

thus earning from the Indian merchants the title of The Shahtoosh King. We sold some of the fabric as shawls, but from it we also made robes for men and women, hostess gowns, mufflers, and scarves. Its fineness is best illustrated by the fact that a fifty-four-inch-wide shawl can be pulled through a wedding ring.

Carol Channing was in Dallas one summer while we were producing the Christmas Book, so we persuaded her to be photographed in bed between butterfly-print sheets designed by Hanae Mori, the famous Japanese dressmaker. We advertised a "wall of wine" as a room divider, filled with rare vintages, at $5,000; "His and Her" aquaria in which we replaced the usual sand with a bed of cultured pearls; a "His and Her" sauna; "His and Her" Jaguars — "His" a Jaguar roadster, "Hers" a jaguar coat. We showed a "His and Her" bathtub, with the lady decorously wearing a wedding ring, and were promptly sued by a French dealer claiming a worldwide patent on the idea, which we refuted by referring to nineteenth-century sketches of the same thing. Despite our innocence, we made an out-of-court settlement so I could return to France without hazarding arrest.

A trip to Hong Kong and a ride on a Chinese junk inspired a Christmas catalogue page with the caption "Junk for Christmas." We offered authentic Chinese junks for $11,500, and to the surprise of all of us we received orders for eight, to be delivered to such diverse bodies of water as the Hudson River, Lake Michigan, the Atlantic, the Pacific, and the Mediterranean Sea. The final order came in over a year after the catalogue was issued. A friend called from Mexico and said, "I've just received your catalogue and I want a junk." "What do you mean, you just received our catalogue? It was mailed eleven months ago," I replied. "Well," he said, "mails in Mexico are slow and I just got it, or maybe it's been here and I've just opened it. Anyway, I want one to be delivered in Acapulco in three months, or if you can't make that date, send it to me in Nice." We were fortunate in getting one to him in

Acapulco in time, but when he found he didn't know how to rig it, we had to fly down someone in the Dallas area who had the knowhow. Fortunately, the other purchasers didn't require this bit of extra service.

The optical paintings of Victor Vasarely had interested me for some time, so on one of my trips to Paris I arranged to visit him at his studio. I asked if he would design a scarf for us, which he declined on the ground that he didn't want to get into the fashion business. I asked what the difference was between printing on paper and on silk. He smiled wryly and admitted, "It's more difficult to print on silk." I showed him the previous year's catalogue and his eye was stopped by the "His and Her" page. He said, "If I were to do a scarf for you, why not do a 'His and Her' scarf, in two-color variations, one for Her to wear, and the other to be framed for Him?" I replied that he should have been a merchant. He consented, and we silk-screened his design in Switzerland in a limited, numbered, and signed edition, which was shown as our "His and Her" gift of that year's catalogue. It caused international attention in the art world and brought orders from collectors in France, Italy, Finland, Spain, and Japan, as well as in the United States. Selling at $350 in a lucite box, at $425 framed, it was the most expensive scarf ever marketed.

Edward Marcus thought up an idea for a 1955 *Life* story on unusual Christmas gifts, a jewelry-studded stuffed tiger. We were deluged with letters of inquiry from readers, including one from a seven-year-old boy, Robbie Jinson of Troy, New York. His letter read:

Dear Mr. Neiman-Marcus,

How much is your Life Tiger? Not the diamonds, I am a tiger collector, not diamonds. I am seven and have 5 tigers. Not real. Just play. I love tigers, especially yours. Please send the letter — the how much it costs without the diamonds letter — right away. Also, can you charge

233

it or do you have to pay right away. I have my garden money, so please send letter right away before I lose it.

Your Friend,
ROBBIE JINSON

I answered Robbie's letter immediately and sent him a stuffed plush tiger head for his collection, with the following letter:

Dear Robbie:

Thank you so much for your Christmas card and your note.

I am very pleased to hear that you are a tiger collector, and I am sending you a mounted tiger head for your collection.

Your Friend,
STANLEY MARCUS

I received a phone call in London one day from a stranger who said he had an idea for our catalogue. I've made it a practice to see anyone who has a merchandise idea, for I never can tell when something unusual and worthy will show up. I made an appointment with him at his flat opposite the British Museum, and learned that his idea was a genuine Egyptian mummy case. I asked if it were a case for a man or a woman. He replied that it was a woman's case. I told him that we weren't in the archaeological business, and that the case would not be of interest to us. On second thought, as I was leaving I asked whether he could match it with a male mummy case, so we could have "His and Her" mummy cases. He replied somewhat disgustedly that he had no idea when, if ever, he could come up with another case. Two years later in Dallas I received a call from London. "I found him," the voice said. "You found whom?" I asked. "I found the male case you wanted," the voice replied. I had forgotten about the whole incident, so it took me a few minutes to unscramble the conversation and realize what he was talking about. We made a deal on the phone. A whole series of mishaps then occurred. We had decided to have the cases photographed in London since we were approaching our press deadline. The photographer chosen didn't want to shoot the picture, for he resented the fact they were being shipped out of England. We picked another photographer, but the insurance underwriter would not approve the security of his studio. Finally we found a third photographer without any chauvinistic hangups or insecure premises just before the expiration date of our thirty-day export permit. Since we had recently opened a new store at Bal Harbour, Florida, we had them shipped from London to Miami to be exhibited at Christmas in the new store.

A few nights later, I was awakened by a telephone call from the manager of our Bal Harbour store. He was very agitated and excited by the discovery that one of the cases contained a mummy! He wanted to know what to do with his unexpected guest. "Get a doctor the first thing in the morning to examine the mummy and provide you with a death certificate, for it is against the law to import corpses, mummified or not, or to transport them across interstate lines, without a death certificate. Then call the customs inspector and tell him that we have unwittingly imported a mummy, but we think we have cured the situation by getting a death certificate. After you've done all this, put the mummy in cold storage, and above all, don't talk about it." Our "His and Her" mummy cases made front-page news all over the world and were taped for TV for both the BBC and U.S. networks. We didn't have a very good prospect list for mummy cases, but we did call them to the attention of several Miami art collectors, hoping they might give them to the local museum. Two weeks before Christmas, we received a call from a man who identified himself as a brother in a philosophical order that might have an interest in acquiring them. "Would you send them out to the West Coast on approval?" This had all of the earmarks of a prank, so we declined, but politely offered to send one of the cases to Dallas, which was halfway, if he would like to examine it. We also suggested that he bring an adequate down payment with him. He arrived a week later,

235

was satisfied with the one case he saw, paid the deposit, and promised to pay the balance on the delivery of the other case in California. It came up to their expectations, and they paid off promptly. We had made our first sale of mummy cases, but we weren't encouraged sufficiently to install a mummy case department.

As soon as one Christmas is over, we start going through the anguishing process of trying to think up the next year's big item. Somehow, I seem to think more fancifully when I'm airborne, and on a transatlantic trip I came up with the idea of "His and Her" camels. A camel is a fairly ludicrous beast to most of us, obviously not designed by the Lord but by a committee, and the idea of offering a pair of camels seemed inordinately funny to me. I tried it out on my wife, who was not at all amused, nor were my associates. Undaunted, I went ahead with the idea, for I felt confident that the press would love it — and they did. So did the daughter of one of our good customers in Fort Worth, who wanted to buy a lady camel for her mother's Christmas present. We arranged for TV coverage of the camel's arrival at the Dallas airport on Christmas Eve and it was broadcast on the late news that very night. Later, we learned that the recipient-to-be was watching the ten o'clock news with her daughter, and when the announcer reported the story of the camel to be delivered the following morning to a local woman as a gift, she said, "I wonder what darned fool is going to get it?" The next morning she found out. The happiest part of the story is that she became very fond of her camel, and had it reproduced, by us of course, in a gold and jeweled pin. The camel still roams her estate and is in good health, according to last reports.

In 1971, I conceived the idea of a gift page for those who were nostalgic for life as it used to be in the "good old days," so I proposed a pair of rose-colored glasses and a clock that ran backwards. Tom Alexander added the final fillip by putting in a pair of tickets for *No, No, Nanette,* which was experiencing a successful revival. The idea of getting a clock made to run backwards seemed simple enough, but the best clockmakers of Switzerland all assured us that it was completely impossible unless we were to build a special backward-clock factory. We were about to abandon the whole idea when our costume jewelry buyer said, "Let me take a crack at it. I have a clock repair man here in Dallas who is a wizard." In one week she came up with a clock that her man had rigged up to run backwards, much to the subsequent embarrassment of the entire Swiss clockmaking industry.

Once we offered a twenty-four-hour cruise in Caribbean waters on the T. S. *Hanseatic* "for you and 598 of your closest friends" for $35,000. The offer was bought by a Miami charitable organization which then proceeded to sell out all of the space at a considerable profit.

One of the newspapers carried a story in 1972 of an industrial designer in Atlanta who was engaged in designing think-tanks. It occurred to me that privacy was probably the hardest thing to achieve in this busy life, and that a miniature think-tank, or privacy capsule, would be an interesting gift suggestion for our customers "who have everything." We commissioned the designer to draw such a unit which we could put in our catalogue to be made on special order to meet the exact requirements of the recipient. It permitted a one-way view of the outside world and offered numerous options ranging from film projection to music, dictation, and typewriting equipment. Completely soundproof, it could be entered solely by the insertion of a sterling silver punched card placed in the entry slot. It was priced at $80,000 and up, depending on specifications.

Inspired by the Metropolitan Museum's purchase of its now-famous $1,000,000 Greek krater, we decided to offer our customers a pair of genuine Greek "His and Her" kraters, "not painted by Euphronios nor made by Euxitheos, these kraters have been authenticated by archaeologists and have been exported legally. No skulduggery or clandestine meetings were involved in their acquisition." Our price for the pair was $5,000; Richard Flasje in the *New York Times* suggested that they were just the thing for Thomas Hoving, director of the Metropolitan. I'm sure that Hoving has heard about all he wants to hear about kraters.

These are just some of the ideas that have helped our catalogue to become the best-publicized Christmas book in the world. We usually sell from one to a dozen of these bizarre offerings, but the important thing is that they help sell millions of dollars of gifts from our under-$10 and under-$20 pages, thousands of dresses, sweaters, neckties, pitchers, cigarette boxes, and toys of good quality and taste, which are sent as gifts all over the world.

As a promotion device for our catalogue and gift-wrapping service, I once sent to a list of top business leaders a large box filled with Neiman-Marcus gift-wrapped packages, one inside the other. The final package contained our Christmas catalogue. My basic premise was that a letter soliciting the gift business of a major corporate executive wouldn't get past his secretary's desk, but that an imposing box surely would be brought to his attention. My idea worked fine with three hundred and twenty-two of the recipients, who applauded our sales ingenuity. Many of them opened accounts and sent in orders for Christmas gifts. It backfired in the case of Billy Rose, who was then writing a newspaper column. He wrote,

Neiman-Marcus Co.
Dallas, Texas

Gentlemen:

May I register a complaint?

Yesterday afternoon I was sitting in my office, minding my P's, Q's, manners and business, when an expressman walked in and handed me a box big enough to house a midget. It was wrapped in Santa Claus paper, and there was a fancy sticker pasted on top with Christmas greeting from Neiman-Marcus.

"Gosh," I said, "I didn't know they cared."

I stopped what I was doing and ripped off the wrapping, and there in a sea of silver excelsior I found a dozen gift packages, each looking like what the well-dressed Christmas tree will wear.

I picked up the phone. "Don't call me for the next 10 minutes," I said to the switchboard girl. "I'm in conference."

Having spent a couple of years in Texas, I of course had heard a good deal about your Aladdin's lamp of a store and so, as I untied the fluffy puffs of ribbon on the first box, my head began to swim (Australian crawl, mostly).

Box Number One contained several cubic inches of exactly nothing.

"Evidently a mistake in the shipping department," I thought, and went on to Number Two. It was filled with grade A, supercrinkly tissue paper.

Number Three, however, contained an impressive collection of diamonds — that is, little cards with pictures of diamonds which you were willing to let go for a fraction — say, six-fifths — of their value.

Number Four was a heavier box, and I scissored it open with renewed hope. But you gentlemen packed it, and you know what was in it — a mail order catalogue!

Well, by this time I realized I had been hoaxed by an advertising gimmick, and so I filed the rest of the package in my wastebasket. And by the time I had cleaned up the mess of excelsior and cardboard, I was ready to go down to Macy's basement, buy a pair of socks and say, "That's for Neiman-Marcus."

Now, it's generally conceded that you gents run one of the smartest stores in the country, and it's probably presumptuous to tell you how to run your business. But it does seem to me that your Christmas promotion stunt violates the first rule of salesmanship — never build a customer up to a let-down.

Next Christmas if I'm still on your list, send me a postcard or if you want to spread yourself, a wall calendar. As I see it, it's better not to play Santa Claus at all than to put on false whiskers and come down the chimney with nothing but hot air in your bag.

Sincerely,

BILLY ROSE

Despite the success of the promotion, I think Billy was right, and if we were ever to repeat it I would enclose a small gift in the final package.

To enhance the appearance of our catalogues, we have commissioned covers by some of the leading illustrators and artists of the world, including Steinberg, Vertès, Bemelmans, Ben Shahn, André François, Robert Indiana, Ib Antoni, Björn Wiinblad, and Ronald Searle. The cover designs are usually reproduced in gift-wrap papers, posters, and in our newspaper advertisements. But despite all of our collective efforts to find the best merchandise, to buy the best photography and printing, despite the accolades we have received from the press, I've never been completely satisfied with any catalogue we've ever published. I can always see how we could have done it better. Some day before I retire, I hope we produce one of which I can say, "This is *it*."

Texas under Three Economies

Historians neatly divide the centuries into convenient compartments which they label "periods," so it comes as somewhat of a surprise, as I review the years of my life, to find that I, too, can discern three distinct "periods" of modern Texas history and the effects of each of these on the molding of its people and their economic and political attitudes.

From the beginning of its colonization until about 1932, Texas had essentially an agriculturally based economy. By 1905 cotton was the money crop, and its annual success or failure determined whether a large part of the population ate well or poorly. Cotton was grown on small farms by individual owners or by tenant farmers, and it was picked by nearby blacks who enlisted all the members of their families to help. Since wages were based on the poundage picked, a big crop meant lots of cash to the pickers, everybody ate "high on the hog," and debts incurred during the previous year were paid off. If the crop was poor, due either to the devastation of the boll weevil or to the wet weather inducing root rot, then debts remained unpaid, belts were tightened, and business was adversely affected.

Farmhands bought groceries from their local country stores on credit and paid off after the next crop was picked; they operated similarly with the doctors, undertakers, and clothing merchants.

243

Similarly, the latter depended on the banks and the wholesalers for their credit. A poor crop or a low price per pound gave the whole economic system a severe case of constipation. Dallas, the largest inland cotton port, reacted to the vagaries of the cotton market through its banks, cotton gins, cotton compressors, cotton merchants, and foreign cotton-buying organizations, all of which were the chief employers of the community.

The goat and sheep ranchers in the southwestern part of the state and the cattle raisers to the west were equally dependent on the weather and on prices for their products set by the world market. On the whole, ranchers were well capitalized, and unless drought or hoof and mouth disease afflicted their herds, they were more affluent than their more numerous counterparts in cotton. They, too, had the habit of settling their outstanding debts once a year.

Texas was also politically Democratic and economically conservative. Religiously, it was Protestant, essentially Baptist and Methodist, with a minority of Catholics heavily concentrated in small towns settled by German, Czech, and Polish immigrants. There was a sprinkling of Jews, who for the most part were later migrants to Texas, coming into the state in the last quarter of the nineteenth century. They became active in the mercantile and professional life of the larger cities. Religious bias existed in Texas as in other areas, but it was directed more strongly against Catholics than Jews. It reached its climax in the twenties with the reactivation of the Ku Klux Klan, which scared the blacks and tried to intimidate the white majority into further discrimination, commercially and socially, against Catholics and Jews. Aside from the intellectual blight it created, the Klan had little effect other than to make it more difficult for Catholic construction firms to bid successfully on public projects. The blacks already knew "their place" in the social order — which was at the bottom — and the Jews had already segregated themselves into their own social clubs as the result of the "no Jews" policy of the fashionable country clubs.

A course on the history of Texas was a year-long subject given early in the school life of every Texas child, with emphasis on the facts that Texas, the Lone Star State, was the largest state in the Union; that Texas had served under six flags: the Spanish, French, Mexican, Republic of Texas, Confederate, and the United States, and that in the terms under which Texas gave up its sovereignty as an independent republic to become a member of the Union, it reserved the right to divide itself into five separate states. Texas history, like all histories, glorified its heroes and the motivation of its wars; it made the bodies of its heroes out of solid granite even though they may have had feet of clay.

The history books emphasized the very size of Texas and the self-sufficiency of the land, which produced cotton and wheat, cattle and fruit, tomatoes and spinach in greater quantities than any other single state in the country. The accomplishments of the early settlers, the story of the Alamo and its heroic defenders, the story of Judge Bean and the law west of the Pecos, and the reiteration of the fact that we were the biggest all served to create in the mind of a child the idea that there was something special about being born a Texan. Even the outside world shared in the Texas mystique, and when a Texas boy went east to college, which relatively few did in those days, he would usually be called "Tex" by his collegemates and queried whether he rode a horse to high school. Great was the disappointment when they learned that the Texan had never been on a ranch, or seen a cowboy, or even ridden horseback.

Nineteen thirty-two ushered in the beginning of the second stage of Texas's economic life. The Depression, the wearing out of the cotton-producing soil of North Texas, and the growing competition of rayon had put a severe dent in cotton's domination of the state's economy. With the discovery of the great East Texas oil pool and the oil finds in South Texas, petroleum displaced cotton as the single most important economic factor in the state. Oil had previously been found in West Texas, at Mexia in North-Central Texas, and in Southeast Texas near Beaumont, but the "Dad" Joiner discovery in East Texas was hailed as "the largest reservoir of oil ever found in the United States." The East Texas area had been largely discounted by the major oil companies, so the scrubby land was owned in small pieces by farmers, florists, under-takers, lawyers, doctors, shopkeepers, and others of diverse oc-cupations. As soon as the Joiner hit became known, the East Texas countryside was flooded with option dealers and wildcatters. The big oil rush was on. Simultaneously, the West Texas producers began a process to reactivate their wells, many of which had dropped in flow to the point that they were no longer profitable producers.

Dallas, midway between East and West Texas, became the hub of oil activities. Title companies, law officers, and banks were suddenly overloaded with their burgeoning new industry, and as royalty money began to flow to the newly rich landowners, many decided to move in from the farms to take up residence in Dallas. They bought large houses, fine clothes, and automobiles, but they were given a chilly reception by the old guard "cotton families," who regarded them as nouveau riche. It was a half-dozen years before the best clubs accepted them as members, but gradually, as in other societies, they became assimilated into the community. "They" were the big money in town, "they" gave the biggest parties, "they" bought the finest clothes, and "they" observed the proper decorum during the probation period imposed on them. Finally, the descriptive phrase of "new oil rich" was changed to the simpler and less patronizing "oil wealth."

The Dallas banks seized the leadership in oil financing for the entire southwestern region. More highly capitalized than the banks of Houston or Oklahoma, they were in a position to handle larger loans than the local banks located even closer to the oil plays. Fred Florence, the energetic and resourceful president of the Republic National Bank, conceived the idea of lending money on estimated oil reserves still in the ground, thus revolutionizing the whole concept of oil financing. He employed petroleum engineers, who scientifically estimated the life of a given well, and the bank made loans against future oil runs. Florence was a banker of extraordinary ability and perception; he possessed a calculator type of mind, an ability to read people as well as figures, and an approach to all problems of "how can it be done?"

The independent oil producer played a very useful and important part in the search for oil; he wildcatted in areas where the major companies wouldn't hazard an investment, he followed hunches as well as geological advice, he proved out structures which had been hypothetical. Aided by the depletion allowances and intangible cost chargeoffs, he was willing to gamble against great odds. He lost most of the time, but when he won he made it big. Undaunted by dry holes, he would drill, and drill again. One independent, D. Harold Byrd, sank twenty dry holes before hitting oil, thus earning the name of "Dry Hole Byrd."

In the late forties, shallow production, less expensive to drill, became harder to locate, and expensive deep-well drilling put a severe strain on the independents. In the early fifties interest rates started to rise and the banks began to demur against the long-time payouts which the much deeper wells required. The assets of most independents were tied up in oil; diversification of investment to most of them had meant buying shares of Standard Oil of New Jersey or Gulf. When the squeeze came they could turn only to the major companies, the giants of the industry, who were waiting at the door to buy them out.

When the majors took over, they closed the offices of the independents and simply added another computer to handle the statistics of the oil runs and royalty payments. Basically nothing changed: the oil was still being produced, the independents had cash or stock instead of oil, but the free-spending oilman with depletion benefits was replaced by the big oil corporation with its banks of computers. We have never been successful in selling a mink coat to a computer, and the president of a big oil company, a professional management man, has never been half as good a customer as a wildcatter from Odessa.

This change in the oil economy had an adverse affect on our business, and for several years we and the state went through a mild recession. During the war, Texas began to experience its first important industrialization with the building of aircraft and munition plants and electronics factories. Thus, as oil was phasing out as the dominant element in the economy, industry furnished new sources of employment and gross product. Enter Phase Three of the Texas economy, the scientific-industrial era.

The new wartime industries continued to manufacture for the government but some also had surplus capacity to devote to peacetime products, such as transistors, petrochemicals, and automobile air-conditioning units. New manufacturers and assembly plants moved into the state, attracted by the combination of weather conditions, tax laws, and a friendly and ample labor market. Some of these new companies brought with them groups of scientists holding Ph.D. degrees. This time the country clubs didn't post barriers to the newcomers, but welcomed them — that is, unless they happened to be Jewish scientists.

Each of these phases left an imprint on the state and its people. The agricultural era gave the state a feeling of self-sufficiency, pride in its history, an illusion of superman, an attitude of "nothing's too big for us to do," a political and religious conservatism. The petroleum era exposed us to great riches quickly attained without obvious evidence of extraordinary ability, a more materialistic society, antilibertarian attitudes. The scientific-industrial era brought fresh, inquiring minds into the state, willing to challenge some of the old shibboleths in education and government, to replace self-satisfaction with some self-criticism.

248

Religious and political conservatism gave way imperceptibly as the labor vote in Houston helped elect a liberal congressman, as the Unitarian and Congregationalist churches attracted larger memberships. The Methodist church retreated from its earlier asceticism, secularizing its control over its leading educational institution in the state, Southern Methodist University. The fundamental Baptist groups maintained their traditional rigidity, leading the late Tom Knight, a brilliant, eccentric, top-notch Dallas lawyer to coin one of his scathing witticisms, "Methodists are Baptists who have learned to read and write."

Texans responded fervently to the McCarthy charges, encouraged by the statewide press and the *Dallas Morning News* particularly, which fanned embers of suspicion and the flames of patriotism. Texans had demonstrated their patriotism in the two major wars of the century and had distinguished themselves on the battlefield. McCarthy's "soft on communism" allegations fell on willing ears, and many Texans, among others in the country, became superpatriots, 110% Americans. The *Dallas Morning News* saw a Communist under every bed, as did McCarthy, and to document its charges, exhumed Roosevelt at regular intervals and rattled his bones across the stage. Many of our ills, the *Dallas Morning News* maintained, could be attributed to the late President, whom they fought when he was alive as well as when he was dead. The paper, which exercised great influence and authority in Dallas and North Texas, became an ultraconservative journal, opposed to social progress, the United Nations, the Democratic party, federal aid, welfare, and virtually everything except the Dallas Zoo, which was a favorite cause of its late publisher, E. M. (Ted) Dealey. My friendship with him dated back many years, but we disagreed on almost everything, from art to politics.

All of this was the paper's privilege, except for the fact that it rarely exposed the other side of the coin on its editorial pages. It carried Walter Lippmann's column sporadically; it rarely gave equal coverage to both sides of controversial questions. It spread a venom which helped poison the minds of a large segment of the community.

It didn't use its editorial power against an English professor, John Beatty of SMU, a former officer in military intelligence, when he waged an anti-Semitic campaign using "secret" documents which he flourished but never exposed. It encouraged a retired army officer, General Edwin Walker, who was to the right of McCarthy, by its failure to challenge his extravagant claims of subversion in high places. It supported the successful congressional candidacy of Bruce Alger, the first Republican representative ever elected from Dallas, who was opposed to federal aid and numerous other pieces of legislation sponsored by his own party. It was reported that even Eisenhower couldn't abide his negativism.

Ironically, he went to Washington at the time Sam Rayburn was the Speaker of the House, and Lyndon Johnson the Majority Leader in the Senate, and he alienated both of them and the entire Texas delegation so completely that he became an ineffective representative in the Congress. Rayburn and Johnson were bestowing benefits upon the state with federal projects, but since Alger and the *Dallas Morning News* were so vehemently opposed to federal aid, they saw to it that Dallas got none. Both Rayburn and Johnson were bitter about the attacks of the *Dallas Morning News* on them, and Rayburn was particularly incensed about the efforts of the oil fraternity to unseat him. With indignation he told me, "They claim that I'm against the $27\frac{1}{2}\%$ depletion allowance, but single-handed I've saved it for them, using my own methods to do it. Get them off my back!"

It was in this atmosphere that Adlai Stevenson came to Dallas in 1963 to speak at the Dallas Civic Auditorium on United Nations Day. The superpatriots had organized picket lines with anti-UN posters that they carried into the auditorium. I had been asked to introduce Stevenson, which I succeeded in doing despite some heckling from the audience. At the conclusion of his speech, I was advised it would be better to take him out the rear exit to avoid hostile demonstrators gathered in the front. However, as we attempted to enter his limousine he was spat upon and whacked over the head with a placard inscribed "If you seek peace, ask Jesus." I jerked him by the arm and pulled him into the car, whereupon the crowd rocked the car in an effort to turn it over. For a moment it looked as though they might succeed, but the chauffeur gave it the gas and we escaped. All of this occurred to a distinguished ex-governor of Illinois, a defeated candidate for the presidency, because he had dared to come to Dallas to discuss the accomplishments and failures of the United Nations.

Some years earlier, when Lyndon Johnson was making a speech in behalf of his reelection to the vice-presidency, I accompanied Mrs. Johnson and him from their suite at the Baker Hotel across the street to the Adolphus Hotel. The Republicans had organized a troop of partisans, patriotically uniformed in red, white, and blue costumes, who formed a jeering cordon through which the Johnsons had to walk. They were spat upon, too, and subjected to taunting and insulting remarks. That afternoon Johnson spoke at a shopping center, and I was one of the few Dallasites who sat on the platform with him, a matter which he recalled on numerous occasions.

In 1946, on my first postwar European trip I was asked by an old friend and former MGM publicist, a colonel on Eisenhower's staff at SHAPE, "Jock" Lawrence, if I didn't want to meet the general. I replied that I would, but I hated to take up the time of so busy a man. "Nonsense," he said, "he'd like to meet you. I'll arrange it for next Tuesday morning." On my arrival at headquarters, Lawrence was not there, but another officer ushered me into the general's office and introduced me as "Stanley Marcus of Neiman-Marcus." Ike obviously had not been briefed, so he looked at me, smiled, and quizzically repeated "Neiman-Marcus" several times, as though he was trying to determine whether it signified a law firm or a team of acrobats. When I realized his quandary,

251

I explained that Neiman-Marcus was one of the finest specialty stores in the country, and that I was on a mission to reestablish our buying connections in Europe. "You'll have to pardon me," he said. "I've been away from the U.S. so long, and even when I was there, I never had occasion to visit stores. I always shopped at the base PX." He asked me to explain in more detail about our operation, after which I said, "General, I hope you will decide to seek the nomination for the presidency, and if you succeed, I hope you will be elected." He thanked me but was noncommittal about his intentions. As I left, I said, "General, if you do decide to go for the nomination, and get it, and if you are elected, I hope that as an ex-Texan, you will buy Mrs. Eisenhower's inaugural gown from us." He laughed and replied, "If I do, I will." He was true to his word, and when he was elected we furnished the inaugural gown, made by one of our leading dressmakers, Nettie Rosenstein.

I supported Eisenhower and raised money for his campaign, not on the basis of his promise, but because I mistakenly preferred him to his opponent. I worked in behalf of Rockefeller in 1960, and when his attempt fell through, I switched to Kennedy and Johnson. Nothing I had done publicly up to that time caused so much reaction among our customers. The fact that Kennedy was a Catholic was not discussed, but worse than being a papist, he was suspected of being against the oil depletion allowance, which was a cardinal sin in the petroleum and country clubs of the state.

Letters poured in closing charge accounts; the writers had the effrontery to challenge my right to support John F. Kennedy. I answered each of them, asserting that it was my privilege to vote for the candidate of my choice, that it was contrary to our democratic system to invoke economic sanctions against those with whom we disagreed, and that I felt confident that they had no desire to emulate the tactics of dictatorship countries in attempting to coerce me. I received very few replies, but I did have the satisfaction of a contrite apology from the wife of a prominent

252

oilman at a country club party (at which I had encountered a frigid reception), who said, "I appreciated your letter. You made me see my position in a new light. I'm ashamed of myself." We lost some sales — how much it was impossible to determine — but most of the accounts were reopened within six months. The vast majority of our customers either didn't care or were staunch enough supporters of the two-party system to accord me the right to support whomever I chose.

One disgruntled patron who had closed her account but continued to shop with us, paying cash, when asked by her salesperson why she didn't charge a large purchase instead of writing a check, replied, "No, I won't charge it. I'm mad at Stanley Marcus because he's supporting Kennedy."

When Kennedy was elected, rumors flew again that I would be offered the ambassadorship to France. The recognition I received for my efforts were appointments to a trusteeship of the National Cultural Center and to Mrs. Kennedy's Committee for the Acquisition of Paintings for the White House and an invitation to the famous White House dinner at which Pablo Casals performed. I disagreed so vigorously with Roger Stevens, chairman of the Board of Trustees of the National Cultural Center, about the size and estimated cost of the proposed Performing Arts Center in Washington that I was not reappointed.

Following the Stevenson incident, President Kennedy's plan to visit Dallas seemed ill-advised to me. The community, instead of being chastened by the disgraceful attack on Stevenson, became even more hard-nosed. The John Birch Society attracted new members; General Walker continued to fly the United States flag upside down whenever he disagreed with the administration's foreign policy. As Patrick J. Owens, executive editor of the Pine Bluff, Arkansas, *Commercial* later reported about the atmosphere of Dallas, "One powerful impression was of a society in which all ideological questions had been settled. A man was a true American and a patriot — and thus held the prevailing views on everything from the oil depletion allowance to the race issue — or he was an outsider and probably a Communist. The overwhelming impression I got of the people in Dallas was of fear bordering on hysteria. These were people honestly concerned that Communists and fellow-travelers had gained control of the federal government, or soon would do so."

The historical conservatism of the city had been fanned to a raging fire by the combination of a number of elements: the far right daily radio "Facts Forum" program by Dan Smoot sponsored by the ultraconservative wealthiest man in town, H. L. Hunt; the John Birch Society; the oil industry's hysterical concern for the preservation of what they considered a biblical guarantee of their depletion allowance; the "National Indignation League" founded by a local garageman, Frank McGehee, in protest of the air force's training of some Yugoslavian pilots at a nearby air base; the consistently one-sided attacks on the administration by the *Dallas Morning News* and the semiacquiescent editorial policy of the *Times Herald,* which had previously been a middle-of-the-road, fair newspaper. For the lack of courageous firemen in the business and intellectual segments of the community, the fire raged on and established the heated atmosphere which prevailed immediately prior to Kennedy's visit. A dubious compliment to Dallas was paid by the late George Rockwell, commander of the American Nazi party, when he said that Dallas had "the most patriotic, pro-American people of any city in the country."

Dallas's business leadership didn't want Kennedy's visit, but it accepted the fact and made every effort to preclude any repetition of the disorders attendant upon Stevenson's appearance a month before. I had to be in New York on business during the preparations for the President's trip, which was just as well, for my anti-Kennedy business associates took charge of the whole affair and froze me, a known Kennedy supporter, out of the program. A telephone call reached me in New York a week before the event from the vice-president, who said, "Stanley, we need more

TEXAS UNDER THREE ECONOMIES

money to make proper arrangements, and that crowd in Dallas isn't doing enough to get it. We need $25,000 and we need it right away." To which I replied, "Lyndon, I'll raise it for you, but try to get the President to cancel his plans. I am apprehensive of the kind of reception he'll receive." "I have the same concern that you have," he replied, "but what you and I think isn't worth a damn. He's determined to come." I wasn't the only one so concerned, for it was reported that Adlai Stevenson had telephoned from California to the White House to warn the President not to make the trip. Johnson, who was scheduled to speak at a dinner for Kennedy on the twenty-third of November in Austin, reportedly ended his proposed but canceled speech with, "And thank God, Mr. President, that you came out of Dallas alive."

I was at luncheon at the Pavillon Restaurant in New York on November 22 with a visiting Swedish merchant when I was summoned to the phone. It was my New York office reporting a teletype message which had just been sent from my Dallas office — "President Kennedy has just been assassinated in Dallas." I broke the news to the shocked luncheon guests, who no longer had appetite for the dishes or wine before them. I had been right in my advice, but in my deep concern about the President's visit I had envisioned only the possibility of humiliation, not assassination.

I attended the funeral in Washington. As I watched the procession marching down Connecticut Avenue from a suite in the Mayflower, and as I observed the precautionary guards on the rooftops of all the buildings, I couldn't help but realize the impossibility of complete security. A determined assassin could easily have wiped out the mourning heads of state and other dignitaries with a bomb or a machine gun.

Returning to Dallas, I found a citizenry partly in shock and partly indignant at the level finger of guilt being pointed at Dallas. All agreed that the *Dallas Morning News* had used poor judgment in running an advertisement placed by an unknown out-of-town person attacking Kennedy the morning of his arrival. The *Dallas Morning News* agreed it had erred, but gave the disclaimer that the persons authorized to accept such advertisements were either at lunch or out of the city. They were sorry, but the President was dead. Of course, no one could claim that the advertisement triggered the assassination, but its appearance was symptomatic of the *Dallas Morning News* and its editorial stance. In my opinion, the *Dallas Morning News*, the most influential paper in the region, a publication with a long tradition of fairness and objectivity, had misused its trust and given the right wing an aura of respectability, and in doing so shared responsibility for the state of hate which existed in Dallas on November 22. It was indeed ironic that the bullet came from the Left instead of the Right.

Throughout the month of December, meetings were held by all types of citizen groups to try to determine what Dallas should do — if anything. Many were enraged by the worldwide guilt with which Dallas was charged. "It could have happened anywhere," they said. But it did happen in Dallas. Some risked the wrath of their neighbors by admitting that something was wrong in the city. The influential Citizens Council was more concerned with the pragmatic effects of the adverse publicity the city was receiving from the international press. "Will this hamper our ability to get new industries and attract conventions?" they were asking themselves. A few of the intellectuals gathered together to try to find out *what* was wrong and *how* to go about rebuilding the community.

At a meeting of the Board of Directors of the Citizens Council, in answer to a proposal that the city should engage the services of a public relations firm to restore luster to the tarnished name of Dallas, I suggested that we first come to an understanding of our deficiencies and that we not spend money for propaganda but for a positive action program, such as sending our orchestra on a worldwide tour or endowing a chair at SMU to be headed by an eminent sociologist to study the development and evolution of the spirit of absolutism which had prevailed. My proposals were effectively ignored.

In the month following the assassination of Kennedy and the murder of Oswald, Dallas was flooded by newswriters, columnists, TV and radio crews from all over the world. The national press was all too happy to lambast Dallas as a citadel of hate. The foreign press came to prove their preconceived conviction that the assassination and murder were part of a group plot. Despite a lack of sustaining evidence, they reported the stories on the basis of that thesis. As the one name in town with which most of the writers were familiar, I was deluged by requests for interviews and TV tapings — to the point that I could do no work at all.

In our New Year's editorial in 1964, published in paid space in both papers, I decided to tackle the subject. I knew what was wrong in the city, but if I had published my piece under the heading of "What's Wrong with Dallas?" it would have been received with indignation. Instead, I headlined it "What's Right with Dallas?" and got maximum readership. The wire services picked it up here and abroad with very favorable editorial comment. The local response was even better than I had anticipated, producing well over a thousand letters of applause and less than a dozen of disagreement. The Reverend Thomas A. Fry, Jr., of the First Presbyterian Church said that my statement "represents the opinions of most of the ministerial leadership." "The *Times Herald* quoted extensively and approvingly," reported the *New York Times;* "the *Dallas Morning News,* considered the more conservative paper, made no editorial comment." The *New York Times* went on to say, "Some conservatives, both Republicans and Democrats, said privately that Mr. Marcus' advertisement overstated his case. But they also expressed a resolve to show moderation and not to surrender all platforms to extremists. . . . Two questions will not be quickly answered, however: Will Dallas residents accept the rebuke implied in Mr. Marcus' statement? And if they do, can they effect a change?"

257

WHAT'S RIGHT WITH DALLAS?

There has been a great deal of discussion about Dallas in recent weeks in both the domestic and foreign press. Some reporters have done a "quickie" on our city and others have stayed long enough to make less superficial studies. The truth of the matter is that no one can get to know a city in a day, a week, or a month. Those of us who have lived here for a lifetime are so close to the picture that we too sometimes fail to see either some of the pertinent details or the entire composition.

We think there's a lot right with Dallas. We think the dynamic growth of this city in the past thirty years has been no accident; that the factors that motivated this growth are still present and can continue to contribute to the development of Dallas as one of the major centers of distribution, banking, specialized manufacturing, insurance in the country. We think Dallas' leadership which has devoted itself unselfishly to community problems and needs is unique in the country. We think that our local government has been distinguished among all American cities by the integrity and honesty of its elected and appointed officials. We think that our citizens are friendly and kind hearted human beings who extend genuinely warm welcomes to newcomers to our city.

All of this doesn't mean that there aren't things about Dallas that couldn't be improved. As Erik Jonsson, our distinguished fellow citizen, said recently, "I have always believed that individuals, corporations, and communities should have a regular stock taking of what they are and what they are trying to be, and how they would accomplish their objectives. I do agree that this is a good time to do that stock taking. It is year end and this is traditionally a time of reflection and introspection." We concur with Mr. Jonsson that a city, like individuals or business institutions, must take an honest look at its inventory and be willing to consider its faults as well as its 'assets. A city like the individual or corporation can't stand still—it must go ahead or fall behind.

Here seems to us to be some of the areas for community improvement—areas in which each of us as citizens, taxpayers and voters can exercise both individual and collective influence. One, Dallas has a slum problem that it hasn't faced up to as yet. We've talked about it for years and we've done relatively little to improve blighted areas which won't disappear by wishful thinking. We have not solved the problem of low cost housing. Two, this community has suffered from a spirit of "absolutism" in

recent years. This was expressed most cogently in a recent editorial of the St. L Post-Dispatch:

"What should concern Dallas and every other city is that the extremists far right and far left have this in common, that they alienate themselves from main stream of American democracy by an absolutism of political temper whic fundamentally hostile to our principles."

"It is the absolutist, whether of left or right, that democracy has to fear. is the man who thinks that he alone possesses wisdom, patriotism and virtue, recognizes no obligation to accept community decisions with which he disagrees, regards any means as justified by the end. who views the political process a power struggle to impose conformity rather than a means of reconciling differen

"Democracy is a method of reaching a consensus. Those who reject the conse reject democracy."

The rejection of this spirit of "absolutism" and the acceptance and insistence all citizens on toleration of differing points of view seem to us to be essential the future health of our community. We believe our newspapers have an impor contribution to make in regard to this matter and we hope they will lead the by the presentation of balanced points of view on controversial issues.

Third, we are still a young city and much of our time and energy has b devoted to physical growth which has been phenomenal. Now, the time has come w more attention needs to be paid to the quality of our endeavors than the size them. This applies to our schools and colleges, our symphonies, operas, and muse It applies to the quality of support that we as citizens give them as well.

Finally, we think that Dallas should forget about its "civic image" as such. best public relations comes from doing good things and by not doing bad things. U have more "fair play" for legitimate differences of opinion, less coverup for obvious deficiencies, less boasting about our attainments, more moral indignation all of us when we see human rights imposed upon. Then we won't have to worry ab the "Dallas Image"—it will take care of itself.

HAPPY NEW YEAR

The *St. Louis Post-Dispatch* editorialized, "What should concern Dallas and every other city is that the extremists of the far right and far left have this in common, that they alienate themselves from the mainstream of American democracy by an absolutism of political temper which is fundamentally hostile to our principles. It is the absolutist, whether left or right, that democracy has to fear." The *San Francisco Chronicle* stated, "The absolutism of spirit which Marcus says Dallas has suffered in recent years is nothing on which Dallas has world rights. It just happened to promote there a climate in which the American political crime of the century could occur."

Marguerite Higgins in her syndicated column said, "And whereas a year ago, Marcus would surely have been the target of fierce attack in his call for soul-searching and self-criticism, his New Year's message has been greeted by a wave of approval, as if he had put into words what many felt but did not know how to say. . . . Important elements have taken the first step towards change — the admission there is something to correct."

And change did occur — by slow stages and in interesting ways. The *Dallas Morning News* retained its conservative editorial policy, but it began to publish material from some of the more liberal columnists, thus offering its readers plural viewpoints. Joseph Dealey, president of the *Dallas Morning News* (Belo Corporation) was quoted a month after the assassination by the AP as saying that he did not believe that Dallas's political climate brought on the assassination, but that the assassination undoubtedly weakened right-wing elements in the city — if only because it left them floundering without the adversary they saw in Kennedy. "I think now opposite sides will give better acceptance to each other's opinions because of the sobering nature of the event," he said. "If a man even suspected he had contributed in any way to the assassination, no matter how indirectly, it would be a terribly sobering thing." The *Dallas Morning News* had sobered up indeed.

Five years later I read an article in *Ramparts* on subversive groups of the Right that concluded with "The latest plot to surface was formulated in Dallas in September, 1966 — its target was Stanley Marcus of the Neiman-Marcus store, a pro–United Nations liberal who somehow has managed to thrive in rigidly conservative Dallas. According to an informant who was present, several Minutemen decided to ambush Marcus outside of Dallas, because another assassination in Dallas would be too much! Again, there was a leak and the plan fell through."

13

The Growing of a Family

Y OU AREN'T MAKING ANY EFFORT to encourage Dick [our son] to come into the business," my wife commented when he was finishing his sophomore year at Harvard. "No," I replied, "I don't have any intention of doing so. If he wants to join the store, that will be fine, but if he would prefer some other occupation, that's all right, too." Dick had worked at the store during a few summers, in the receiving rooms, in the housekeeping department and as a stock boy. In his receiving room assignment he would unpack all sorts of goods, including huge cases of china from England. One night as we sat down to eat he picked up the dinner plate and exclaimed, "Why, this is Wedgwood! I just unpacked five thousand pieces of it today." "Yes," his mother said, "you've been eating off this same pattern of Wedgwood since you were six years old, and this is the first time you've ever noticed it."

Dick was a good worker and earned the esteem of his associates and superiors in his various summer jobs. From their earliest days, our children had been taught good store manners: politeness, courtesy, no presumptiveness because their name was Marcus, respect for the handling of merchandise, and an understanding that we paid for what we bought just as customers did. Both Jerrie, his older sister, and Wendy, his twin sister, had sold behind the counter as well, for their mother and I believed that retail selling was one of the most enlightening and enriching experiences a person could possibly have.

One Christmas season, Wendy decided she would like to work at the store during her holiday vacation. She was assigned to a job in the gift-wrap department on the afternoon shift. I was supposed to bring her home with me when the store closed, but one evening I forgot about her completely. We were sitting down to dinner and her mother asked, "Where's Wendy?" Just then the phone rang. It was one of the store guards calling to say that while he was on his rounds, he had come across a girl who claimed she was our daughter. She was still working, unaware that the store had closed. We assured him that she was our daughter and I immediately returned to the store to bring her home.

At dinnertime we used to play a game we called "perception." I would ask the children to look at a painting on the wall for ten seconds, close their eyes, and then tell me what objects were in the picture. It always enlivened a family meal and it was a splendid exercise in observation. We encouraged them to handle "touchable" objects of art to get a tactile understanding of the pieces. Our small Rodin and Moore sculptures have now gained a rich patina from the hands of three generations of Marcuses, since our grandchildren are now doing the same thing.

We always encouraged our children to meet and talk with our dinner guests, so at an early age they developed a presence and an interest in the varied people who came to our home — musicians, writers, actors and business associates. Wendy had the good fortune to find a stimulating teacher early in her high school career. She was greatly interested in government, so when Abe Fortas came to dinner, she sat at his feet and listened avidly to discussions of politics, government, and the law. He urged her to consider going to law school after college and cited his wife, Carol, as an example of a woman who had made a success as a lawyer. Wendy joined Jerrie, who was already at Smith, and majored in government in preparation for a Washington career.

During a college summer vacation, she worked in the office of Senator John Sherman Cooper, who took a great interest in her and went out of his way to encourage her by letting her write a speech for him and by taking her onto the floor of the Senate. Wendy came away from that summer convinced that if she wanted to get anywhere in government as a legislative researcher, she needed a law degree. So, on her graduation from Smith, she applied to several law schools and was accepted by Harvard among others. During one of her law school summers she worked in the office of the Majority Leader, Senator Johnson, and the following summer worked on his campaign staff at the Los Angeles convention.

When Dick finished his sophomore year, I decided it was time to have a serious conversation with him about his future plans. I told him he had to make a decision about what occupation was apt to give him the greatest happiness in life, and that just because I was in retailing it wasn't necessary for him to follow in my footsteps unless he really wanted to more than anything else. I assured him I would back him if he decided he could find maximum happiness as a poet, an architect, a philosopher, a lawyer, a scientist, a teacher — anything except a loafer — that, he would have to do on his own with no help from me. He said he wasn't sure in his own mind, but that he'd like to try working on a ranch one summer and in a bank the following one. At the conclusion of his banking summer, he said, "I have decided I want to come into the store." "That's fine," I replied. "I have found great happiness in the retail business and I can only hope you will, too. Do you want to go to Harvard Business School?" "No," he said. "I'd prefer to spend a year working in another store." I arranged for him to be interviewed by Bloomingdale's for a position in their executive training program. He was accepted, and although they had taken him as a courtesy to me, they offered him a permanent job at the end of it if he chose to stay on. He declined with thanks, spent another few months at Saks Fifth Avenue, and returned to Dallas to start his first assignment.

Jerrie, two years senior to the twins, went to Smith at the age of seventeen without any motivation more serious than having a good time and finding a husband. She was successful on both scores, but somewhere along the way she was intellectually awakened. A summer in Italy with a Smith-sponsored art class, an exciting teacher the following semester, and an Amherst senior combined to make her final two years stimulating. She married Fred Smith, the Amherst man, the summer following her graduation. She has emerged as a young woman with great civic and cultural leadership, interested in politics and education and a participant in community affairs. She is not just a clubwoman; she has taken active positions in political campaigns in support of liberal candidates. Against my advice, she has co-founded a local magazine, *D*, and I think she may prove me wrong.

Wendy, who has a wanderlust quality she may have inherited from me, had arranged to take a job with an American law firm in Paris when she finished law school in 1963. In fact, she was about to leave for Paris when President Kennedy was killed. Instead, her first impulse on hearing the news was to go to Washington to offer her services to the Johnson family, whom she knew quite well as the result of her two summer experiences in the Johnson offices. In Washington she was immediately engaged as assistant to Liz Carpenter, Mrs. Johnson's press secretary. During the year she worked in the White House she performed a variety of duties, including traveling with the two Johnson girls and handling the press for them. She met hundreds of the important personages visiting the President and Mrs. Johnson, impressing them to a point where I would receive letters every week from friends commenting on how much they had enjoyed meeting Wendy at the White House. I soon found myself being identified as "the father of Wendy Marcus."

After a year she felt that it was time to move on to her legal job in France, which had been held open for her. She went to work for the firm of Coudert Frères and fell in love with Paris, that is, until she fell in love with a journalist with the *New York Times*, Henry Raymont, and returned to the United States to marry him. When she announced she was going to give up law to become a housewife, I said she was merely proving what I had long suspected, that higher education was really wasted on women, and that she should think of the male candidate whom she had displaced at Harvard Law School. She was indignant, but several days later came to me with the news that she had just taken a position as the legal researcher for the law section of *Time*. Belligerently she said, "I hope you're satisfied." I replied, "I am if you are." This was a fresh experience for her in which her legal education was put to good use and from which her legal experience was perceptibly broadened.

Being the child of successful parents has its drawbacks as well as its advantages, at least so thought one of our daughters, rebelling at the responsibilities and reputation the Neiman-Marcus fame imposed upon her. I reasoned with her, "Let's assume that I hadn't been successful and that I was a minor employee of a company and had less financial ability to provide education and travel opportunities for you. Do you think you would be happier?" "No, I guess I wouldn't," she replied. "Then you must learn to recognize that one pays for success, and sometimes, as in your case, the child has to pay some price, too. Nothing in life comes without a price tag. Finally, we have to determine whether the values of success are worth the price we have to pay for it. This isn't an easy question to answer, and many times your mother and I have discussed this same subject. Actually, I prefer the words 'accomplishment' and 'achievement' to the word 'success,' for the latter is too identified with the concept of monetary reward. I don't belittle the advantages of money, but the achievement of the best within one's own abilities, together with recognition accorded by one's associates, is the greatest reward of life. However, achievement in any field, whether in business, writing, painting, or the law, exacts a similar price. So what I think we are really talking about is whether it's better to be an achiever or a nonachiever. Think it over and some day give me an answer." She never did give me the answer, but now that she is married with children of her own, I know she understands what I was talking about.

In 1968, Dick married a charming, talented girl, Heather Johnson, a commercial artist, who has done much to give his life full dimensions. He has passed through various positions in the store, from buying to merchandising to store management, with success at all stages. Having lived through the problems of a family-dominated business, I must admit I leaned over backwards to avoid any charge of nepotism so far as Dick was concerned and no doubt I have expected higher standards of performance from him than I have from others. When my brother Edward decided to retire from the store to devote his full time to his extensive real estate interests, I had no idea who his replacement might be. I was not sure that Dick was ready or that he possessed the combination of qualities necessary to fill the job. We interviewed candidates from all over the country, and when we had talked to the last one, one of my associates said, "You've got the best-qualified person in the entire country right here in the store. You're being unduly tough on him just because he happens to be your own son." I made a reappraisal of Dick, concluding that my associate was right, and recommended that Dick be named president. I moved to the position of chairman of the board and chief executive officer, thus enabling me to give Dick on-the-job training in the problems and techniques of administering the affairs of an expanding business. He has responded to his new responsibilities even better than I might have hoped, earning the respect and cooperation of the entire organization. By the time of my retirement, he will be well qualified to carry on the objectives of Neiman-Marcus in the manner enunciated by his grandfather.

One Christmas my father gave me a first edition of *Huckleberry Finn* which he inscribed, "There has never been any disappointment in your relations with me. I hope to carry to the end that love which I hold most precious of all things." I can say no less about our three children.

I am confident my devoted wife regards my deep commitment to my life's work, Neiman-Marcus, with a mixture of pride and jealousy. After all, a business can be as demanding as a mistress, and no woman shares a man's interest with a business or another woman with equanimity. There's always a new store with new starting problems, or an old store with old problems. There are new buyers who have to be broken in or older ones who need redirection. When business is dull, new solutions have to be evolved; when business is good, there's not enough time in the day to take care of all the demands.

I have to talk so much during the day that sometimes when I get home at night I feel all talked out and become uncommunicative. With many members of the family in the business, it becomes somewhat difficult to remember to keep all of them familiarized with decisions, new appointments, visitors who have dropped in, resignations, births and deaths, and on occasion I forget to relay such information to Billie, for which there is never a satisfactory explanation. Despite my deep involvement and communication failures, she has been proud of my achievements and has contributed importantly to my success.

The requirements made of the wife of the head of a corporation, and especially of the wife of the chief executive officer of a fashion specialty store, are not to be underestimated. She has to entertain and be entertained; she is constantly on show and is expected to wear the latest in fashion; she is supposed to know the happenings in both the fashion markets and the stores. With it all, she gets no tax allowance on her clothes, as do actresses.

We entertain a great deal, usually for visitors who come to

Dallas from all parts of the world. One night there might be a small dinner party for Sean O'Faolain of Dublin, or a visiting designer from Rome, or a fellow merchant from Paris, followed a few days later by a luncheon for seventy-five honoring Prince Rainier and Princess Grace of Monaco. Or we might be visited by friends from New Delhi who extended great hospitality to us when we were in India, or we might have a party for a very dear friend like Björn Wiinblad from Copenhagen. We have learned to be cautious in extending the invitation "Next time you are in America, come to see us in Dallas" — for they usually do. One year in Europe we uttered these words to a couple we had just met, and upon our return two weeks later they were in Dallas awaiting us.

Billie is a marvelous hostess. Her flower arrangements, which she does herself, are better than those of any florist; her table decorations, built usually around some interest of the guests of honor, are ingenious and beautiful; her menus are carefully planned around the capabilities of whoever may be cooking for us at the time. Birthday parties for our children, and now our grandchildren, have been her particular joys. Our annual family Christmas Eve party, with small presents she individually gift wraps, is her year-end finale.

As an expert gift adviser to others, I have always tried to make my Christmas gifts to Billie exciting and memorable. One year I made her presents into a treasure hunt, leading from a pair of bedroom slippers by her bed to a myriad of other gifts in every room of the house. Another year I selected twenty-six gifts from A to Z, each packed in a box with the appropriate letter. Once I chose a gift from each of the eight countries we had visited that year. I know her taste so perfectly that rarely have I made a wrong selection. The joy of giving to Billie over the years has been in her genuine responsiveness whether the gift be large or small. She enjoys possessions but never has she hinted or connived for anything. She is a most appreciative person.

Vacations unadulterated by any business considerations have always been difficult for me to take, for there is hardly a place in the world that doesn't offer some buying or business opportunities or obligations. If we go to Europe, I always feel compelled to check the shops in search of new ideas or to visit some of our leading suppliers. In Mexico there are handcrafts to search out; in California there are customers to see; even in the desert I have found merchandise ideas worth bringing back; in the Orient I can't resist visiting the antique shops conveniently located near the shrines. All in all, Neiman-Marcus is difficult to flee from. I doubt if I have had two months of pure vacation in my forty-eight years of work.

Billie is very understanding and puts up with my insatiable appetite to see everything a new place has to offer, but at times she says, "I've had enough. If you want to see five more shops and three more galleries, go on by yourself." In my most uncommunicative moments, she accuses me of being a loner, which I guess is partially true. This comment will invariably shake me up and make me more loquacious, temporarily at least. I do know that I sometimes "lock out" the outside world just to be able to concentrate on a thought, thus satisfying my urgent need for privacy but antagonizing those around me. I can scarcely list this as an attractive social trait. A drop in hearing in one ear has caused me to use a hearing aid, and while that device is most helpful, it does give me a subconscious excuse for being apparently inattentive. It was Winston Churchill, I think, who admonished a friend turning on his hearing aid at a cocktail party, "You are a fool, sir, not to take advantage of a natural infirmity."

271

14

Collecting

T HE *New York Times* column "Topic of the Times" once devoted its space to the subject of collecting and led off by saying, "The wish to accumulate material seems to be one of the more important drives in human existence . . . in most people the collecting urge is just a passing step in the process of growing up." If this be true, then I've never grown up. I was bitten by the bug in early childhood and I've never recovered from the infection. I'm glad I haven't, for collecting, next to my family and business, has brought me continuous joy and satisfaction, allowing me to get to know other collectors all over the world, and leading me to rich and varied experiences.

Collecting has meant much more than the mere acquisition of things; it has brought knowledge about the objects I've collected, their use, the motivations of the people who made or used them, and the history of the times in which they were used. Frequently I've been asked, "How do you start collecting?" Invariably my answer is to start buying things you think you like, cautiously, until you develop some critical standards of quality and value. Don't be afraid to make mistakes; all collectors make them. But *do* have the courage to put your money down and make a commitment, for until you take this first step, you are not likely to start learning. Above all, buy what *you* like, after getting the

275

best advice available, but don't buy on the basis of possible appreciation in value. If that comes later, then so much the better. Trade in your mistakes or give them away.

My adult collecting started when I was at college, stimulated by the "Gentleman's Library" at the Harvard Union consisting of representative works of English writers of the sixteenth to nineteenth centuries, and subsequently by Mr. Winship's seminar "The History of the Printed Book," held in the Widener Room. The first inspiration led me to form a "reading library" of the works of English dramatists, novelists, and poets in contemporary bindings, though not first editions. The second started me off in the direction of collecting books of typographical importance from the fifteenth through the twentieth century, with particular emphasis on books designed and printed by America's leading typographer, Bruce Rogers.

My preoccupation with Bruce Rogers has continued to the present and has resulted in the accumulation of one of the more complete collections of Bruce Rogers's books, leaflets and ephemera in the country. There's no great value to the collection but it has been great fun to check my list against the several B. R. bibliographies and to then search for missing items in bookstores I visit and in book dealers' catalogues. Reading book catalogues is, in itself, a delightful distraction, and even more so when you are looking for something in particular. Some Rogers books privately printed in small editions for wealthy patrons and his great Bible, printed at the Oxford University Press when he was living in London, are still to be added. Some day I hope to find the missing items and complete the collection.

I do have a unique Rogers book that is in great demand for all exhibitions of Rogers and Max Beerbohm material. Its acquisition came about as a result of a fan letter I wrote to Sam Behrman, the playwright, in 1955, following his profile of the art dealer Lord Duveen in *The New Yorker*. I've always followed the practice of writing a note of appreciation to actors for a performance I've enjoyed, to writers for books or articles I've liked, and to public figures for speeches or actions I've admired — whether I know them or not. So it was that I wrote to Mr. Behrman after I read his Duveen profile. I received a very warm acknowledgment from him, asking me to lunch with him at "21" on my next visit to New York. I accepted his invitation and we did lunch together a few months later, hitting it off as though we had been long-lost acquaintances. I inquired what he was planning to do next, and he told me that he was leaving for Italy the following month to do a *New Yorker* profile on Sir Max Beerbohm at the latter's villa at Rapallo. I casually mentioned that we were going to nearby Portofino for Easter, expressing the hope he might join us and our daughter Wendy for a *zuppa de pesce*. "Great," he said. "Would it interest you to meet Sir Max?" "Who wouldn't like to meet this last of the Victorians? Besides which, I've just bought a trial proof of his *The Happy Hypocrite*, designed by America's preeminent typographical designer, Bruce Rogers. He might be interested in seeing it." We set a date for the day before Easter.

We drove over from Portofino to Sir Max's modest little villa in Rapallo, and were ushered into his tiny sitting room by Mrs. Jungmann, his nurse and companion, whom he subsequently married. There we met Sir Max, a frail, delicate, little man with a black skullcap on his head and a shawl around his legs to protect him from any drafts. My lasting impression of this ninety-year-old man with the translucent skin of a three-day-old infant was that of fragility. It seemed as if a heavy wind or a hearty handshake might completely destroy his eggshell-like body. After a few minutes of conversation, I told him of the book I had brought along so that he would know that there were still people in the United States interested in him and his writings. I told him of Bruce Rogers's significance in the printing world, and explained that as a trial proof, there were only a half-dozen pages set up. He glanced at it, and I asked if he would be kind enough to autograph it for me. He replied, "I didn't sleep well last night and I don't think I have

the strength to do it today. Leave it with me and I'll mail it to you."
There was nothing I could do but acquiesce, so we departed, leaving my precious little book behind.

Months went by with no sign of my book. Then one day, in a plain brown envelope, the book came back. Not only had he autographed it, but he had added to it! On the flyleaf he wrote:

Dear Mr. Stanley Marcus,

Here is the book that you left with me, I have dared to amend, here and there what seemed to me to be a lack of continuity in the narration.

Yours very sincerely,

MAX BEERBOHM

Rapallo
1955

He added words, phrases, and whole sentences, all in his own typical, small hand. I couldn't have been more delighted with his emendations. I then hastened to Connecticut to pay a personal visit to Bruce Rogers to solicit *his* autograph in the volume. Curiously and sadly, both men died within a few months. Sam Behrman wrote later:

You will be interested to know that Mr. Shawn [editor of the *New Yorker*] was tremendously impressed by the photostat you sent me. He couldn't get over that Max, at his age, should have accomplished this ingenious thing. You own the last bit of writing that Max ever did. My final chapter will make this clear.

On this same trip to Italy I paid a visit to another ninety-year-old man, Bernard Berenson at I Tatti, in my capacity as a member of the Board of Overseers of Harvard University. The property had recently come into Harvard's possession and it was suggested that it might be nice if I paid my respects to B. B., which of course was a very pleasant assignment. I was greeted by the famous Nicky at the villa with cordiality; shortly thereafter, Mr. Berenson was brought in. My association with the university apparently made little impression on him, for he showed no inclination to even ask questions about his alma mater. He said, "You're from Texas, aren't you?" Without awaiting an answer, he continued, "Now let's see. Texas, as I recall, is somewhere between New York and California. You know, when you reach my age, and when you've been gone as long as I have been, you tend to forget a lot of things." When I confirmed the location of Texas, he said, "You had a very fine leader there who became a United States senator, didn't you?" While I was trying to identify whom he was describing it came to him. "Houston was his name, I think." Sam Houston was the first president of Texas, subsequently becoming one of the state's first senators when Texas joined the Union. That was the extent of his conversation. Six months later, he, too, had passed away.

As I became increasingly interested in both contemporary and primitive art, I started collecting books related to these fields for quick and easy reference. I am called upon to make numerous speeches before various groups on art, corporate responsibility and business ethics, and I have tried to build a working library that will provide me with reference material on most of the subjects on which I am working. I have been asked on many occasions, "Have you read all of these books?" To which I answer quickly, "No, but I know which one to go to for the information I need."

In my study of book catalogues, I became impressed with the number of books which had been privately printed for presentation as Christmas remembrances. This was often a rich man's hobby, and frequently printers would indulge in this activity in their spare time. I started a collection of them fifteen years ago and have built up a library of about a thousand different volumes. Many of the titles are the well-known Christmas stories and legends, such as Clement C. Moore's *A Visit from St. Nicholas*, O. Henry's *Gift of the Magi*, Milton's *On the Morning of Christ's Nativity*, and Thackeray's *Round About the Christmas Tree*. Others are stories or articles which the publisher of the volumes wanted to distribute to his friends. Usually, they are printed in small editions limited to fifty to two hundred copies; many are typographical gems.

My latest field of interest has been miniature books, the size of which is limited to three inches in height. I think I must have started on miniatures at the time my wife began to comment about the burgeoning collections which were claiming every bit of free space in the house. I figured I could smuggle in five miniature books without detection, but soon they began to require housing in the form of miniature bookcases, which in turn began to demand shelf space. Miniature books have been printed almost from the beginning of printing; they have been printed in almost every country, either to meet some practical purpose or as virtuoso performances by the printers. Their subjects vary as widely as those in standard-size volumes, ranging from the Bible to propaganda from the Third Reich, from dictionaries to Shakespeare. Many of them were printed for travelers in coaches, where space wouldn't permit a full-size book; others, on the subject of etiquette or daily prayers, were made for children to carry with them. Printers vied with each other in seeing who could use the smallest-size type face, almost like Paganini daring a fellow composer to top one of his Variations. They are being produced today by a wide number of printers in this country, Europe, and Japan, with Hungary taking the leadership in the sheer number of titles being published.

Several years ago when we were in Holland, I looked up an American, Jack Levien, who was producing charming miniatures. He asked if I had ever met a Mrs. Irene Winterstein of Zurich, who had a superb collection. We were on our way there, so I phoned her and said I should like to see her collection. She invited us to her home and showed us her books, which she had been collecting since she was seventeen years old. Consisting of over four thousand volumes, it must certainly be one of the largest and finest collections in the world. One of the pleasant consequences of collecting is the opportunity it affords to meet others with similar interests everywhere you travel.

Painting and sculpture had no consuming appeal for me in my undergraduate days, so I failed to take any of the excellent courses Harvard offered in art history or appreciation. Consequently I was unaware of the exciting ferment occurring in the art field in the mid-twenties. I was vaguely aware that something called the Museum of Modern Art had been formed, about which there was considerable controversy, but I didn't become interested in the museum until some years later. I did feel some affinity for the field of graphics, for it was a printing medium, a relative (however distant) of book printing.

So I backed into art collecting accidentally. For some reason beyond my recall, I became aware of masks, and as I read about their use by different societies, I started to acquire a few. Billie gave me my first one, a Noh mask from Japan. Then my father and mother bought me a couple of Javanese masks at the Javanese pavilion at the New York World's Fair in 1939. From then on, I started to buy masks of all cultures — American Indian, Northwest Coast Indian, Mexican, and African. About this time, I happened to run across a refugee German dealer who had a tiny shop in the East Forties in New York. This beaten, shy man had little capital and few customers, but he had a wealth of knowledge and taste which he generously imparted to me. He guided me wisely and I told other collectors about him. One day Jacques Lipchitz discovered him, and a few days later Rene d'Harnoncourt (Nelson Rockefeller's primitive art adviser) came to his shop. Julius Carlebach was "made," and in a short time he moved over to Third Avenue to a greatly enlarged store; years later he made his final move to Madison Avenue and Seventy-ninth Street, where he occupied former branch banking quarters, replete with a vault and a steel door. From an intimidated, penniless immigrant he rose, through hard work, kindness, and study, to become one of the city's leading primitive art dealers. He was always gracious and fair in his judgments of works bought from other dealers, unlike one or two others of his fellow refugee competitors.

It was only natural to move from masks to African wood sculpture and pre-Columbian terracotta figures, and then to Asiatic and Middle Eastern archaeological pieces. One day Carlebach showed me two cubist paintings by Diego Rivera which Lipchitz had traded him for an African mask he found irresistible. They were painted around 1919 when Rivera was living in Paris, painting with Picasso and Braque, and I bought them. They are totally unlike any of the oils painted by Rivera in Mexico.

About the time that Vincent Price was appearing on TV on "The $64,000 Question," he was in Dallas and we gave a party for him. We purposely sat him facing the wall on which the two paintings were hung, for we were curious to see whether he would be able to identify them. The painter had discreetly signed them with his initials in the lower right-hand corner; they were indiscernible except by close scrutiny. Throughout dinner Vincent was courteously polite to his dinner partners, but I could see that he was agonizing over the pictures. Finally, after coffee was served and we left the table, he pulled me aside and said, "You've got to tell me who painted those two pictures. I simply can't figure them out." "You're paid $64,000 for being an expert; try real hard," I replied. "Well, it isn't Juan Gris, or Marcoussis," he said. "It's not any one of the major cubists. It's not Metzinger or Gleizes." I put him on his honor not to approach the paintings closely enough to read the initials, promising I'd reveal the identity of the painter before he left. Later in the evening I told him that they were by Rivera. "My God, of course, I should have recognized them," and he then proceeded to tell me all about Rivera's attempts to stifle his natural style while working with the Parisian cubist masters.

Our paintings and sculptures multiplied as did our pre-Columbian archaeological collection. On any important purchase, Billie has been a participant in the decisionmaking. She has a good eye, and above all she is a superb curator and a master in placing works in proper juxtaposition. I am inclined to make the selection based on judgment, and then afterwards try to place it. We agree on most things in art, although each of us has pet likes and dislikes. I've kept her from buying Chagalls, at a time when we could afford them, because I didn't care for or understand his work, and she in turn restrained me from buying Francis Bacon's paintings twenty years ago because she found them depressing. Each of us still holds to our original opinions, but we respect the right to mutual dissent.

She valiantly holds me on a leash, reminding me, "We're running a home, not a museum." Our collection is certainly catholic in taste, ranging from archaeological and primitive art of many cultures to twentieth-century painting and sculpture of all national origins. We go through a weeding process at intervals, but we like almost every piece so much that we find it painful and difficult to eliminate any. I may be willing to take out a pre-Columbian figure, but she will object, saying, "We bought that when we went to Oaxaca with the Tamayos." Then I will demur about withdrawing something else on the grounds that it has a relationship to an object from another culture. So the collection grows and grows — but Billie won't permit me to add another room to the house.

When we made our first trip to the Middle East, I found a few small terracottas of females with the hands cupped underneath the breasts, which were identified as fertility figures. Later I found similar figures from Greenland, Rome, Greece, Africa, Mexico and Costa Rica. In my innocence I thought, perhaps, that I had made an important archaeological correlation, but very quickly I learned that the archaeologists had been aware of this dissemination of the fertility idea almost all around the world. It fascinated me to see this demonstration of the power of an idea, so fundamental to man, to transcend thousands of miles during a period of at least eight thousand years. I started to collect them wherever I could find them, so that today we have an assemblage of these figures dating from about 6400 B.C., the Haçilar culture, to Syrian-Hittite, 2000 B.C.; Luristan and Amlash, 1600 B.C.; Greco-Roman, 200 B.C.; Mexican 600 B.C.–A.D. 600 and African, early twentieth century. Throughout man's history, until the present time, the reproduction of his species, his crops, and livestock has probably been his single most driving objective. It represented survival, and to achieve it he propitiated his gods. Now, for the first time, irrigation and science have stepped in to help him regulate his crops and his herds, and education is beginning to teach him the hazards of overpopulation. With the advent of "the pill," it is possible to regulate the sizes of families, so I have added it in a lucite case to the collection of fertility idols, not in frivolity but seriously, for it is truly the "idol" of our century.

I've never had time to go on an archaeological dig, though I've seen several in progress in Israel and Egypt. The dramatic discoveries are exciting to read about, but the actual digging under the boiling sun must be sheer drudgery, requiring patience and dedication. However, archaeological discoveries can be made away from the field, and I made one in an air-conditioned gallery in Beverly Hills. A few years prior to my "find," we had purchased a forty-eight-inch terracotta representation of Tlaloc, the Mexican god of rain, which we gave to the Dallas Museum of Fine Arts. At the time of the purchase, I had asked the seller what he knew about the piece. He said he had been told that the Tlaloc had been found facing a semicircle of three large terracotta frogs about eighteen inches tall and two forearms with hands about twelve inches tall standing in between the frogs. He was unable to tell me the whereabouts of the frogs and the arms, but promised to let me know if he was able to get any information.

Several years went by with no news of the missing pieces, and I had just about forgotten about them. On a trip to Beverly Hills, I went in to see a favorite dealer, Harry Franklin, and there in his gallery was a large frog and *one* forearm. "Where are the other frogs and forearm?" I asked. Somewhat surprised, Harry replied, "I don't know anything about another forearm, but there is one other frog which I have sent down to the County Museum for consideration by the acquisition committee."

The Dallas Museum was delighted by the news of the reappearance of three-fifths of the missing figures, purchased them from Franklin and reunited them with the Tlaloc in its pre-Columbian gallery. Perhaps someday the other frog and arm will show up, and they too can be added to complete the lot. This adventure might be labeled "Archaeological Discovery Without Sweat!"

A great practical joke was played on me by one of my business associates, the late Joe Ross, a vice-president of the store. I had purchased a large oil of a standing nude figure, back facing, by our friend Saul Schary, an American painter, and had placed her at the head of our stair landing. Several years later on Christmas Eve, Billie and a bachelor friend, Ben Eisner, and I stayed up until about 3 A.M. setting up Dick's electric train and assembling the girls' dollhouses. When we were all through, I started up the stairs, passing the painting, and only after I was in my bedroom did I realize that something was unusual. I didn't know just what it was, so I retraced my steps to the ground floor. I started back up, slowly this time, and looked at the pictures lining the walls of the stairwell. When I got back up to the landing I looked at the nude, and there she was in her usual position — *but,* she had turned around and now her front side was facing. Obviously I was flabbergasted, for I had never heard of a painting turning around. Just then Billie and Ben broke out in laughter and told me that I had been pranked by Joe Ross, who, together with the other executives, had commissioned Schary to paint this reverse picture for me as a Christmas present.

On my trips to New York and abroad, I visited art galleries at lunchtime and on Saturdays to train my eye and to look for objects of art which might be suitable for one of our stores. I purchased a large bronze sculpture by Hajdu which graces the second floor of our downtown Dallas store, paintings by Kepes, Brō, Maeda, the Japanese, and many others. I met up with Stanley Landsman, the light and glass sculptor, whom we later commissioned to do important sculptures for our Houston and Atlanta stores. Flying to New York one day in 1951, I picked up a copy of *Time* and came across a story in its art section of an exhibition opening that very day at a Manhattan gallery. The paintings, by Marcel Vertès, whose murals were hanging on our second floor, bore the captivating title "Imaginary Portraits of People When They Were Very Young." I was so intrigued with the concept that I went directly from the airport to the Kleeman Gallery to see the pictures. There on the walls were Churchill at the age of one year, Bernard Baruch as an adolescent, curly-haired Einstein with a violin in his hand at the age of eight, Gypsy Rose Lee at the age of four — provocatively raising her skirt, the artist's wife at the age of seven, Eleanor Roosevelt at the age of six, and Wally Warfield in a simple basic black dress at the age of eleven, looking adoringly at her Prince Charming, the Duke of Windsor, also aged eleven, and fourteen other notables. I couldn't make up my mind between several of them, so Mr. Kleeman said, "Since you're having such a hard time choosing, why don't you buy the whole collection?" "Make me a good price and I will," I replied. He did and I bought the entire collection.

We brought it to Dallas and showed it in the store to an invited audience as "The Neiman-Marcus Collection of Imaginary Portraits," by Marcel Vertès. The artist came to Dallas, delighted in having sold out his entire show and pleased with the knowledge that the collection would be kept together. We've declined many offers from the subjects, their families, and museums to buy single paintings, though we do send the collection on loan to other cities.

Several years later, Vertès wrote to say that he would like to buy back the portrait of his wife, "No," I replied, "I won't sell you your wife, but I'll trade her to you for another imaginary portrait." "Who shall it be?" he asked. I told him we would take a public opinion poll and let him know. The overwhelming choice of our customers was for a portrait of President Eisenhower. Vertès painted a picture of Eisenhower as he imagined him to look at the age of one, with the dove of peace in one hand and a rifle in the other. The paintings have brought great joy and amusement to hundreds of thousands of viewers who get a chance to see them on visits to our downtown Dallas store.

We asked Alexander Calder to design a large mobile for our first suburban store and it was an object of great curiosity, being the first Calder hung permanently in Dallas. An elderly customer was reported to have gazed at it shortly after it was suspended and remarked, "If they think that they're going to catch flies with that, they're crazy!"

The most sales-productive work of art I ever bought was a tapestry made up of hundreds of pieces of fur by an artist-artisan from Strasbourg, France. We hung it in our fur salon, where it caused so much attention and requests for a sales price that we put a $10,000 ticket on it, hoping to discourage any potential purchaser. We discovered that people would come up to examine it, get in a conversation with one of the members of our fur sales staff, and end up buying a fur coat. It became known as our fur trap. I was disturbed to learn one day that a man from Detroit had bought it during my absence from the city, but fortunately his credit proved not to be good and the tapestry was rehung. We have now taken it off sale in the belief that it serves a far greater value as a conversation piece.

One of the many dividends from collecting is the inspiration you give, sometimes unwittingly, to others who start collecting. Very good friends of ours in Baltimore were going to Africa, so I asked them if they would try to pick up some African sculptures for us. I gave them an illustrated book, marking the photographs of pieces we wanted. Until that moment, neither Janet nor Alan Wurtzburger had ever evidenced the slightest interest in any form of art. Not a single picture adorned the walls of their beautiful home, "Timberlane," in Pikesville, a suburb of Baltimore. They were unable to locate any desirable pieces in Africa, but when they stopped in London on their way home, they spent several days at the British Museum to study the wonderful African collection there, met some top dealers, and bought their first African sculptures. They worked on their collection until they had it well rounded and gave it to the Baltimore Museum of Art. They then proceeded to duplicate the same systematic approach to pre-Columbian terracottas and Oceanic sculpture, giving these collections as well to the Baltimore Museum.

Their home was located on a beautiful, rolling piece of land, surrounded by towering trees. For their next art project, they decided to build a modern sculpture garden which would include large-scale works of all of the top contemporary sculptors of the world. They enlisted the aid of a landscape designer, James Rose, who assisted them in placing their sculptures to the best advantage of both the works of art and their surroundings, making their sculpture garden one of the most beautiful in the world. The sculpture then went the way of their other collections — to the Walters. It has always been a source of gratification to witness how a simple request resulted in the "turning on" of two people who never knew that they could be interested in art.

Traveling to Europe by ship one summer, I was talking with a shipboard acquaintance about art, great paintings we had missed, what to look for in Paris, and the usual chitchat art collectors indulge in, when Nate Cummings, then president of Consolidated Foods, came up and listened to our conversation. "How do you know what to buy?" he inquired. We explained that the best thing to do was to visit museums and galleries, determine what period of art and which artists you liked, and start buying cautiously from that point. "Can you make any money on art?" he next asked. "I understand a lot of paintings by Renoir and Cezanne have gone way up in price." We admitted that prices had risen spectacularly on

288

many painters, and that money could probably still be made, though neither of us had ever bought paintings or sculptures with that objective in mind. Nate turned to me and asked, "Would you be willing to go around to some galleries with me to help make some selections?" I assented readily and the following week I introduced him to the art world. I discovered quickly that Nate wanted to buy a lot of pictures, requiring more time than I could afford to give him. I therefore recommended a reliable art consultant who could devote a week to shopping the art market with him, but I expressed my willingness to pass on his selections and help him make final decisions.

Our apartments were on the same floor at the Plaza-Athenée, so every night Nate would call me to come over and take a look at his finds of the day. His living room would be filled with canvases from a dozen galleries, and I would go through them, pointing out the ones I liked and giving reasons for my preferences. His first purchase was a Degas, starting him off on a collecting career from which he derived great satisfaction, met a wide variety of people, and, buying at the time he did, made a handsome paper profit, at least.

One of the best "collecting" stories I have ever heard was told to me by my late friend Albert Lasker, the great advertising man, on his patio at La Quinta, in the California desert. "You know, my wife Mary was formerly in the art business before our marriage, so she tried to get me interested in buying paintings. The only art I had ever bought was to illustrate our clients' advertising, and I had no compelling desire to put any art on my walls. Every Saturday, Mary and I would have lunch at the old Ritz garden in New York and on one particular Saturday, Mary told me of an auction to be held that day in which there was a very choice Renoir which was likely to go for a song, since the balance of the collection wasn't good enough to pull out the usual complement of dealers. She suggested we stroll over and take a look at it.

"When we came to the Renoir, it was surrounded by a group of people whom I quickly identified as art dealers. I realized then that it wasn't going to sell for a bargain price, but I asked Mary what she thought it could be bought for, and told her if she could get it for that figure to buy it. The auction room was crowded, so we had to take seats on opposite sides of the room. When the painting came up, it quickly passed Mary's price, so I started bidding on it. I noticed that the dealer Paul Rosenberg was one of the leading contestants for the picture, and I figured that if the painting was worth so much to him, it was worth 10% more to me. I kept topping his bid, and finally it was knocked down to me.

"After the sale was over, Mary came up to me and said, 'Well, I was wrong about the price, but some crazy old fool kept bidding it up.' I told her that I was the crazy old fool. It was the first picture I ever bought, and it excited me so much I've been buying ever since." Mary and he did buy, and they built a great collection of paintings with superb examples of van Gogh, Renoir, Matisse, Picasso and Toulouse-Lautrec, which Mary loaned to the Dallas Museum of Fine Arts to help our program of art education in Dallas.

Another great story of Albert's had to do with an eminent French art dealer who had moved to New York prior to the war and set up a distinguished gallery on East Fifty-seventh Street. When the draft went into effect, the dealer was panic-stricken lest his frail son be assigned to a job beyond his physical capabilities. He begged Lasker to intervene and get him a job he could perform with honor. "It was a request I wouldn't have honored for my own son, but this man's family had undergone such tragedy in Europe, I yielded to his importunities. After much effort, I succeeded. The dealer was almost hysterical with appreciation, asking, as a favor, if I would come to see him at his gallery. When I arrived, he said, 'Mr. Lasker, I know I imposed on you by my request, but you've saved my wife's and my life by the thing you've done. I want you to know that we shall always be indebted to you. Do you remember the large Braque which hangs upstairs in my living room and which I have always refused to sell you? Well, in appreciation, I just wanted to tell you that *if* I ever decide to sell it, I shall *offer* it to you first.' " Albert concluded, "I didn't know how to thank him."

Like a couple of million other men, I have had a one-sided love affair with Sophia Loren. When a business visit to Rome necessitated setting up an appointment with her husband, Dr. Ponti, I was elated, for I thought I might have the good fortune to find her visiting her husband's office. But I had no such luck, for she was in Geneva. As a preliminary to our business discussion, I commented to Dr. Ponti that we had two interests in common: one was my admiration of his wife, to which he merely shrugged his shoulders, as if to say well, doesn't everyone?; the other was that we both collected the paintings of Morlotti. With that he grew quite excited, insisting I go out to his villa to see his collection of over forty canvases by this contemporary Italian painter. This joint interest in art led to a meeting a few years later with the glorious Sophia, who, great as she is and looks in pictures, is even more beautiful and lovelier in person. I shall never part with our Morlotti!

Noncollectors frequently make the mistake of attributing more knowledge to those known as collectors than is deserved. One such instance occurred when I received a call from the president of Southern Methodist University asking if I would go out to see a collection of Spanish paintings of the eighteenth century which were being offered as a gift to the university. I disclaimed any expert knowledge of Spanish painting, but the president said, "The rest of us have less knowledge than you, so take a look at them and let me know what you think of them." The donor was Algur Meadows, an old friend and customer, who had bought the paintings at a time when his company had the oil exploration concession in Spain. At that time he didn't know anything about paintings, but he was never a man to turn down a bargain. Spanish friends had introduced him to a man who had been represented as a great expert on Spanish art and who had written a catalogue of the collection.

I asked Al the provenance of the pictures. *"Pro* what?" he asked. I explained the meaning and importance of a provenance, to which he replied, "Oh, the man who wrote the catalogue sold them to me." This, of course, immediately aroused my suspicion and I so reported to President Tate, urging him to call in two or three of the recognized experts in Spanish painting in the United States. The president was reluctant to take this step for fear of offending Mr. Meadows, who, in addition to offering the paintings, had also pledged to build a gallery to house them in the new Fine Arts Center at the university, and to endow the building with a million dollars. I explained I was in no position to question the paintings but I was apprehensive about their provenance, and that if the pictures should turn out to be spurious both the donor and the university would have egg splattered in their respective faces. Tate was unwilling to risk losing an important benefactor and preferred to take the gamble that the paintings were genuine. He was a pragmatist.

The building was built, the paintings were installed, and the community was grateful to Mr. Meadows for his munificence. Between the time Mr. Meadows acquired his Spanish paintings and the time he gave them to SMU, his first wife died and he remarried, and the new Mrs. Meadows was more interested in contemporary painting. Hence the gift of the Spanish collection to SMU. There was some mumbling around town about the authenticity of the Spanish collection, but no one was in a position to challenge the pictures forthrightly until a new curator, Bill Jordan, a first-rate Spanish painting scholar, came to the Fine Arts Center. I presume he had some deep-seated doubts.

In the winter of 1967, the Dallas Museum of Fine Arts and the Fort Worth Museum of Art held complementary exhibitions of Picasso's works honoring the ninetieth birthday of the artist. It was a dramatic affair to which art critics, collectors, and dealers from all over the country came. Among the dealers was Klaus Perls, the president of the Art Dealers Association of America, who was asked by Mr. Meadows to come to see his collection of contemporary paintings with the idea of valuing them for insurance purposes. Mr. Perls, with two or three other dealers, did go and proclaimed the paintings fakes. Mr. Meadows was indignant at first, but as he meditated on the matter, and possibly after calling in other dealers who confirmed the indictment, he decided to remove them from his walls. Simultaneously, questions about the Spanish paintings came out in the open, and with Mr. Meadows's blessing, the same Spanish painting experts whom I had recommended earlier were called to Dallas to examine the pictures. They pronounced them "unauthentic."

At this point Mr. Meadows chose a brilliant course of action. Instead of crying about having been bilked, he took it like a man and said, "I have made a mistake. Fortunately I am a wealthy man and I can afford to rectify my mistakes, and I shall." He employed the services of the Wildenstein Gallery and, with the assistance of Bill Jordan, proceeded to build a collection of choice, genuine, Spanish paintings. Simultaneously, he replaced his collection of fake contemporary pictures with ones of unquestionable authenticity. It was a brilliant recovery from the depths of adversity.

In the case of his personal collection, he had been taken in by a dealer named Fernand Legros, who was selling "names" below the market. The whole story is chronicled in Clifford Irving's *Fake*. In both cases, Mr. Meadows had invited victimization by his lack of knowledge of the art field and by his attraction to bargains. Those of us who have been collecting a long time recognize that a bargain in art, as in diamonds, as in furs and as in automobiles, is a rarity indeed. Mr. Meadows learned sadly that being an authority in *oil* did not necessarily mean that the expertise carried over into *oil paintings*. He paid a price for his lesson, but he learned it well, coming out of the affair with great dignity and public esteem.

15

Deep in the Heart
of Fashion

IT REQUIRES COURAGE to portray a role on the stage; likewise, it requires supreme egotism to design new products for a national or worldwide audience. I'm referring to creative designers, of whom there are relatively few at any given time. Most so-called designers aren't designers at all — they are adapters, skilled in using the design of a creator to make adaptations and variations thereof.

As I wrote in *Fortune* in 1940, the American fashion trade has historically used Europe as its fashion laboratory, and has contented itself with making reproductions and adaptations to meet the requirements of American women. It's not that Americans, per se, lack creative ability; rather, there has been little economic necessity for them to create. Paris, the hub of fashion for most of the twentieth century, designed for the individual, experimenting with new ideas, fabrics, construction; the United States, dedicated to manufacturing rather than dressmaking, found it more profitable to modify French originals for machine production. All of this was true until World War II; it is much less true since then, for "couture" is dying in all countries, giving way to ready-to-wear production. Paris still has the lead as the most important design center, for the newest, finest fabrics are produced in France and nearby Italy, and its garment industry has not yet reached the gargantuan size of its American counterpart. Fashion creativity moves in inverse ratio to the scale of production.

Fashion, which formerly started with the top of the social order, now originates in the "streets" as often as not; today it rises to the top rather than filtering to the bottom. The strongest fashion of our generation, blue jeans, is a good case in point, and incidentally, represents the USA's most important contribution to fashion in our history. Young English designers first recognized the fashion vitality being expressed by the young and made clothes to fulfill the demands of that market. Italy, despite its fabulous textile production, has added little to the enrichment of fashion aside from its continued leadership in knits.

I don't mean to belittle the contribution of the adapters; they keep the factories of the world busy, they dress millions of women. There is creativity in "adapting," for new hybrids are developed with a silhouette borrowed from Dior, a sleeve from Saint Laurent, and a new idea from a Givenchy print. Adapters may have no ability to develop a new trend, but they can spot one immediately and make the most of it. With fashion piracy laws as weak and ineffective as they are, the original creators seldom reap the financial rewards to which their creativity entitles them. Sketching is not permitted at any of the couture shows, but Harry Shacter, who put together the lines for Ben Zuckerman in the latter's heyday, could sit through a Paris collection, and after the showing reproduce from memory fifty models, although he paid the minimum entrance fee, or "caution fee," as the French call it, which at that time was the purchase of a single model. That's one reason why the French couturiers have had to depend more and more on their perfumes, neckties, and boutiques to sustain themselves.

The best designers are like great architects, working with new materials and constructions to create new forms and shapes; some good designers may have one idea in a lifetime, repeating it ad nauseum in countless variations until the public finally tires of it. The minor designers are more like interior decorators, taking a form and changing its look with color, flowers, and ornamentation. It's conceivable that any good architect can build one great building; it takes a great architect to do hundreds of noteworthy structures, employing new concepts, arriving at fresh solutions. And so it is in dressmaking. The greatest are never content with what they have done; they move on to new silhouettes, new methods of cutting fabric, and new ways of creating distinction for their customers.

Over the past fifty years I've been acquainted with most of the designers, here and abroad, the greatest, the not-so-great, and those in between. Some have been modest, shy people, others flamboyant and aggressive. My comments about them are strictly limited to those with whom I've had a personal acquaintance or some direct business experience; I do not intend to make this a documentary of the many talented designers throughout the world.

At the top of my list, I would have to put Madame Vionnet, who designed on the cutting table rather than in the sketchbook. She introduced the bias cut as a new way to make dresses, utilizing the fabric's stretching qualities. As Diana Vreeland wrote in the catalogue for the Metropolitan Museum's exhibition *Inventive Clothes 1909–1930*, "Consisting of intricately cut bias triangles and rectangles, skillfully mitred, a Vionnet dress could be slipped over the head and become form fitting without any side or back opening. Never before did well-shaped bodies have a more beautiful showcase. . . . Vionnet was an architect. Her creations were a total work of art. She was a pure creator. . . . Vionnet is without a doubt the most admired and important one-dress maker of the twentieth century." I met Madame Vionnet only once; awed by being in her presence, I could only stammer my admiration for her work. She impressed me as being a serious, no-nonsense, creative genius.

Coco Chanel revolutionized clothes in a different way. She recognized the social changes occurring as an aftermath of World

299

War I and created simple dresses of jersey, to be worn with cardigans and berets. She made little suits of Linton tweeds from England, to be worn with white silk shirts, and borrowed the convenience of pants pockets from men's trousers for her skirts. Having stripped clothes down to a basic simplicity, she then proceeded to adorn them with copies of her lavish personal jewelry, given to her by her lover, the Duke of Westminster. She had two vogues, one when she started in 1915, and the other when she came out of retirement in 1954. In the '50s and '60s, her little tweed suits became a worldwide mass fashion, with copies selling for $75 to $400. In 1957 we invited her to Dallas to receive the Neiman-Marcus Award for Distinguished Service in the Field of Fashion. She came, accompanied by the president of her American perfume company, the tall, gregarious, loquacious, encyclopedic, and charming Gregory Thomas. He told me privately that Mademoiselle Chanel was eager to visit a ranch, so we gave a Western party at my brother Eddie's Blackmark Farm, with a ranch-style dinner and roping and bronco riding exhibitions. It turned out that she didn't like the taste of the barbecued meat and the highly seasoned beans, so she dumped her plate surreptitiously under the table. Unfortunately, the contents hit the satin slippers of Elizabeth Arden, who was seated next to her. We topped the party off by putting on a bovine fashion show, with the show cows all adorned with headdresses in the latest fashion colors. She loved the spoof.

I had been introduced to her by my dear friend Marie-Louise Bousquet, long-time Paris representative of *Harper's Bazaar*, at a luncheon at Chanel's apartment. At that time I could understand conversational French, but she spoke with the rapidity of a machine gun and I was soon lost in a sea of words, rescued only by the interpretations of Marie-Louise whenever she could get in a word. It would be an exaggeration for anyone to claim that they had ever had a conversation with Chanel, for she conducted a one-woman filibuster. Supreme egotist she was, but with justification.

Balenciaga was a shy man, shunning publicity and public exposure. He was a dedicated artist, exploring new fabrics, searching for new silhouettes, influenced always by his Spanish heritage. His taste was as flawless as I've ever seen; his clothes were consistently the most beautiful and luxurious in Paris. On one of my first postwar trips to France, I called on him with the idea of obtaining the exclusive representation of his perfumes for the United States. In my efforts to persuade him, I described the kind of advertising campaign we would undertake, which would assure him an important income from the sale of his perfumes in America. He listened patiently to me and replied, "No, Mr. Marcus. All of that publicity would make my name quite common. I should not like that. I prefer to sell my perfumes only in Paris." Either I had overkilled in my selling enthusiasm or I came to see him five years too early, for subsequently, perhaps when he was more in need of money, he did sell the franchise for his fragrances to an American distributor.

Christian Dior had been, successively, a painting dealer, a designer of hats for Agnès, and a designer of clothes for Piguet and Lelong. Backed by the cotton textile fortune of Marcel Boussac, he started his own house after the war, not in small quarters as most designers are forced to do, but in a resplendent mansion on the Avenue Montaigne. Dior was a quiet man of superb taste with diverse interests in gardening, art, the theater, good food and wine. He had an associate, a Madame Bricard, who served him in a fashion coordinating role. She had the greatest sense of luxury of any woman I've ever met, and I liked to take her to luncheon for inspirational purposes only. Her ideas of luxury would have made Madame de Pompadour or Marie Antoinette look like strict amateurs. One day, following luncheon at Maxim's, and after she had made some interesting suggestions for our Christmas catalogue, I said, "Madame Bricard, you've been very kind to give me these ideas. I'd like to send you some flowers. Who is your favorite florist?" She replied, without a smile, "Cartier."

Elsa Schiaparelli was the daughter of a professor of Oriental languages and the dean of Rome University. Forced to earn her own living, her first contribution to fashion was the invention of a hand-knit pullover incorporating *trompe l'oeil* designs, which met with instantaneous success. She was more editor than designer, I suspect, using a staff of young designers to feed her ideas, which she culled and developed into her collection. One of the young men she employed, who decorated her boutique, was a tall young fellow named Hubert de Givenchy, who later rose to fame in his own *maison de couture.* "Schiap" was keenly aware of the value of publicity, creating at least one costume for every collection that, by its drama and bizarreness, would get prime news attention in all of the fashion magazines — colored taffeta gloves ending in gargantuan leg-of-mutton sleeves at the shoulder line, huge surrealist appliqués of jeweled gold kidskin on the backs or fronts of coats. In my opinion she wasn't a great designer, but she was one of the most interesting and exciting. She was always au courant. She was among the first of the Parisian designers to exploit her own perfume with success. "Shocking" she called it, named after the Mexican-inspired color shocking pink, which she featured in her collection.

Above all, she was a wise woman, interested in fashion but not buried in it, as were some of her contemporaries. She was a worldly woman, aware of the changes being brought about by modern technology. I recall a conversation with her in 1954, shortly after the introduction of the jet airplane. "The jet plane is going to have a profound effect on the fashion business in Paris," she said. "Women who used to come here for a four-week visit to have clothes made are going to come to Paris for four days instead. They won't have time for fittings, but they are going to want to pick up something ready-made so they can jet off to Ethiopia, Ceylon, Angkor-Wat, and places they never would have dreamed of visiting previously. The couture business is finished. I am going to close my house."

She was able to retire on her perfume income to a life of privacy in her interesting house on the rue de Berri, surrounded by her extraordinary collection of paintings and objets d'art. She was an inveterate collector, possessing a fine eye for the esoteric in jewelry and antiques. When there wasn't space on the wall for a new painting, it would be propped in a chair or against a table. "Never mind whether you have a place for something; if you like it, buy it," was her philosophy. My wife has contended that my first visit to Schiaparelli's home corrupted me completely, as far as acquisitions are concerned.

Yves Saint Laurent, Dior's designated heir and his first successor, lived up to all of his patron's predictions, but he yearned for his own house, and left the House of Dior to go into business under his own name. He was first backed by a wealthy Atlanta businessman, who subsequently sold his interest to Dick Salomon, head of Charles of the Ritz. While the Dior business was directed towards the Establishment customers on both sides of the Atlantic, Saint Laurent appealed to a much more avant-garde audience. He became an interpreter of the social changes taking place, and designed clothes for the women with young, slim bodies and fat pocketbooks. His clothes set major fashion trends, and after tiring of being copied, he decided to make his own copies, to be sold at lower prices in his own series of boutiques, Rive Gauche.

His successor at Dior was Marc Bohan, a first-rate designer who recognized the characteristics of the wealthy Dior clientele and was content to design for it. He is a steady designer with occasional bursts of brilliance. Hubert de Givenchy, whose closeness to Balenciaga often caused the critics to belittle his collections by describing them as "sheer Givenchiaga," continues to dress a large number of social leaders in refined, understated clothes.

Courrèges, from the Balenciaga atelier, proved to be a designer with a big idea — but only one. His sphere of influence lasted just about two years.

Emanuel Ungaro, a Spaniard, is a talented designer whose

strength lies in his casual, daytime clothes. He, like Givenchy, is devoting more attention to his boutique line, which is distributed to most western countries. He has solved his production problems by having his *pret à porter* clothes made in Italy.

The best, and practically the only successful dressmaker in Italy is Valentino, who probably would have attained even greater recognition if he had been in Paris. He, too, is in the boutique business in a big way.

The most copied designer of our time, aside from Chanel, was an Italian, Emilio Pucci, whom I met on my first trip to Florence in 1948. He was then an impoverished nobleman, a former military air pilot, and an amateur auto racer who still owned the family *palazzo* with his mother and brother, but couldn't afford to light it and to heat more than three rooms of the multiroomed structure. He came to our Florence office to show me some scarves he had designed and wanted to sell. They were unusual in design, brilliant in coloration. I gave him a small order and suggested that they might be made into blouses, or even simple dresses. He picked up the idea immediately and within a few years the Pucci craze had developed into such a financial success that he was able to restore and reopen the entire family home, including the beautiful Wedgwood-ceilinged dining room, originally installed by his grandfather, and the ballroom, which he converted into a salon in which to show his collection. He opened boutiques in Capri, Rome, and Paris as women adopted the Pucci dress as a status symbol.

No shrinking violet, Pucci has the arrogance of the Italian nobility, the resolute determination of a consummate egotist, and a philosophy inspired perhaps by a Florentine of another day, Machiavelli. He is opinionated on most subjects, including fashion design, retail distribution, airline stewardesses' costumes, store architecture, child-raising, perfume, and liver ailments. Having scored an overwhelming success with his first scarf dress and then his printed silk jersey, Pucci was convinced that he was a dressmaker of the first order, and proceeded to design couture collections in solid-color fabrics that consistently proved to be flops. Nothing his friends or associates told him could convince him that he wasn't really a designer; only the customers' refusal to buy anything but his prints would get the message over to him.

Pucci was a man with an idea at the right time. Postwar fashion was hungry for a color explosion, and his exotic, vivid color combinations were timed to perfection. Whether he designed his first print or not, I don't know. He did come up with an original idea, and as he gained experience in dress manufacturing, he had the good fashion sense to transfer his designs to silk jersey, which he made up in simply constructed dresses with round, square and shirt-collar necklines. His close social contacts with chic Italian women in Capri and the ski resort of Cortina enabled him to anticipate the trend for pants, teaming them up with his scarf-printed shirts. He introduced stretch yarn in ski pants, and made the ski pant itself into an everyday slack. He performed the function of a skillful manufacturer, taking a hot idea and exploiting it through all the possible variables. Not only did his prints have a tremendous vogue for an extraordinary time span, but they received the highest accolades from shoplifters. In every shop selling Puccis, stock shortages attained disastrously high percentages.

Pucci is charming, gracious, and entertaining when he chooses to be. He is an indefatigable worker and traveler, who thinks nothing of flying to New York for dinner, back to Rome the same night to attend a session of the Italian parliament (when he was a member), and then to Japan for a two-day presentation of his fashions at a Tokyo department store. During the years of his ascendancy, he not only made a fortune for himself but also for the countless manufacturers who copied and imitated his prints. The only fashions of the twentieth century which even remotely approached the degree of universality of his prints are the typical Chanel suit and blue jean Levi's.

Closely akin to Balenciaga is the American designer Jimmy Galanos. Also a shy and retiring man, Jimmy has been unspoiled

305

by his success as America's preeminent designer. He is uninfluenced by what others do, going his own way with single-minded
dedication to quality and beauty. He runs a one-man show; he does
his own designing, his own selling to the wholesale trade, and
finally he goes on the road to visit the stores and help sell his
clothes to the customers. In my judgment, he would have been
equally successful in Paris, pitted against the best of the French
dressmakers.

Charlie James, another American, a mad genius of a designer,
had a short-lived fashion career, but in the few years of his
ascendancy he designed some of the most beautiful ball gowns ever
made, many of which have been given to costume museums for
future generations to study with awe. He perfected a cut and construction with architectural skill, but his personal eccentricities
made it impossible to harness his talents commercially, either for
himself or his business associates.

An American designer I would label "great" was the late
Claire McCardell. She was credited with starting the casual
"American Look" in the '40s, with clothes conceived for comfort
and functional purposes. In 1953, the Frank Perls Gallery in
Beverly Hills took down its modern paintings and hung a show of
contemporary clothes, a retrospective of this American designer's
fashion originals, including her "monastic" dress, "diaper" bathing
suit, garments in which she used rivets and blue-jean stitching,
and the Capezio ballet shoes which she popularized for daytime
wear. I was asked to write the foreword to the announcement of
the exhibition, and I commented,

Claire McCardell, as much as any designer I've ever known, designs
as she pleases. Her clothes are not for everyone, but they are made
for the twentieth century woman, slim in body, youngish in outlook.
She is the master of the line, never the slave of the sequin . . . she
is one of the truly creative designers this country has produced, borrowing nothing from other designers. She is to America what Vionnet was
to France.

Norman Norell was a designer with a long memory. He was deeply impressed by Chanel and Molyneux and everything they ever designed. His own models evolved from his recollections of these two French couturiers, and season after season the variations would reappear. They were wearable and classic and restrained. He helped further the cause of simplicity and good taste, but his memory was better than his creativity. His associate, Andrew Traina, a long-time apparel manufacturer, was responsible for the extraordinary quality of workmanship in the Norell clothes. He was a mercurial man who, after several luncheon martinis, would return to the showroom and, likely as not, give a verbal lashing to the first luckless store buyer he set eyes upon. He would actually tear up their orders if he thought they weren't large enough, or if they had the impertinence to ask that a garment be changed in color or fabric. For sheer meanness I can compare him only to one other manufacturer whom I met early in my career. His name was Moe Solinsky, of the firm of Ben Gershel, who took sheer delight in publicly humiliating new and unimportant buyers or girls bringing in special orders from the New York buying offices. These men were the bullies of Seventh Avenue; they didn't need whips, they had nasty tongues.

Gilbert Adrian was a product of Hollywood, having become one of the preeminent designers for motion pictures. He decided to enter the ready-to-wear business and opened a salon in the heart of Beverly Hills in 1942. Women knew his name from his frequent credit lines on the screen, so he started his manufacturing career with a better recognition factor than any other American designer in fashion history. There will be many who may dispute any attribution of "greatness" to him, but no one can deny that for a period of a half-dozen years he was one of the most influential designers in the United States. He arrived on the commercial scene at a time when we were cut off from Paris; he was the only show in town, and as such, he attracted great attention. He brought in the exaggerated wide-shoulder suit, dramatic, gigantically scaled prints, patchwork ginghams, "baby doll" taffeta evening gowns, and a quality of theatrical costuming.

Among American designers there are a number with varying degrees of talent and creativity. The French-born Pauline Trigère ranks among the top designers, with a distinctive style of her own that she varies but little from season to season. Bill Blass, from Fort Wayne, Indiana, is a sophisticated interpreter of the casual American look whose clothes sell to a wealthy socialite clientele. Geoffrey Beene, a shy native of Louisiana, concentrates on nostalgic clothes for tiny, slim young women. In another category is Adele Simpson, a marvelous and generous human being, who doesn't attempt too much innovation, but concentrates her efforts on making clothes that middle-to-high-income women with less than perfect figures can wear with comfort and satisfaction. Mollie Parnis, an old-timer in the fashion business, edits the several designers she has working for her and comes up with clothes for the more dressy occasions in the lives of her well-to-do customers. Interestingly, both Simpson and Parnis have satisfied the fashion requirements of two First Ladies in the White House, Mrs. Johnson and Mrs. Nixon. Anne Klein was a gifted designer with a compulsion for perfectionism. She had two designing careers, one as a designer of junior clothes and a second as a designer of deluxe casual clothes. She comprehended the requirements of a large business and established a design studio quite openly admitting it would take many talented people working under her direction to achieve her objectives. Thus it is difficult to judge where her designing began and where her editing of other collaborators ended. This is a compliment to her skills as a creator and director. Her coordinated casual clothes were indicative of her understanding of contemporary American life. She was a real pro.

Bonnie Cashin has made a distinct contribution to American design, expressing herself in tweed and leather and combinations of the two. She has led the crusade for functional clothes and makes an authoritative statement uninfluenced by any designers from other countries. On the other hand, there is a visible effect of her "layered look" on the designers of Paris. Donald Brooks is another designer with creative talent, whose appeal is directed essentially to the "café society" type of customer.

Ten years ago, it was unlikely that a great designer of western clothes would come out of Japan, but that is what happened. A public relations man in San Francisco asked, as a personal favor, if we would look at a collection being brought to New York by Hanae Mori. We were charmed by her, and excited by her beautiful prints and her skillful dressmaking. Madame Mori started out as a watercolor painter and emerged as a fashion designer, using her beautiful paintings in the chiffons and crepes from which her clothes are made. In a period when most designers in the United States and France seemed to have lost a sense of direction, Hanae Mori persisted in making fashionable dresses whose function was to make women more attractive. She is a marvelous human being, a great designer, and an able, far-sighted business woman.

In the field of shoes two names stand out, Evins and Levine. David Evins, the largest producer of fine shoes in the United States, concentrates on refinement in design and perfection in fit. Beth Levine, whose husband Herbert runs the production side of their business, continues to be innovative and creative. She is one of the few designers in any field of fashion who has the ability to work directly and productively from original source material.

When the revolution in men's fashion occurred a few years ago, there was a great rush of women's designers trying to get in on the act. Bill Blass, hampered by mediocre production, never achieved the acceptance he deserved. Pierre Cardin, the man who started it all, had the same difficulties in getting good execution of his designs. Ralph Lauren, a former necktie manufacturer, turned his hand to designing shirts, clothing, and ties under his trademark, Polo, and has had the greatest success of them all. Like many designers, though, Lauren wanted to reach out in all directions and invade women's sportswear as well. This is a well-known phenomenon among designers, which retailers are in a good position to observe. Some are moderately successful; the majority fail for a combination of reasons — lack of time, undercapitalization, and an exaggerated appraisal by the designer of his own designing ability in foreign fields. Never in my experience have I seen a designer who can design everything across the board with equal skill. I know of no dress designer who designs shoes as well as she does dresses, no cosmetician who designs handbags as well as she does makeup, or any bag designer who designs dresses as well as she does handbags. It may work in a small country the size of Finland, but with the economic problems of manufacturing and distribution in a country as vast as the United States, it has not been successful.

The very mention of the name of Finland in connection with fashion brings to mind the name of its foremost fashion designer, Armi Ratia, one of the most extraordinary women I've ever met. She is a warm human being, generous in spirit and action, and completely originative. She, like other Finns, feels competent and qualified to design everything from fashion to prefabricated houses, though she has scored greater accomplishments in the former field than in the latter. Her giant-scaled prints adorned both Radcliffe students and some of the best sofas in Palo Alto in the '60s.

When one of our buyers visited her in Finland to buy her line, called Marimekko, she was questioned by Mrs. Ratia, who wasn't sure that she wanted another American account, "What is Neiman-Marcus? Who runs it? What kind of man is he?" After she received the answers, she then asked, "Does Stanley Marcus own a Charles Eames chair?" The buyer replied, "Why, yes he does. I saw it the last time I visited his home." "In that case," Mrs. Ratia said, "I'll sell Neiman-Marcus." Never before had we faced a problem which was solved by the possession of a piece of furniture.

All designers, like actors, want publicity. They cater to the fashion editors of *Vogue* and *Harper's Bazaar* in hopes of getting color pages of their garments, going to the extent of rushing up special things the editors think are newsworthy. They wine, dine, and dress many of the magazine representatives to get favored representation in the most timely issues of the publications. Some employ public relations people whose job it is to insure maximum exposure in magazines and gossip columns. Many designers, again like many actors, become spoiled by success. They begin to believe their own publicity and in their own infallibility. They become reluctant to admit mistakes in production or design and refuse to accept constructive suggestions from qualified retailers who have firsthand experience in the problems of selling their clothes. Arrogance is a quality to which too many American designers fall victim. Retailers are less prone to this least attractive of human characteristics, for they are subjected to a constant deflation by the daily exposure to a vast number of customers.

In America, *Women's Wear Daily*, formerly edited solely for the garment trade, became customer-oriented when John Fairchild was named editor in 1964 and introduced his Eye column built around the important and not-so-important activities of socialites in New York and Paris. In the past few years, *Women's Wear Daily* has begun to discover the hinterlands by reporting parties and people in Beverly Hills, Dallas, and Chicago. The column was so successful that a second gossip page, Eye View, was added.

To further enliven the paper, Fairchild instructed his writers to do not only a reportorial job on fashion collections, but also a critical one in the news columns. This led, for a time, to an attempt by Fairchild to become a kingmaker, giving extravagant praise to those designers he admired, panning those he did not favor. Many people in the fashion business, myself included, believed he was overstepping the bounds of objective reporting. Those who didn't give *Women's Wear Daily* reporters an inside story or a time lead could find themselves virtually boycotted by the news columns. We refused to bow to their pressures and for several years events in our stores received little attention by them.

In 1969, Fairchild went on a one-paper crusade to force acceptance of the Paris-inspired midi length on Seventh Avenue and American retailers. Those who dragged their feet were labeled old-fashioned; many acceded to the pressure to avoid words of opprobrium in *Women's Wear Daily*. The campaign succeeded so far as manufacturers and stores were concerned, but the American buying public refused to accept the fashion, despite John Fairchild's almost hysterical endorsement. The fashion industry, makers and retailers alike, suffered colossal financial losses as customers, confused by the controversy on lengths, decided not to buy at all. It proved to be the most disastrous season in the history of American fashion. Chastened by his defeat and the criticism heaped on him, Fairchild abandoned his role as self ordained fashion dictator and went back to the job of publishing. Perhaps the new owners of the Fairchild publication, Capitol News, had something to do with the decision.

Of all the fashion markets in which I have worked, the fur market has been the most enjoyable. The manufacturers in the period of the forties were, to a large extent, foreign-born. They had an earthiness, a warmth, a lack of the sophistication characteristic of the dress industry. They were shrewd traders — many of them would cut corners if you didn't watch them; they were interested in their craft, and when you talked to them about a technical matter involving construction of a garment, they knew the answers, unlike the manufacturers of dresses and cloth coats, who contracted the making of their garments to factories in New Jersey and Pennsylvania and consequently were far removed from the manufacturing process. I never went to the fur market that I didn't learn something new, and I never left the market without having been cheered by the wealth of good Middle-European Jewish humor. The entertainment value of a visit to the fur market was better than the shows at Grossinger's, and at no extra cost. These pioneer furriers are almost all gone now, having been replaced by

312

their college-educated sons, who run their establishments much more efficiently but with less humor.

One day a woman came into the store to offer us a line of neckties. They were very bold, brightly colored patterns, and in what I thought was shockingly bad taste, they had her trademark embroidered on the tip of the front of the tie, and, to make it worse the mark was in the form of a crown on top of her initials, C. M. With all my self-assurance as an experienced retailer, I turned her down on the grounds that men wanted small patterns in restrained colors and they would not be pleased to wear a manufacturer's label on the front of their ties, particularly if it had a feminine connotation. I advised her to restyle her line, forget about the embroidered trademark, and use a masculine name. The woman was the Countess Mara, and after listening to my expertise, she ignored it completely, and proceeded to market her ties as she had originally planned. She met with instantaneous success, and we had to go back to her to beg for the line. A Countess Mara became a status-symbol tie; men liked the bold patterns, didn't resent the feminine signature or the royal connotation the label implied, as I had forecast. My logic was good, but in the fashion business, logic can lead to false conclusions.

This was neither the first nor the last mistake I made in fashion judgments. I tend to tire of a popular fashion long before the buying public reaches the same conclusion. I forecast prematurely the end of the gabardine era in the postwar period, the demise of the sling cape and the fur stole, and the willingness of women to continue to buy the typical Pucci prints. I was wrong on all scores, for certain popular fashions maintain a longevity beyond all reason. I had to go back to our buyers and confess I had read the fashion signs incorrectly.

Fairly early in my career I was exposed to the extraordinary Miss Elizabeth Arden. She defied all the rules in building her great cosmetic company except for two fundamental principles: make fine products and sell them aggressively. She was perhaps the first compulsive seller I ever met. The first time I entered her office, she said, "Why aren't your Arden sales better?" and then, before I could answer her, she launched a sales pitch to which I could only reply, "Yes, Miss Arden, we'll be glad to buy more fitted bags and compacts." We had the line exclusively in Dallas, a valuable franchise to preserve, so we were constantly at her mercy.

Although we were her largest customer, she had great difficulty in distinguishing me from Grover Magnin, the San Francisco dean of specialty store operators, despite the disparity in our ages. She irritated me by calling me "Mr. Magnin," so one day I replied, "Yes, Madame Rubinstein," her archrival in the cosmetic industry. She was shocked sufficiently to call me by my own name thereafter.

As our acquaintanceship ripened, she would ask for my advice on business matters — advice she never took. I was concerned about the continuity of her business if anything should happen to her, but death was a subject she refused to contemplate, and any reference to it met with icy silence. I'm confident that she was convinced she would never die, but would merely pass on into a Blue Grass–scented heaven anointed by Eight Hour Cream.

Another compulsive seller, in the same line of business, is the current Queen of Beauty, Estée Lauder. She came on the horizon just as Arden was aging, so I am not aware of any personal confrontation between the two. Had there been one, the effect would have been similar to a nuclear explosion. Mrs. Lauder's success can be attributed to a fine product line, her driving sales ability, her two able sons, and to her adoption and expansion of the "gift with purchase" technique, originated by Charles of the Ritz some years ago. This practice, condemned by many in the cosmetic industry and finally imitated by all, greatly accelerated her market acceptance. When I first met her, she came in swinging like Sugar Ray Robinson; today, some twenty years later, she has the same vitality and sense of urgency. She jabs you to sell more Estée, her fragrance, she hits you to sell more Azurée, her bath line, and she throws an uppercut when she says, "Sell more Clinique, my allergenic line — it's a product for rich women, and all rich women have allergies!" Her sons administer her business wisely, giving her leisure time to enjoy her château in France and her villa in Palm Beach. Hers is a genuine Horatio Alger-ess story.

Only a part of our fashion dealings are with the great designers and the free-spending customers; a large portion of our time is consumed with small makers who need fashion direction and financing, and with discovering new resources.

The over-the-shoulder handbag became a dominant fashion during the war, and in our search for makers who knew how to style them, we came across a husband-and-wife team in Greenwich Village, Bill and Elizabeth Phelps. They were a traveled, worldly pair, who had drifted into making bags of a quality superior to the commercial production of the market. Their difficulty was that they were undercapitalized, so we helped finance them for several years until they got on their feet. We don't like to get financially involved with a maker, but we do so when we think the talent is good enough to justify the risk and when we believe that without aid the designer won't survive. The Phelps experiment proved to be one of our best. In addition to supplying us with the best bags of the type in the market, Bill Phelps made an observation to me following his first visit to our store which has been well worth its weight in gold.

He commented, "You, whether you realize it or not, have followed a time-tested principle in the building of your store. In any old European town, you will find that the cathedral is in a central location. It inspires its visitors by the greatness of its architecture, its stained-glass windows, its carved or gilded interior. Next to it, usually not more than a hundred feet away, is a fine shop where people, stimulated by the beauty of what they have just seen, can make a purchase. One wants to buy after being aesthetically stimulated. Invariably, on the other side of the cathedral, is the best restaurant in town, for after looking and buying, you are apt to be hungry. That's what you have done in this store. You give your customers numerous examples of designs which are not for sale — the Swedish marble escalator walls, the hanging gardens, the blooming orchids, the sculpture and paintings. Having exposed them to all this beauty, you have desirable merchandise easily available for purchase, and then in your Zodiac restaurant on the sixth floor you regale them with the best food in the city."

Of course that's what we had been doing, but we had never recognized the historical origin of this formula; we were following it unconsciously. Now we make a special effort in all our new stores to keep the three elements in balance.

New York was supposed to be the place where all fashion originated; if a manufacturer came from the hinterlands forty years ago, he received very little attention from buyers, who sniffed as if to say, "If you're from Des Moines, you can't be taken very seriously." We learned our lesson in the mid-thirties when a woman from St. Louis, Grace Ashley, put a shirtwaist dress on the market, the distinguishing feature of which was the use of men's dress shirt studs and cuff links instead of the customary buttons. She had picked up the idea from a New York sportswear maker, William Bloom, who had not been successful with the dress at a considerably higher price. I gave Miss Ashley the cold treatment when I learned she was from St. Louis, and was turning her down when she said, "Let me put twenty-four dresses on consignment." While I have never liked consignment deals, I accepted her proposal. The twenty-four dresses sold out within three hours of their arrival. Over the next two years of the life of this garment, we sold fifteen thousand dresses at an average retail price of $35, for a total of over $500,000 in volume. Never again have we held

316

a prejudice against the place of origin. We learned from this profitable experience that ideas are not restricted to any geographical location, and that good merchandise can be made wherever there are talented people dedicated to making the best.

It takes time to look at everything that is submitted to us, but in the fashion business it's impossible to forecast just when and where the next good idea will emerge. I was dining in Beverly Hills one night at the home of my good friend Dore Schary, the motion picture director. He mentioned that his fourteen-year-old daughter, Jill, aspired to be a fashion designer, and asked if I would take a look at her sketches. The child's drawings were imaginative and creative; one in particular caught my eye — a sketch of a glove with a blue bird appliquéd in the palm, illustrating the old proverb "A bird in the hand." I told her I would pay her for the design, and if we used it she would receive a royalty. We sent the idea to Paris where our great glovemaker, the late Roger Faré, made it for our Christmas catalogue. It sold extremely well, she received a nice royalty check, and we had another exclusive merchandise item. We recognized the news value of a catalogue article designed by a teenager, particularly with a Hollywood background, and we were able to get valuable international publicity from it.

In addition to the fashion stories offered by the manufacturing market, we frequently need to supplement them with ideas of our own. Sometimes we may wish to emphasize a particular color or color family, or a type of printed fabric, or combinations of different materials. On other occasions we ask a limited group of designers to work from source material for the development of a collection of clothes or theme, as we did when we took the American Indian as a source of inspiration. We drew upon Indian design motifs, embroidery techniques, beading, and jewelry to make a well-rounded group of clothes and accessories which were wearable by any smart contemporary woman. In an operation of this

317

type, we give the designers the right to sell their special designs after we have introduced them and reaped the benefits of the publicity arising from this creative effort.

In 1947, we believed that the sportswear markets needed stimulation, so we organized and financed a weekend party at the Flying L Ranch, located in the hill country west of San Antonio, to which we invited a select group of sportswear designers from both the East and West coasts. Each was asked to make one costume inspired by the Southwest, to be presented in a show we staged on the runway of this exciting ranch. The eastern designers were not sure they wanted to even recognize the importance of the western group, but after an evening of conviviality, the ice was broken and the regional rivalries were put aside. To judge the show, and to give added publicity, we impaneled a jury of Jinx and Tex McCrary, tennis champion Jack Kramer, the late "Prince" Mike Romanoff of Beverly Hills (born in Oklahoma), and Elizabeth Gordon, editor of *House Beautiful*. Aside from our designer greats and store executives, our audience consisted of local cowboys, who yipped in appreciation of the beautiful mannequins rather than for the exciting clothes shown. The jury selected an "All-American" sports wardrobe, consisting of frontier and Southwestern-influenced designs for flying, riding, tennis, swimming, golf, fiestas and patiowear. The press was there in full force and *Life* reported the event in a picture essay. The show was then taken back to Dallas for presentation to two thousand of our customers on successive nights. I was quoted by a *Life* correspondent as saying,

We wanted to dramatize sports clothes in a sports setting in a great extravaganza that would show purchasable clothes ranging from $15 to $40. We wanted to put the emphasis on lower-priced clothes. We want people to know that though we have cake, we also have bread and butter . . . with a little sugar on top.

No account of fashion in America would be complete without some reference to Tobé, who furnished a fashion advisory service for the leading retail stores of the country. Born in Milwaukee, she came to New York and worked for Franklin Simon during the period when his specialty store was at its zenith. She never forgot the lessons she learned from him, and incorporated them into her own merchandising philosophy, which she imparted at her semi-annual review of the season's fashions and in her personal conferences with her clients. My good friend and classmate Mike Cowles once said of himself, "I may be wrong, but I'm never in want of an opinion." This observation fitted Tobé like a kid glove, for she almost invariably had an opinion on anything related to the field of fashion. On the few occasions when she didn't, she knew exactly whom to telephone to get it. In a way she was a broker of ideas, which she traded in with the dexterity of a futures dealer. Everyone recognized her technique and no one resented it, for she gave information as freely as she took it. She was a great catalyst, bringing together people from different parts of the country, from a variety of related industries, and succeeded in getting them to talk.

She was on the telephone in her bedroom from six until nine in the morning, and by the time she reached her office, she knew pretty well what was happening in retailing across the country. She attended the fashion showings, sleeping through most of them, but awakening in time to catch the three best numbers in the line. Her personal taste was poor, but her analytical fashion skill was great. The best of her talents was her ability to make you think. I acknowledge my indebtedness to her.

Somewhere along the line I met James Laver, curator of prints at London's Victoria and Albert Museum. He was also a prolific writer on the history and theory of fashion, with interesting and original interpretations of the motivations of fashion evolution. We considered him such a unique authority on fashion that he was presented with our fashion award in 1962. In 1969, when a state of anarchy reigned in the fashion industry over the introduction of the midi skirt length, and our own organization was torn by the

319

struggle between those who believed in the miniskirt and others who favored the newer length of the midi, I cabled to ask him for an historian's perspective on this hotly debated subject. I asked him point-blank if the mini was dead. He replied, "I give it at least another two years." Robert Musel, in a UPI interview wrote,

Although his [Laver's] advice was against the weight of expert opinion at the time, Laver was right, a fact that did not surprise him since he says fashion doesn't just happen, it takes account of social conditions and almost always follows two principles. One of these is Laver's rule that an appreciation gap must elapse before a style, once it is finished, can return to favor. This seems to work out at a minimum of thirty years. The other is the *erogenous zone* theory, that there is a constant shift of emphasis, as fashions change, to different parts of the female form.

LAVER'S LAW

The same costume will be:

Indecent	10 years before its time
Shameless	5 years before its time
Outré (daring)	1 year before its time
Smart	———
Dowdy	1 year after its time
Hideous	10 years after its time
Ridiculous	20 years after its time
Amusing	30 years after its time
Quaint	50 years after its time
Charming	70 years after its time
Romantic	100 years after its time
Beautiful	150 years after its time

His forecast was right, the midi was a complete flop, many women continued to wear the miniskirt, and those who couldn't or wouldn't make up their minds went into the pants suit. Pants were bound to come, but the skirt-length controversy made pants acceptable at an accelerated rate. *Women's Wear Daily*'s crusade for the midi resulted in the destruction of the dress business, from which it still hasn't recovered, the popularization of pants, and the undermining of consumer confidence in magazines, stores, and designers. When the smoke cleared Bill Blass commented, "The prime thing we've learned is that we'll never again try to impose a fashion on American women."

16

Strictly Personal

MY BIRTH CERTIFICATE records my name as Harold Stanley Marcus, but the first name was never used. It came about as the result of my mother's desire to memorialize one of her favorite uncles, Hyman Mittenthal. My father probably objected to the name Hyman, so they compromised on a name which would carry his first initial. At some stage in my adolescence, I was impressed with the use of the letter H and signed my name as H. Stanley Marcus. Later, after I had entered business, a good friend suggested that this was an affectation, and that it might prove to be a liability if I were ever to consider running for political office. I had never entertained such an ambition, but I thought the advice was good and I dropped the initial.

On one of my parents' trips to San Francisco, they met a charming man, Albert Bender, who was a guiding force in the Book Club of California, and in recognition of my interest in bookmaking and typography they took out a membership in my name. I was so delighted with the books, printed by the leading West Coast printers, John Henry Nash and the Grabhorn brothers among others, that I decided to start a similar venture in Texas. I found a trust officer at a bank, John Lomax; an architect, David Williams; and a lawyer, John M. Hackler, who shared my enthusiasm for bookmaking; so together we formally founded the

325

Book Club of Texas, dedicated to publishing books for its membership, dealing with subjects related in some way to the history of the state and region, and in a design and format which would encourage printers of the area to higher standards in the field of typography. We issued a handsome broadside to potential members, inviting them to join at a membership fee of $10 annually, which entitled them to purchase the club's publications. David Williams, known locally for his "indigenous" architecture, designed a colophon from some of the early Texas cattle brands, which, in a way, represent the first printing done in the state.

I visited Fannie Ratchford, Wrenn Librarian of the University of Texas, to discuss potential material for publication, and came away with several good suggestions. For our first imprint in 1930, we selected *The Memoirs of Col. Ellis P. Bean*, which had first been published in the appendix to Yoakum's *History of Texas* in 1856. Bean was a young colonist adventurer, who in 1800 set forth from his Tennessee home for Natchez, where he joined forces with Philip Nolan to go to Texas to trade with the San Antonians, subsequently being captured by the Spaniards and taken off to prison in Mexico. Very few printers in Texas had ever printed a book, so it became my responsibility to teach them the fundamentals of pagination, margins, and title page design. We selected the Rein Press in Houston for our first effort, which received glowing reviews from the critics. It had been our plan to publish four or five titles a year, but we had underestimated the time requirements for producing even a single volume without the support of any full-time professional assistance.

As part of our program to educate both the public and the printing industry in the graphic arts, we sponsored exhibitions of the Fifty Prints of 1927 and the Fifty Books of 1927 in Dallas, Houston, and Austin. In successive years — and a single volume a year was the best record we could achieve — we published the *Code Duello*, which was selected as one of the Fifty Books of the Year by the American Institute of Graphic Arts, *Miss Zylphia*

Gant, which was also so honored, *Aeneus Africanus, The Story of the Champ d'Asile,* and *From Texas to Mexico in 1865.*

Miss Zylphia Gant was an original short story by William Faulkner which was a little bit outside of our publication policy, but we considered it such a find we decided to publish it anyway. Idealism yielded to pragmatism. John McGinnis, professor of English at SMU, editor of the *Southwest Review* and of the book page of the *Dallas Morning News,* brought the Faulkner story to my attention, saying it had been submitted for the *Southwest Review* but that he considered it too hot for them to handle. He asked if we would be interested. "Certainly," I replied, "if we can get a transfer of rights from the author." McGinnis suggested we send his bright associate, Henry Smith, an instructor in English, to Oxford, Mississippi, to negotiate with the author. Smith was successful and agreed to write the preface. In 1932, SMU was not the liberal institution that it is today, and the clergy-dominated Board of Trustees fired Smith for his participation in the publication. This was probably the best thing that could have happened to him, for he went from Dallas to Harvard, and then to professorships at Minnesota and the University of California.

My associates in the Book Club were enthusiastic, but they had little time to devote to its problems and were content to leave them all to me. With increased business responsibilities I felt I couldn't carry on, and decided to terminate the club's affairs. Our efforts were not in vain, for a number of able and talented bookmakers, including Carl Hertzog in El Paso and Bill Wittliff at the Encino Press in Austin, have produced notable books in the highest standards of typographic design.

My first venture in the field of music came during the Depression, as we sought ways to help the plight of unemployed musicians. In association with the musicians' union, I helped organize a series of open-air "pop" concerts which were held in the Cotton Bowl at admission prices of 25 and 50 cents. We had splendid turnouts for these bargain concerts, but the gate receipts, which went entirely to the players, were always disappointing. It was only later that I discovered that an official of the local union, who was acting as treasurer for the concerts, was "counting us out" at the box office. Later, when I became president of the Dallas Symphony Society, I made certain that the integrity of the box office was carefully safeguarded.

As head of the symphony, my main responsibility was that of raising money to offset the annual deficit. Our conductor, Antol Dorati, a brilliant Hungarian, employed so many jobless fellow-Hungarians for unbudgeted soloist and instrumentalist jobs that I could never raise enough money for the ever-increasing losses. Off and on for the past twenty-five years, I've had some association with the activities of the symphony, and I've observed that their problems without a Hungarian conductor are virtually the same as mine were. Audience growth has been disappointing; money is still difficult to raise. This situation is not unique to Dallas, but prevails throughout the nation, which leads me to several conclusions. The first one is that the American public, except in a few large cities, is musically illiterate. Sending children to a few symphonic concerts a year is not adequate musical education to build large appreciative audiences. The second conclusion is that symphonic organizations, financially supported as they are today, are fast becoming dinosaurs and will go out of existence. My final conclusion is that if symphonic music is to survive — and there is no biblical commandment that it must — orchestras will have to get massive federal matching-grant financing. In the future, perhaps in twenty-five years, local orchestras will disappear, and may be replaced by regional orchestras, ten to fifteen in number, which will service large geographical areas. Without tremendous funding, even this solution is not possible. This may sound revolutionary, but that's what European countries have done for several hundred years.

One summer in Europe, our departure plans were disrupted by

the cancellation of our sailing date, due to damage to the ship as it left New York harbor. The only space available was on the maiden voyage of the *Liberté*, a week later. With a full extra week, we accepted the invitation of Claude Philippe to join him; Alfred Knopf, the publisher; Alexis Lichine, who was just completing his book *The Wines of France;* and J. P. McEvoy, the writer and an editor of *Reader's Digest* and his wife, on a wine-tasting trip through Burgundy. I had always liked good food, as my girth testifies, but neither Billie nor I knew enough about wines to fully enjoy them. We tasted young Chablis wines in *caves* at the foot of the white limestone hills of Chablis, where the soil is so meager that the workers must carry it back up the slope after a heavy rainfall. We tasted hundreds of new wines from famous vineyards of the Côte de Beaune and the Côte d'Or, learning the trick of how to swirl the wine around the tongue to get its flavor and bouquet before spitting it out on the dirt floor of the *caves.* We ended our tour at a sumptuous Sunday luncheon given by some of the leading wine producers of Burgundy at a restaurant in Beaune, to which each of the growers brought a contribution of his prize vintages. On our drive back to Paris, we passed the four and a half acres of the famous Romanée-Conti vineyards, the smallness of which startled Alfred Knopf. He snorted, "Why I've drunk that much!" You don't get a wine education in four days, but we learned enough to drink wines with greater understanding and curiosity.

Five years later, after I had acquired more knowledge, I was initiated into the Confrèrie des Chevaliers du Tastevin by the New Orleans chapter, an organization dedicated to the study and appreciation of the wines of Burgundy. The next year I organized a chapter in Dallas, with members drawn from all over the state. There were only a handful of genuine wine connoisseurs around, the majority of our fellow-Texans being bourbon and branch water devotees. We had the job of not only teaching them about wines, but we had to instruct the waiters as well to uncork, decant, and serve wine. Planning a Tastevin dinner is an experience in itself, for the menus are based on Burgundian tradition and limited, of course, by the foods which were available in Burgundy in the Middle Ages. Some modernization of the meals has taken place, but not enough, in my opinion, for they are still too lengthy. Every chef regards one of these dinners as a challenge to his gastronomic ability, and a chance to demonstrate his skill. He has to be cajoled into omitting certain spices which will fight with the wines to be served; he has to be persuaded to prepare simple dishes within the capability of his staff and kitchen, and he has to be ordered not to attempt a soufflé for dessert, which can be a disaster when served for seventy-five people. The Dallas chapter, which has now been divided into North and South Texas branches, has unquestionably raised discriminating wine consumption in the area, and improved the standards of food preparation and service in many of the restaurants and clubs of the state.

One of the most famous restaurants in France was La Pyramide, or Chez Point as it was also known, at Vienne. Before the war I never got there, and after the war I was never able to fit a pilgrimage to that gastronomic shrine into my schedule. After several abortive attempts to get there, I said to Billie, "Let's go to France to have lunch at La Pyramide. If we make that the purpose of the trip, we can arrange everything else around that objective." We went first to Antibes to spend a few days there with our friends, the Judas, and made a luncheon reservation in writing at La Pyramide for Easter Sunday, which we confirmed by telephone. We were told to be at the restaurant promptly at 1:30 P.M. We decided to have a real gourmet holiday by driving on Saturday to lunch at another great restaurant, La Baumanière at Les Baux-de-Provence where we had a simple meal of *langoustines* and the specialty of the house, *gigot d'agneau en croute.* I remember distinctly turning down the *bisque d'homard* lest it scald the roof of my mouth, and thus make the next day's repast less enjoyable.

On our way to Avignon we encountered a mistral, and by the

time we reached the Hostellerie de la Poste, I was so chilled that I jumped into bed immediately, shivering and miserable. I took a hot lemonade to warm me, but decided to forgo any evening meal. I kept dreaming all night that I had indigestion, and that I wouldn't get to La Pyramide after all. The following morning I awakened in the best of health, and after visiting the Palais des Papes, we set forth for Vienne with time to spare. Ten miles out of Avignon, our car had a flat tire. Our chauffeur repaired it and we started off again, only to have our motor conk out on us after we had driven another few miles. By that time, I was convinced that we weren't really destined to have luncheon at La Pyramide at all. We called the restaurant to explain our plight and that we would take a taxi, but to be sure to hold our table. We were given an additional fifteen minutes of grace, but with admonitions to be no later. We found a cab and drove up to the portals at 1:41! By all rules of fate, the meal should have proved to be an anticlimax, but it turned out to be as great as anticipated. I can still recall the *turbot au champagne*, the *volaille de Bresse à la crème*, and the superb *gâteaux*, which were miniature French pastries in great assortment. I concluded that Monsieur Point, *le patron*, must have been the originator of French pastry. The food was so delicately prepared and the dishes so well orchestrated that we didn't feel full when we departed. We drove on to Saulieu where we were spending the night at Monsieur Dumaine's Côte d'Or, which at that time had a formidable reputation for its food, too. We tried valorously to eat his specialty, the *galantine de saumon*, but for some strange reason we had no appetite.

At St. Moritz, years later, we met a charming couple from Paris, Zmira and Abdullah Zilkha, and eventually we got around to the subject of food and memorable meals. I commented that one meal which would always stand out in my mind was one served by Christian Dior. Zilkha inquired about the various dishes, and I was able to describe them graphically. "Next time you are in Paris," he said, "promise me you will have dinner with us." We

331

kept our word and had dinner with them at their apartment. To our amazement, the Dior dinner was duplicated exactly. When Zilkha saw the amazement on my face, he laughed and said, "We have Dior's former chef." Now the chef, Monsieur Georges Huillier, is semiretired, and comes in to cook only on special occasions. Last year in Paris we dined with them again, and were witnesses to a brilliant feat of gastronomical "one-upsmanship." The dessert was a marvelous strawberry soufflé. When it was passed a second time, the soufflé was chocolate!

I have had two unfilled desires. One was for Sophia Loren, but my wife and her husband wouldn't let me have her. The other was for a beard, for I have always detested the chore of shaving. When we decided to go to Egypt in 1965, I concluded that this would be the perfect place in which to start to grow one. I knew no one in the country, which would make it easier to go through the first critical two weeks of growth. We were in Cairo only a day when we received an invitation to attend a black-tie dinner at the U.S. Embassy. "Surely you'll shave that stubble off?" my wife asked. I replied, "No, the ambassador will understand my predicament." I survived the first two beard trims by Lebanese and Jordanian barbers, so by the time we reached France, my beard was in pretty good shape. We met a cute young American girl, a friend of Wendy's, who said, "Mr. Marcus, that beard certainly makes you look sexy." Even my wife, who had been skeptical, admitted she liked it. On our return home, when our five-year-old grandchild came running up to me instead of away from me, I knew I had it made.

Commander Edward Whitehead of Schweppes fame was one of our guests during a British Fortnight. He has one of the most publicized beards in the country, so I thought it might be fun to have a dinner party in his honor, restricting the male invitations to those with natural beards. I soon discovered that I didn't know that many bearded men, so I had to call the deans at the university and the medical schools for recommendations from their faculties.

We ended up with fourteen men who had nothing in common except beards and fourteen wives who had nothing in common except husbands with beards. There was a columnist, an insurance broker, two geologists, five men of medicine, one theologian and two actors, aside from Whitehead and myself. Commander White-head was greatly amused by the evening and later reported it for the *Daily Telegraph* in London:

It was a B and B dinner — beards and black tie. Doctorates were as much in evidence as whiskers. It was diverting and, at times, hilarious to hear each man's reasons for having abandoned the time-consuming practice of shaving. As Stanley Marcus put it: "At the rate of twenty minutes saved not shaving, twice a day, in a year, this amounts to 243 hours, or a little more than 10 days, that can be put to better use."

My father was always fascinated by the little editorials which Mr. John Wanamaker used to run over his signature in connection with his merchandise advertising. In an effort to carry out his idea, I engaged a young reporter, Warren Leslie, from the *Dallas Morning News* to write a weekly editorial column on a free-lance basis. I had read a few stories he had written for the paper and was impressed by his writing ability. He called his column Point of View and signed them with the pseudonymn Wales, since he was still working for the newspaper. His pieces caused favorable comment, and as he learned more about the store, he became fascinated with the retail business and finally came to work for us full-time as a sales promotion director. He had difficulty during his first few years in learning that store hours are considerably different than a writer's, and that advertising writing is considerably different than news writing. He accepted my tutelage in the techniques of sales promotion, and soon became a valuable member of our management team. His heart was in writing, though, and after Kennedy's assassination, he left us to write a book about Dallas and the events leading up to the tragedy. He felt that he was uniquely fitted to write this story and that it had to be written quickly, or it would be too late.

After his departure, I decided to write the column myself as a Monday morning President's Letter, over my own signature, and in juxtaposition to our regular advertising. I chose to write the pieces as letters to customers, vendors, salespeople, or friends in reply to communications I had received. This gave me the opportunity to reply publicly to complaints, compliments on the store and individual service, and inquiries about merchandise or fashion. The letters have had a splendid reception and have done much to give a warm human quality to the store. I am flattered by the readership my letters have developed, but I have learned that flattery is dangerous if you inhale it. One of the nicest compliments I received was from the editorial director of the *Dallas Morning News*, Dick West. He wrote an editorial on some phases of the educational problem, and included this paragraph: "Some of the best writing in this newspaper may be enjoyed every Monday morning in the letters composed by Stanley Marcus for the Neiman-Marcus ad on our local news page." I'm sure that Dick recognizes our philosophical disagreements, so his praise was doubly appreciated. Here are a few letters from my files:

November 15, 1973

Ms. Gloria Emerson
The New York Times
New York, New York

Dear Ms. Emerson:

I applaud your article in the October 5 issue of the *New York Times* observing the deterioration of women's apparel. I think you stated the case to perfection, but I am not sure that you came out with the solution. I must confess, as sympathetic as I am to your point of view, that I do not fully know who or where the culprit is. Perhaps it is the stores, perhaps the designers, or maybe even it is the press, ranging from *Women's Wear* to the fashion magazines and all those in between.

We may be suffering from mass production and mass consumption, and certainly mass communication, which places a premium on newness, however badly made the product may be.

It's become fashionable to accept the cliché that customers no longer care anything about quality. I don't believe this is true, and if it is true, as some think it to be, then I think that more of us in the fashion trades should raise our voices more vocally to protest its universal acceptance. There is no question that much apparel has deteriorated in quality faster than the prices have risen. We, for one, are going to attempt to impress our manufacturers with the fact that we are still interested in quality and that we will no longer accept "junk" from them simply because it is chic. We have just given instructions to our buyers going to Europe that they are no longer to buy a couple of the so-called "haute" lines in Paris which deliver badly made clothes of sleazy fabrics. There is no glory in having "le dernier cri" if the quality is more suitable for the Gum store in Moscow than for us.

Sincerely,

Stanley Marcus

October 21, 1972

Miss Wilma Osborne
East Liverpool, Ohio

Dear Miss Osborne:

I'm sorry you felt that I stepped on the collective toes of all home economics teachers when I wrote Miss Lori Smith on October 3rd urging her to concentrate her college work in the field of the humanities in preparation for a career in retailing. I can assure you I have the greatest respect for home economics, *but* I still cling to the proposition that a liberal arts education is, in our judgment, the best qualification for future Neiman-Marcus executives.

A local and very successful businessman challenged me on the same subject and contended he wanted young men joining his organization to have a background in accounting and business management. I don't disagree with him, provided those subjects are studied in graduate school.

335

A student who gives up two electives a semester to study accounting or finance or advertising has to sacrifice other courses in history, literature, physics, or languages. He can learn the technical subjects after he enters business, but rarely will he go back after graduation to pick up an acquaintanceship with Ovid and Shakespeare, Cicero and Browning, Pasteur and Caravaggio.

Our society needs more *fully* educated men and women, or at least that's what Neiman-Marcus needs.

Sincerely,

STANLEY MARCUS

January 12, 1971

Mrs. _____
Nashville, Tennessee

Dear Mrs. _____:

Until I received your letter, I thought we had performed virtually every service imaginable. We have delivered live ducks a hundred miles away from a fond grandparent to his grandson, we have climbed the rocks on the coast of the Pacific to fit a mink coat on a leading star of the screen, we have searched the world for a forty carat emerald, we have dressed the living and even the dead, but never — no never — have we had the request to locate a male companion for a lonely woman.

Not that we shrink from a challenging task, but since all Neiman-Marcus services carry a satisfaction guarantee, I'm afraid the risk for us is too great, particularly when you specify that you are looking for a "companion — between seventy and seventy-five — who is completely and absolutely finished with sex."

Frankly, I wouldn't know where or how to search for such a man, nor do I think I would believe him if I found him, nor would I recommend that you put too much faith in any man who claims to answer your specifications.

Get interested in a hobby and join a local club devoted to your hobby, and in all likelihood you'll meet a man who will share your interests.

Mrs. ——, we do a large mail order business, but we've never filled a *Male* order.

Sincerely,

STANLEY MARCUS

336

These letters appearing weekly in a half-dozen cities produced a tremendous amount of mail directed to me personally. I probably receive more letters of complaints and compliments than any other retail executive in the country, which I relish, for it gives me insight into the weaknesses and strengths of our organization. Furthermore, I answer all of them myself whenever possible, for I believe a personal letter deserves a personal answer.

I received a letter from a woman in New York asking me to select a cowboy shirt for a friend of hers, a Mr. Picasso, who lived near Vallauris, France. I replied that since I was going to the south of France the following week, I'd be glad to take it with me and deliver it. At last, I thought, I'll meet the great Picasso. The customer was delighted with this bit of personal service and sent a card to accompany the gift.

When we reached Antibes, I tried to phone Picasso but got no answer. We drove to his villa, which was surrounded by a high wire fence enclosing a vicious-looking dog. The bell at the gate produced no answer, so I decided to brave the dog and opened the gate. The dog proved docile and shied away after I brandished a large stick. I knocked on the door; finally it was opened about a foot and a woman stuck her head out, demanding what I wanted. I told her I wanted to see Mr. Picasso. *"Il n'est pas ici,"* she replied, starting to close the door. *"Mais j'ai un cadeau pour M. Picasso,"* I said, holding up the package in evidence. With that, she grabbed it from my hand and said, *"Picasso est parti pour deux semaines,"* and slammed the door in my face.

I had performed my duty, but I had failed to accomplish my mission. At luncheon with our friends the Judas and the Weintraubs, I told my sad tale, with which they commiserated. Bill Weintraub had just bought a new Leica and asked if I knew how to load it. I assured him that I did and proceeded to insert the film. He returned later in the afternoon in great glee. He had visited the ceramic shop in Vallauris that handled Picasso's ceramics and had found Picasso there in great spirits, sporting the new cowboy shirt he had just received as a gift from a friend in America. Bill took numerous photographs of the artist and couldn't wait until the film could be developed. He asked me to unload the camera, and to our mutual horror, we discovered that I had not engaged the film properly. As a result there were no Picasso pictures, for which failure I was never forgiven.

In 1950, I received an invitation to attend the twenty-fifth reunion of my class at Harvard. I had not gone to any of the interim reunions and had no intention of attending this one until I ran into a classmate, Mike Cowles, who urged me to do so on the ground that if I didn't, I would be depriving my children of one of the greatest times of their lives. He was the chief marshal of the class and asked me to serve as an aide. I yielded, and he was right. It was a great party for the children and for Billie and me as well. I found that some of the fellows I hadn't liked in college had turned out to be first-rate human beings; I discovered interesting classmates whom I had never known in college.

On the first night of the reunion, the children were taken to a party separate from their parents. Someone came up to our table, having just come from the children's gathering, and said, "I've got the best story of the reunion. Wendy Marcus and John Lodge's daughter Beatrice have just been having a conversation about their fathers. Beatrice said, 'My father is governor of Connecticut, and he is *going* to be President of the United States.' 'That's nothing,' Wendy replied. 'My father is president of Neiman-Marcus *now.*'"

When Jerrie was first married, she and her Air Force husband were stationed in Taiwan, and she wrote me a letter questioning the pace of my life. I replied,

Dear Jerrie,

I caught your remark about my "supersonic pace," and I wondered whether it had been prompted by my letters or by what you have actually observed yourself.

338

There is no question that I lead a very busy and full life, partly through choice and greatly through circumstance. The operation of a successful business which requires a high degree of personal leadership is demanding. When we were at Easthampton this summer, we stayed at an inn operated by Henri Soulé, the owner of the Pavillon, generally regarded as one of the finest restaurants in the world. Well, we saw very clearly that it wasn't the finest simply by virtue of the fact that he had good recipes, or by the fact that he had a good staff. It was the finest because Mr. Soulé is a perfectionist. We watched him as he thumped every melon and examined every chicken.

The thing that has made Neiman-Marcus the great institution it is, recognized all over the world, has been the high quality of merchandise, decor, housekeeping, and service we have been able to maintain. None of this has come easily. Your grandfather before me was a great perfectionist, and it was through his and Aunt Carrie's remarkable set of ideals that the course of this business was set.

The great painters, writers and doctors have never found a substitute for intensive work. Fortunately I like my work and I have the ability to shed my problems when I come home. I live by a motto, "Don't worry about something you can't do anything about," and this has saved me from unnecessary worry and fretting. I have been blessed with a rugged and strong constitution, which, thus far, has permitted me to carry a stronger load than others in our business. This may be unfair to them, but I don't think anyone would benefit if I slackened my pace.

I am writing all of this in detail, so that you can have a little better understanding of what goes to make up my "supersonic pace." I certainly realize that Mother can't run as fast as I can, and I am going to help her go at a slower pace even to the point of eliminating some of my outside activities. She has a tremendous desire to want to participate in my interests, which is wonderful. There are some things, though, which we shall have to sort out as being of lesser importance. There are some trips which she may have to skip; there are some short trips she won't take because of the costs involved. You know, it's a peculiar thing in America — our tax laws make it legal for a businessman to deduct the traveling expenses of his secretary, but not those of his wife.

In these days of high taxes and large obligations, we have to conserve somewhere. I am confident Mother and I are going to be able to work this out, so that she will be able to maintain a pace within her physical capacity.

In all of this, I haven't mentioned the pressures of obligations, familial and financial, which have been great and which will continue to be with me for several years to come. To provide one's children with the best education possible, to give them the opportunities to travel, to clothe them and a wife and oneself, to maintain a home that is not only comfortable but adequate for the large-scale entertaining required of us, at today's tax rates, is not easy. Perhaps this will give you a better idea of "What Makes Stanley Run."

Devotedly,

DADDY

A few years later I was elected to the Board of Overseers of Harvard, which proved to be one of the most interesting and rewarding experiences in my life. I met men from many different industries and professions during my term, and as the result of one acquaintanceship, I suspect, I was invited to become a member of the Board of Directors of the New York Life Insurance Company. There, too, I have had valuable relationships with a diverse group of associates. I am confident that the fact I was from Texas influenced my selection by both institutions, for both were striving for geographical representation on their boards. I had earned a good name *and* I was from Texas.

Being a Texan certainly didn't have anything to do with being invited to the People's Republic of China in the spring of 1972, for there was little evidence in Canton that very many trade officials had any idea of what or where Texas was. When President Nixon removed the ban on trading with China, I made an immediate effort to get a visa through the Ottawa Embassy of the People's Republic of China. My eighteen letters went unanswered, and after our State Department advised me that they couldn't help, I decided to try less orthodox methods. I wrote to my friend

Bruno Kreisky, chancellor of Austria, to see if his ambassador to Peking, Hans Thalberg, with whom I had worked at the time of our Austrian Fortnight, might help. I negotiated with a former member of the Department of Justice who was setting up a Pakistani trading company to do business with China. The Canton Trade Fair was opening in mid-April and I was determined to be among those American retailers present.

One day I received a phone call from a man I hadn't seen in years, the former head of the Civil Aeronautics Bureau, Del Rentzel, who wanted to know whether I had any interest in China. "Have you been reading my mail?" I asked. "I'm very much interested." He went on to explain that he was setting up a trading company to sell American goods to China, and that it seemed sensible for them to have a client who wanted to buy merchandise from China. He said that he thought he could get me invited to the fair. Within two weeks my wife and I were en route to China. We were pleased by our reception, although we entered the country two days after U.S. planes had bombed the port of Haiphong. The only incident to mar our visit came about when the chief of the textile section asked us to meet with him and his staff on our second morning in Canton. He spoke at great length, condemning our bombing activities. "Your country doesn't have any business in Vietnam in the first place," he said. I agreed with him, but quickly pointed out that others among my countrymen would disagree with me. "Why don't you do something about it?" he asked. I explained that the only way any citizen in our country could take action was at the ballot box, and that I intended to vote against those who were perpetuating our blunderous adventure in Vietnam.

In making my application for admission to China, I had stated that our company was one of the most important retailers of fine-quality merchandise in the country, and that it was therefore to our mutual interests for us to receive an invitation. My interrogator had evidently seen my letter, for he turned to me and said, "If

341

you are as important as you say you are, then you must know President Nixon and members of his cabinet, and I want you to take this message I have just given you back to them." I admitted that I had met President Nixon and a few members of the cabinet, but that I had no intention of being a messenger boy, since there were more proper channels through which the President could be informed. "I have come here as a result of political agreements reached by Chairman Mao and our President which can lead to the establishment of peaceful relations between our two great countries. My objective here is to conduct deeds of trade, for as Chairman Mao says in his *Little Red Book*, 'Deeds are better than propaganda,' and if I don't get busy buying merchandise, I won't be fulfilling my mission." With that the meeting was terminated and I went back to work.

My purchases were mainly in the field of antiques, including superb eighteenth- and nineteenth-century Manchu court robes, porcelains, pewter, K'o-ssu tapestries, jewelry, and wood carvings.

We were not allowed to go past Canton on this trip, but on our second visit in November I put in another request to visit Peking. "Why do you want to go?" I was asked. "Because I came here to buy antiques and there aren't any left to buy. The Japanese have bought everything for sale," I replied. "You should have come earlier," I was told. "You should have sent out your invitations sooner," I retorted. "You've brought me here under false pretenses. I am confident I can find the antiques I want in Peking." "Let's discuss this at the end of the fair," he suggested. "No," I said. "Unless I can go to Peking tomorrow, I shall leave the fair and go to Sotheby's in London and buy Chinese antiques there." "What's Sotheby's?" he asked. I explained that Sotheby's was a great auction house and that they were having a sale of Chinese antiques on November 24, a few days away. "Come back tomorrow," he suggested. The next day, he said, "You are right, Sotheby's is having an auction on the twenty-fourth. You can leave for Peking tomorrow."

342

I was reviewing some wartime letters from my WPB days and came upon one to Billie in which I had written, "I've just met a young congressman from Texas who impresses me greatly. I think he's going places and when I return I want to give a luncheon so he can meet some people outside of his own constituency. His name is Lyndon Johnson." I did give the luncheon for him about a year later and introduced him to a hundred of the leading citizens of Dallas. I wrote later, "I've just met Lyndon's top aide, John Connally, who is smart and tough. I believe he will be more sensitive to the requirements of vested interests than to the problems of the poor and less fortunate." Both of the prophecies turned out to be fairly accurate.

When Johnson was a senator he used to come to the store to shop for Lady Bird, his daughters, and his secretarial staff. He had fixed ideas of what he liked and was not subject to persuasion, except by Billie, whose sense of fashion and taste he admired and respected. He did not like dark colors for the women who surrounded him, but leaned towards yellows, oranges, reds, and greens. He rejected all full skirts in preference for tight narrow ones, even when the fashion shifted away from the latter. He would not buy heavy fabrics or prints unless they were in black and white. Lady Bird was a very careful shopper, watching her budget with exactness, taking voluminous notes of what she had bought so that she could coordinate her clothes with accessories already in her wardrobe. After she had made her selections, the clothes usually had to be sent down to the ranch for her husband's final approval. Sometimes she would call in advance of her visit to see if Billie could come downtown to help her shop. She must go down in history as one of the great women of our times. She has a basic integrity seldom found in men or women.

I was impressed by Johnson's genuine concern with people and their welfare, which manifested itself in the legislation he sponsored from his early days in Congress right through the first few years of his presidency. I was disappointed when he got sucked into the Vietnam vortex and failed to deal with the American people and the Congress with full candor and honesty. He failed in this regard as did his predecessor and his successor.

All of us have our idiosyncrasies, and I have many. One is a violent antipathy for the misuse of the first person pronoun following a preposition. Once I broke off with a lovely girl I was courting when she said "between you and I." Not long ago, I received a thank-you note from a budding young executive, who wrote, "Thank you for sending such a fine ice bucket to Mary and I." It's hard for me to have a sanguine opinion about his future with us. Another anathema is small talk, for which I have absolutely no talent. This is certainly no virtue, for the world is full of nice people who indulge in it. Life is too exciting and my interests are too many for me to "make" conversation. There is no time for small talk. Time is a precious possession and I attempt to make the most of it by not wasting it, for it is irreplaceable. One of the ways I cover so much ground is by using time judiciously. I have scant regard for an associate who apologizes, "I just don't have time to do everything," for we all have time to do everything we want to do if we organize our time properly.

After my first few years of European travel, long before the Common Market encouraged the free flow of goods between countries, I could look at a man in a railway compartment and determine his probable nationality by examining the style of his shoes and the cut of his suit. One of my colleagues and I used to make quite a game out of this exercise. This led me into the bad habit of dissecting women's wardrobes, not to identify their national origins, but to figure out what they had paid for their various articles of apparel. I do this so unconsciously that I don't realize I'm guilty of staring at them. My wife accuses me of scrutinizing them so intensely that I virtually undress them mentally during the ascension of an elevator to the thirtieth floor, but I assure her that I redress them completely before the elevator comes to a stop.

One evening in a Hotel Pierre elevator I was giving a well-dressed woman the "eyeball" treatment. When we arrived at the lobby she walked out and took the first taxi. We took the next cab, and on arriving at our destination found she had reached the party just before us. We were introduced to the lady, who was Rosalind Russell. She said, "You were giving me a 'going over' to the point I thought my slip was showing." I apologized and explained that this was an occupational bad habit I was trying to overcome. I'm afraid I'll never fully succeed.

During my life I have received many honors from my peers in business and in the community and decorations from a half-dozen foreign countries, but no accolade compared to that rendered me prior to our Far Eastern Fortnight in an advertisement which was run in the local papers by my associates in the store:

A LETTER TO THE PUBLIC

FROM THE BUYERS AND EXECUTIVE STAFF

OF NEIMAN-MARCUS

This letter is published without the knowledge of our President. It is inspired by a meeting which was held in the store last week. At that time each buyer presented the merchandise which he had developed for our Far Eastern Fortnight beginning Monday, October 15. It was the first time each of us had had the chance to see what everyone else had done.

It was one of the most exciting days in the experience of any of us at Neiman-Marcus. Always, of course, we try to maintain the standards of quality and taste for which our store is known. But the things that have been developed for the Fortnight seem to us — as professionals — so imaginative, so really beautiful, and so typical of what N-M is and should be that we are taking this space to say so. Much of what we all saw cannot be found anywhere else in the world. You can't even find it in the Orient.

We think there are some credits due. We deserve some, even if we do say so ourselves; so do our manufacturers who have done an absolutely brilliant job of translating ideas from faroff places into wearable and beautiful things for today's life. Our several executives who have traveled the Far East have been enormously helpful.

The prime credit, however, must go to our president, Mr. Stanley Marcus, whose ten week Oriental trip produced most of the ideas that resulted in all this excitement. He personally directed the presentation which will be made to you Monday by every department in the store. This kind of creative leadership on the part of the Marcus family, father and sons, has welded together the team that makes Neiman-Marcus what it has been since 1907 and is today. It is a very personally led tradition.

This ad has been paid for by the buyers and executives of Neiman-Marcus, some seventy contributions in all. It was done this way because the corporation would never have run it, Mr. Marcus would never have permitted it; and then we wouldn't have been able to say these things we wanted to say.

17

Critical Decisions

In the late forties, Jack Lait and Lee Mortimer wrote a series of books, *Chicago Confidential*, *Washington Confidential*, and *New York Confidential*, all of which contained bits of local scandal about notable people in those communities. Curiously, they were not sued for libel. In 1952, they published a successor, *U.S.A. Confidential*, covering many of the cities not included in their earlier works. In this book they devoted several pages to Neiman-Marcus employees, charging our mannequins and Man's Shop salesmen with acts of moral turpitude. We were incensed by these allegations, and felt a strong obligation to defend the moral integrity of the members of our staff who had been intimidated. We believed also that if we permitted the stories to go unchallenged, many young people might be discouraged from seeking employment with us.

I consulted Abe Fortas, our Washington lawyer, and told him that we wanted to file a suit against the authors and their publisher. After investigating the facts, he rendered the opinion that certain of our employees had been libeled and that we could institute a class libel suit in their behalf. I recall him saying, "Before you make a decision to undertake this action, I must advise that libel suits are messy, troublesome, and expensive. Don't go into it unless you are prepared to live with it for a couple of years." Despite the forewarning, I felt that someone had to stand up against such scandalmongers and fight them in the courts. I made the decision to prosecute.

In 1952 we sued in behalf of our employees for $7,500,000 in what was one of the first class-action suits in the country. The publisher settled out of court within a few months, agreeing not to print any more copies of the book. The suit against the authors dragged on for several years, during which time I was subjected to intimidation, insinuations of blackmail, and harassment of various types. Finally, in 1955, we made an out-of-court settlement with the authors for $10,000, the publication of half-page advertisements of retraction in several newspapers across the country, and letters of apology to each of the individuals who were listed as plaintiffs. This settlement was a far cry from the $7,500,000 damages asked, but it did accomplish the objective of vindicating our staff. The cost of the advertisements, the cash payment, and the defendants' legal fees took all the profit out of the book for both the authors and the publisher. They wrote no more books of this type.

The class suit itself and the unique terms of settlement were considered so unusual that they were incorporated into the case books of many of the country's law schools. I've met many young lawyers who have said that their first acquaintance with Neiman-Marcus came about through their exposure to this case in law school. Now I can understand why more people don't sue for libel, for as Abe Fortas had predicted, "Libel suits are messy, troublesome, and expensive."

At 1:35 A.M. on Saturday morning, December 19, 1964, I was awakened by the incessant ringing of the telephone. We had retired an hour before and I was in deep sleep. It took me a few seconds before I could comprehend what the voice on the other end of the line was saying. "Mr. Marcus, we have just discovered a little fire in the store, and we wanted to alert you. There's no necessity for you to come down, but we'll call you back as soon as we get it under control." I turned over and went back to an uneasy sleep. Forty minutes later the phone rang again, and this time I was fully alert to our store superintendent's message. "The fire is spreading," he said. "I think you'd better get down here at once!" I jumped into warm clothes, drove at high speed on the deserted, icy streets, and arrived at the site of the burning building within fifteen minutes after the second phone call.

Smoke was billowing from the upper floors, flames were licking the early morning air from the second-floor windows. It was obvious before I entered the building that a major catastrophe had occurred. The fire chief confirmed my fear that all of the floors had been damaged by fire, smoke, or water, and estimated that it would take several hours to extinguish the fire. He permitted me to go on an inspection trip as far as the third floor, but no farther, because of the hazardous conditions. A few firemen had been overcome by smoke, but fortunately no one had been injured. By this time it was 4 A.M. and five cups of coffee later. My brothers and many of our executives had arrived on the scene with questions about the cause of the conflagration, the extent of the destruction, and the condition of our stocks. The air was full of contradictory ideas and suggestions. I recognized that in an emergency situation such as this it was necessary for strong leadership, and as chief executive it was my job.

I commandeered a small office on the ground floor, removed from the center of the firefighting activities and smoke-laden air, and called all of our senior people together. I said, "We have an emergency, and we are going to have to make some fast decisions. Time won't permit us to discuss the pros and cons of every question. I'll listen to anything you have to recommend, but I am ready and willing to make final judgments. I may make some mistakes in judgment, but I'll have to take that chance. We have been put out of business just a week before Christmas, and thousands of people are depending on us to supply them with Christmas gifts. Bob, you get hold of the radio and TV stations, and ask them to tell our customers that we shall reinforce our staff of salespeople

351

at the Preston Center and Fort Worth stores, so that they can complete their Christmas shopping. Buy commercial time as well to carry this message, and also tell our customers that most purchases made the day before the fire are already at our service center, and are undamaged. As soon as you get access to our alteration department, determine how many garments are there which had been promised for delivery today, and if they are undamaged, offer to send them out, subject to the customers' satisfaction."

I continued, "We are covered by 'use and occupancy' insurance, which will safeguard us against financial loss while we are closed, but even that can't protect us from the loss of the customers who have to go elsewhere to shop in the meantime. Therefore, our number one objective is to get back into business at the earliest possible moment." It was then 4:45 A.M. I turned to our construction supervisor. "Call our contractors, and tell them to get down here at once and start building a barricade around the building. Telephone Eleanor LeMaire in New York, and ask her to send two of her store designers to Dallas on the first plane they can catch, and tell them to come prepared to stay for the duration. We'll need them to determine what, if anything, can be reused, and after that, they can start designing permanent installations." By 7 A.M., before the firemen had left the premises, the construction crew was erecting the protective barricade around the building. Miss LeMaire suggested on the phone that it would be useful to get Alvin Colt, our Fortnight designer, to come down to help with establishing temporary decor. A call to Colt revealed that he was on a cruise in the Caribbean, his first vacation in four years. "Find out the first port of arrival, and pull him off the ship," I ordered. He was located that morning in Granada, flew back to New York minus his wardrobe, and was in Dallas by ten o'clock that night.

By that time the insurance adjusters showed up, and together, we were able to make a preliminary investigation of the condition of the merchandise stocks. They concurred that the entire stock, with minor exceptions, had to be considered unsalable. Bill Bramley, our vice-president and treasurer, told them that we would not consider offering for sale any piece of merchandise which had been exposed to smoke, even though it showed no visible damage from fire or water. (The rejected stock proved subsequently too large for even Filene's Basement to absorb, so it was sold by the insurance company in separate lots to a half-dozen fire outlet stores across the country.) They agreed, so I turned to George Baylis, our general merchandise manager, and instructed him to get our buyers to New York by the following Monday morning to buy replacement stocks for delivery in two weeks, not knowing whether a reopening could be accomplished by that time or not.

One of our merchandise men reminded me that we had a number of wedding deliveries scheduled for that day, and since the bridal and attendants' gowns were all stored in our bridal shop, they were either smoke- or water-damaged. He made the brilliant proposal that we call in the entire wedding garment stocks from our Fort Worth and Houston stores, rent a suite of rooms at a hotel, and notify every bride to come and make another selection. By eleven o'clock in the morning this plan had been executed, and we re-outfitted the fifteen bridal parties without losing a single bride. Helen Corbitt, our food director, set cooks to work in her own apartment to meet our Christmas party catering commitments.

By 11 A.M., Bob Jeffrey, our controller, had organized a fleet of trucks to start moving the inventory out of the building to the salvage warehouses. Another group of trucks carried off water-soaked furniture and carpets. Engineers and contractors began an appraisal of the physical damage caused by the fire and started to establish a reconstruction schedule. By that night we had demolition workmen in the store, pulling down plaster walls and sagging ceilings.

Throughout the meetings, I was called out to talk to the press, do radio and TV interviews, and pose for innumerable photographs wearing a fireman's helmet. By cooperating with the reporters and helping them make their deadlines, we scored the most inclusive

353

and sympathetic press in the history of fires. We even had coverage on European TV. Our total loss was about $12,500,000. The cause of the fire was never determined.

By 11 P.M. I called it a day and went home, carrying with me the acrid stench of smoke in my clothing, my hair, and my nostrils. For years the slightest smell of charred wood was enough to send a shiver through my body, creating instant recall of that fateful day in 1964.

When Miss LeMaire and her designers arrived, we had a long discussion about our alternatives. We could either return the store to its prefire condition, or we could take advantage of a bad situation and redesign the fixtures and decor of every department, ending up with a completely modern-looking store. Even though I knew the latter choice would prove more difficult and expensive, I nonetheless took that option. Under normal conditions, it takes a year to design the interior, six months to finish the shell of a building (and that's about all we had left), and another six months to build new fixtures. Through the Herculean efforts of the LeMaire organization, our contractors, and our own staff, we were completely rebuilt in eleven months. Equally remarkable, by a scheme devised by Miss LeMaire and Alvin Colt, we were able to reopen the first three floors on January 15, 1965, twenty-seven days after the fire. Occupancy of the fourth floor followed a week later. Miss LeMaire figured that if we could create an attractive decor in the center of each floor, permanent reconstruction work could be started around the perimeter. The second stage involved closing down the center, and occupying the perimeter spaces. She felt the colorings of the interim areas should be verdant and springlike, the antithesis of fire and smoke. Colt, using theatrical techniques and employing scenic designers, gave the store a stagelike quality. Since the floor coverings and furniture were to be used for a short period of time, he bought the least expensive and most effective things he could find, compensating for their quality by a lavish use of fresh flowers, and large-scale live plants. Our manufacturers in this country and abroad cooperated to the fullest extent in restocking us. One sweater mill in Scotland turned over its entire production for one week to manufacture replacement stocks for us. Our customers poured in on reopening day to express their congratulations on our speedy recovery.

During the days following the fire we were deluged with cables and letters from all over the world — from retail colleagues, customers, and even the President of the United States. I was deeply touched by the generous concern of local retailers and banks who offered trucks and manpower, storage facilities, and personnel to help us in our time of need.

In the New Year's message for January 1, 1965, I stated:

Smoke gets in your eyes, but not in your hearts . . . when you find a whole city, a nation, a world coming to your aid at a time of disaster. Most people and institutions have to die before their friends say all the nice things they've been storing up for years. Obituaries are read by the living, not the dead about whom they are written.

Not so for Neiman-Marcus. We have had a liberal opportunity to learn the depth of affection and regard in which our institution is held by our customers, employees, vendors, fellow merchants here and abroad, and by the citizenship in general.

I assured our readers that we, like the legendary phoenix, would arise from the ashes, and thanked them all for the "greatest vote of confidence imaginable."

One wag took advantage of the fire by sending out a New Year's card that read,

This is to inform you
That a gift being held for you
at
Neiman-Marcus
Was destroyed by fire
Happy New Year
Pat Donahue

355

Another customer got hold of a two-inch square of mink. He singed it around the edges, tacked on a Neiman-Marcus label from one of his wife's dresses, and gift-wrapped it with his card, which was inscribed, "I know you've always wanted a mink coat, so I decided to buy you one this year. This is all that's left of it after the fire at Neiman-Marcus."

With a brand-new downtown store and three thriving suburban stores, we started to look for new markets. A recurring problem was that of capital; the solution was either the sale of a large amount of common stock, which would reduce family control and make us susceptible to raids or merger with another organization with larger financial muscle. I was concerned, as well, with the problems of succession in a family business. In selecting my successor for the chief executive position, I did not relish the responsibility of choosing between my brothers. Furthermore, I had obligations to our stockholders, and to my own estate, to make an unbiased decision. Thus, by a study of the alternatives, I came to the conclusion that all interests would best be protected by going the merger route. My brothers and the other stockholders concurred, so we started to look for a prospective mate.

We had offers from three or four of the leading retail firms in the country and from one wealthy man who wanted to buy us to start a conglomerate. All of our prospects were insistent that my brothers and I stay in the business, and they all promised autonomy of operation. We were just about to make a deal with one of them when I received a call from Ben Sonnenberg, who asked if we would be willing to talk to Ed Carter, president of Broadway-Hale of California. I had known Ed for a number of years and liked him, but I said to Ben, "But they don't know anything about specialty store operation." To which he replied, "That might be all to the good, for they'll have to leave you alone. The others you are considering all know something about specialty stores, and they might find it difficult to keep their hands off you." With some reluctance, I agreed to see Ed and have preliminary dis-

356

cussions with him. We hit it off extremely well, for we had mutual interests in community affairs, art, music, and the philosophy of retail operation. He promised autonomy of operation, as had the others, but somehow I believed him. He said, "We don't want to interfere with you in any way in the running of this business. There are only two stipulations I would make: first, make your business finer if possible; second, build more stores.

I felt I needed some outside counsel, so I called my old friend Nate Cummings in Chicago, and said, "Nate, we are considering a merger, and since you've been through a lot of them in Consolidated Foods, I want to check with you to see if you think I have all the factors properly evaluated." "Yes," he said, "I've been through eighty-seven mergers. What are your factors?" I replied that price, the quality of the stock we would take in exchange for ours, and compatability seemed to me to be the three dominant considerations. He replied, "You're right. Those are the three most important, but you have them in the wrong order. First of all, price is not important. They are all going to pay you within a dollar of the same price. Second, you wouldn't be talking to anyone who didn't have a good quality of stock to exchange. Third, if you are planning to stay in the business, then compatability is of overwhelming importance." When I rearranged the factors as he suggested, Broadway-Hale came out on top, and I recommended to our Board of Directors that we merge with them.

That was a little over five years ago, and I have never had reason to regret that critical decision. If I were doing it over again, the only thing I would do differently would be to have merged five years earlier. It was a good deal for both our stockholders and for Broadway's. It gave us the financial ability to enter into a large and significant expansion program. And it relieved me of having to name my successor by myself. I would imagine that in the whole history of American corporate mergers, this is one of the few in which neither of the parties has suffered any disillusionment after five years of association.

18

Credo

I N COLLEGE I TOOK A COURSE in medieval history in which the German Reformation and Martin Luther occupied three pages of the textbook and twenty minutes of classroom discussion. It was years later, at an exhibition of the works of the great American artist and humanist Ben Shahn, that I came across a poster he had painted to advertise the motion picture *Martin Luther*, which he simply titled *Credo*. It was only then that I understood what Martin Luther was all about. Luther said, "I have the right to believe freely. To be a slave to no man's authority. If this be heresy, so be it. It is still the truth. To go against conscience is neither right nor safe. I cannot . . . will not . . . recant. Here I stand. No man can command my conscience." It seemed to me then, as it does now, one of the noblest statements ever made by man. I bought the painting, and whenever the pressure against freedom of expression gets too great, I reread it for sustenance.

Of all the controversies in which I have been involved, the "long hair" episode proved to be the most savage in the reaction it engendered. It all started in 1966, when three teenage musicians were ejected from a Dallas high school because the principal said their hair was too long. I didn't know the boys and I personally disliked the fashion of long hair, but I was appalled by what I thought was a violation of the boys' constitutional rights. I read the newspaper account of the incident on my way to the airport and telephoned them before my flight to offer financial aid in fighting the decision in the courts. My secretary, unaware of my call, told me we had never received so many phone calls in a single day on any subject, and that the vast majority of the messages were highly critical of my position.

The protest against my support of Kennedy was mild in comparison to the flood of letters, telegrams, and messages condemning my offer of assistance to the three boys. The attacks came from all sides: from schoolteachers siding with the principal, ministers, conservative older people, doctors, lawyers, friends, and even relatives — from residents of Dallas and nonresidents alike. In retrospect, I realized that I had touched a sensitive nerve in the populace — the insurgency of youth — and it was glad to have someone of stature to lash with their pent-up indignation. Some of the letters were so similar in wording that I was forced to suspect they had been inspired by some common source. More charge accounts were closed than on any of the other occasions when I took an unpopular stand.

Typical of many of the letters was this one from a Dallas woman:

Dear Mr. Marcus,

I was shocked and horrified to read that you upheld those who defy school rules. You evidently are not aware that *dress* does make a difference in attitudes, behavior, and even human morals. You should stick to merchandising and allow principals to do their job without interference.

Yours truly,

AN IRATE CITIZEN

I received a card with a Dallas postmark,

Dear Stanley,

It would be impossible to estimate the loss in volume to your firm from your asinine remarks about "civil wrongs and liberties." Your remarks hurt all the merchants in Dallas. Why don't you keep your trap shut?

E<small>D</small>

I had no way of identifying "Ed."

From one of the city's most respected and competent physicians came a copy of a letter addressed to a school board member:

I do not agree with Stanley Marcus regarding the "Mop-tops" in W. W. Samuell High School. Mr. W. S. Lanham, the Principal, has my wholehearted support. Educating is more than text-book instruction.

Mr. Marcus has been quite successful financially, by helping people appear well groomed, and I doubt that he would think of employing these strange looking students in his store. If he wants to be of real help, let him furnish wigs instead of lawyers.

Yours very truly,

An oilman wrote with obvious restraint,

Dear Mr. Marcus:

I have been a customer of yours and all my family has traded with you ever since we came to Texas. I have always thought well of you and considered you a man of wisdom and good judgment.

I am disappointed in you and your attitude toward a school principal who is trying to uphold standards.

I want to thank you for the courtesy given to me and my family over the last several years and I also thank you for the business given my company. However, since I don't agree with the stand you have taken, I will not be trading with your company in the future.

Yours truly,

A solicitation card for a trial subscription to *Venture* magazine was returned with this notation written on the side:

363

I wouldn't *venture* into your store one more time for anything — until Stanley begins to keep his nose out of other people's business.

There were many letters from ardent students of the Bible who tried to prove by scriptural reference that I was misguided, as in this letter:

Dear Mr. Marcus:

I am writing concerning the three boys with whom the principle ordered to get their hair cut. As a mother of three teenage boys, I was very disappointed. You of all people encouraging the boys to rebel against rules and regulations. The Lord never meant for boys or men to go around looking like women. He created them male and he expects them to look like it. The Bible says in 1st Corinthians 6:9: "Know ye not that the unrighteous shall not inherit the kingdom of God? Neither fornicators, nor idolaters, nor adulterers, *nor effeminate* nor abusers of themselves with man kind." Would you as a father (if you are father), sanction any of the other things mentioned in this scripture? Yet in God's eyes men or boys going around looking like women are equal to the others. So you are encouraging them to go against mans' rules and God's also. I speak as a mother.

Sincerely,

Mrs. L. R. Gordon

To which I replied,

Dear Mrs. Gordon:

As a taxpayer and citizen, I feel that I had every right to give "unsolicited" support to the boys whose constitutional freedoms were being abused by the administrative action of the principal of the W. W. Samuel High School. Frankly, I don't like long hair on boys any more than you do, but I do think that the preservation of the freedoms guaranteed by our Constitution is of utmost importance and that whenever they are abused by the government or by administrators, that it is the obligation of good citizens to put up a fight.

Historically, man has worn long hair and short hair. Many religious books depict the leading characters of the Old Testament and the

364

New Testament as wearing long hair. George Washington and Benjamin Franklin wore long hair. I suspect that our civilization, just as theirs, will survive the changes in hair fashion.

I do appreciate your writing me and giving me this opportunity of expressing my opinion more fully.

Very sincerely,

STANLEY MARCUS

One writer, after expressing her shock at my audacity in expressing my opinion, asked, "Could it be you are a Communist and like to see some of the breakdowns in the ways of our youth?" She closed by stating, "I want you to know I will never again patronize your store. If I were you, I'd certainly reconsider your views and get back on the track of the right. Hoping you will apologize for such nonsense, yours truly." I felt this charge deserved a special answer and I wrote her,

Dear Mrs. Fordyce:

It's quite surprising that my attempts to protect our Constitution and the freedoms granted to its citizens have led you to raise the question as to whether I am a Communist. I can assure you that I am not and never have been and never will be.

I don't like long hair on boys any more than you do, but I have a profound respect for the United States Constitution and the privileges of freedom that it guarantees its citizens. Your decision to close your account is certainly your privilege, but may I call your attention to the fact that such an action is exactly the kind that the dictatorship countries use when people disagree with those in power. They retaliate by economic sanctions. This is not the democratic way of doing things. You have every right to disagree with me, just as I have a right to disagree with the school administration, without fear of retaliation. I am sorry that you have taken this decision, but this, of course, is your privilege.

Sincerely,

STANLEY MARCUS

365

A few, but very few, rallied to my support publicly. One letter came from a Methodist pastor,

Dear Mr. Marcus:

I am not high-school age nor do I have long hair. However, I feel that our society is doing a great injustice to our youth in demanding conformity in areas which have nothing to do with our legal structures.

I am currently involved in directing a youth program in a Methodist church. It is my opinion that our young people must be allowed to exist as real persons, individuals, and not as cogs in a vast social machine.

Sincerely,

I was especially heartened by two letters from conservative Republicans. The first came from a former Republican county chairman,

Dear Stanley,

This is just a brief note to congratulate you in speaking up recently on "the long-hair" matter. It would seem that if any damn fool wants to wear his hair long it should damn well be his right to do so. No other person is harmed by it — no other person's rights are abused thereby.

The community needs more persons like you to declare themselves. We are slowly being strangled in Dallas by the noose of conformity.

Sincerely,

MAURICE CARLSON

The other letter sent to the *Dallas Times Herald* came from a man I didn't know.

Gentlemen:

As Sam Goldwyn would say, I was thunder and struck at the bigoted, fatuous attack made by some of your more provincial readers on the man who has probably done more to bring international recognition to Dallas than any other civic leader of this city, Mr. Stanley

Marcus. And merely because Mr. Marcus exercised his constitutional right of concerning himself about the constitutional rights of others less fortunate than himself — just as we are doing in Viet Nam today — in providing assistance to the three long-haired high school musicians.

I would assume that these readers and the Board of Education would bar Dr. Albert Schweitzer, Dr. Albert Einstein, George Washington, Patrick Henry, Thomas Jefferson, Robert Browning, Lord Byron, Bach, Brahms and Beethoven, Leonardo da Vinci, Michelangelo, all those mentioned in the Holy Bible, including, with all due respect, Jesus Christ, Virgil, Homer and Socrates — from Dallas High Schools, since all of the aforementioned had long hair.

Educators are supposed to be concerned with what can be put IN a student's head, not the length of hair ON it. The crew-cut tyrants of their time, the Roman Caesars, would never have been known to us were it not for the accounts of the long-haired Virgil and Homer, which have long outlasted the achievements of the Caesars.

Of course individual liberty can always be punished as was done by the Nazis in World War II in shaving the heads of the French Underground who were fighting for the principles we were, or as Delilah did to Samson in the Holy Bible; but I trust your readers and the Board of Education do not intend to employ such barbaric procedures, although their attitude would seem to open the door to same.

As I trust that Mr. Stanley Marcus, one of the all too few truly Renaissance men of our time and town, who has done more to widen the world of Dallas than any other single citizen of the City that I can think of, will not be further vilified by those, who it would appear — should spend more time in the "adult" high school classes, poring over the Constitution of this country, the Holy Bible, and classical history — and less time in the local barber shops with the Police Gazette.

(A SHORT-HAIRED REPUBLICAN)

The case did go before a federal judge who ruled in behalf of the school board. On petition for writ of certiorari to the United States Court of Appeals for the fifth circuit, Mr. Justice Douglas, dissenting, wrote a thoughtful opinion which expresses my objectives for having become involved in the dispute.

367

It comes as a surprise that in a country where the States are restrained by an Equal Protection Clause, a person can be denied education in a public school because of the length of his hair. I suppose that a nation bent on turning out robots might insist that every male have a crew cut and every female wear pigtails. But the ideas of "life, liberty, and the pursuit of happiness," expressed in the Declaration of Independence, later found specific definition in the Constitution itself, including of course freedom of expression and a wide zone of privacy. I had supposed those guarantees permitted idiosyncrasies to flourish, especially when they concern the image of one's personality and his philosophy toward government and his fellow men.

Municipalities furnish many services to their inhabitants; and I had supposed that it would be an invidious discrimination to withhold fire protection, police protection, garbage collection, health protection, and the like merely because a person was an off-beat, non-conformist when it came to hair-do and dress as well as to diet, race, religion, or his views on Vietnam.

I would grant the petition for certiorari in this Texas case and put it down for argument.

I came out of this experience battered and bruised, but unshaken in my conviction that citizens who feel deeply about the civil liberties guaranteed by the Bill of Rights have an obligation of citizenship to speak out loudly, if we are to preserve them.

Edward and I had been waging a battle within our own organization to effect changes in the manner of handling black customers. The more conservative members of our managerial staff opposed us on the grounds that we would alienate our white clientele, particularly our most important customers. Finally, when the courts ordered desegregation of the Dallas public schools for September 1961, the local business leadership met and decided that all efforts must be made to prevent a repetition of the Little Rock disorder. Sam Bloom, the head of a local advertising agency and a great humanitarian, was commissioned to design a program to educate the

368

public well in advance of the day the children would be confronted with a new and strange set of conditions.

We all agreed that children should not be the first to meet desegregation, but that the adult community needed to desegregate itself beforehand. "Don't leave it for the children to do" became the phrase used with hotels, restaurants, and stores to encourage them to cooperate. The chain hotels, like Hilton and Sheraton, were feeling the pressures from some of the national organizations, which would not schedule conventions in any of their hotels so long as they practiced segregation in some of them. Acting on the theory that if all the hotels acted in unison none would be hurt, they all agreed to eliminate any restrictions on the basis of color. Once the hotels came into line, most of the independent restaurants went along too. The department and specialty stores opened their restaurants to blacks and eliminated some of their previous practices designed to discourage black patronage. The minute we decided to desegregate the store eating facilities, it became obvious that we would have to desegregate toilets as well.

It's one thing to make an executive decision; it's another to get wholehearted acceptance of it by an entire staff. We held numerous training meetings, trying to break through generations of prejudice, to give us confidence that black customers would be served in our stores well and graciously. To the great credit of our employees, we were successful in our efforts. Still, a few of our most conservative managers predicted dire results; they honestly thought the roof would cave in. When "D-day" occurred in the store, everything went smoothly; the roof didn't cave in, nor did any other calamitous consequences occur. Several charge accounts were closed by women who said they wouldn't shop in the store in view of the fact we were not only selling to blacks, but employing them in sales positions as well. Within a month the accounts had been reopened. The communitywide campaign was a success, and school desegregation took place without incident. Dallas is a conservative city, but in this case many of us thought that the public was way ahead of the city's leadership.

Inspired by the action of the Levi Strauss Company of San Francisco on the subject of equal employment, and by a letter that its president, Walter Haas, had sent to its suppliers, I drafted a letter for distribution to all of the companies with whom we did business. I submitted it to our executive committee and I am very proud of the fact that my associates gave it unanimous approval. We sent it out in the form of a New Year's message to some five thousand vendors all over the United States. We received about ten replies in disagreement, but hundreds of letters expressed enthusiasm for the statement of principle.

HAPPY NEW YEAR:

As we start a New Year, I should like to express my appreciation to you for having served us so well during the past year. As one of America's fine specialty stores we are dependent on manufacturers and suppliers who can *understand* and *appreciate* the principles of *quality* for which we stand.

1967 will have been a good year for most retailers and manufacturers, but it was a bad year for our country. We witnessed riots and civil disturbances in many of our major cities which threatened to disrupt the nation. *None* of us can feel secure in our business, however prosperous or well managed they may be, if we have disorder and destruction in our land. A large part of the problems facing our cities is caused by poverty and discrimination which lead to frustration then to violence. Steps must be taken beyond those contemplated in current programs, and in our opinions the *business community* must assume a *greater* degree of *responsibility* than it has heretofore.

Specifically we feel that despite obvious difficulties, a greater effort must be made to create job opportunities for members of minority groups. I am sure that you have given thought to positive ways in which businessmen can work to help *correct* the situation.

The Federal Government, as you know, requires that every one of its suppliers of goods and services certifies that it is an equal opportunity employer. We believe a *private* company should do *no* less, and we maintain an equal opportunity policy in our employment program.

It is our intention to include notice on each of our purchase orders that we expect our suppliers to follow fair employment practices as a condition of the order. We shall, in our purchasing activities, look with *favor* upon those companies which are taking *positive* steps toward employing and training people of minority groups.

In implementing this policy, we will continue to buy primarily based on quality, service and price, but this *additional* factor of an *affirmative* equal opportunity employment policy will also be considered by all of our buyers. In the future we would rather do business with a company which is actively and sincerely pursuing a policy of equal opportunity, than to continue to do business with one which is not.

In our belief that the private sector should take the *lead* in this country, we recommend our policy to you and *hope* that you will implement it with your own suppliers.

Again may I thank you for what you've done for this past year. With the opening of our new store in Houston in the fall of 1968 we look forward to achieving new sales records, to which I hope your company will be an active participant.

Sincerely,

STANLEY MARCUS

This letter was not a grandstand play for applause, even though we received it, but was an act of conviction.

In a recent TV interview with Murphy Martin of station WFAA, he wound up by using the last few minutes to throw some names and subjects at me, asking for instant reactions. I am borrowing his device, for it seems to be a good way in which I can express my own personal credo on diverse subjects.

Religion: I have no sense of religion; I'm not concerned whether there is a deity or not. I make no efforts to proselytize and I have resisted all attempts at being proselytized. The metaphysics of religion I understand, but reject.

Ethics: The ethical concepts of all major religions interest me greatly. I subscribe to them and make them part of my life.

371

Conscience: With Martin Luther I say, "No man can command my conscience."

Public Relations: The best public relations are based on good deeds. Executives should be their own spokesmen on the occasion of bad news as well as on good ones.

Free Enterprise: To my mind, it's the best of all systems thus far developed. I am saddened, though, by some businessmen who worship at its shrine but then do everything they can to destroy it by collusive price-fixing and bidding.

Education: Events of the past year in business and government demonstrate the need for the inclusion of the subject of ethical conduct in all of the various fields of study.

Truth: Truth is the elusive but vital ingredient for intellectual discussion and decisionmaking. Its attainment is hampered by the four stumbling blocks enunciated by Friar Roger Bacon:

1. The influence of fragile or unworthy authority.

2. Custom.

3. The imperfection of undisciplined senses.

4. Concealment of ignorance by ostentation of seeming wisdom.

The Most Important Public Document: The Bill of Rights.

Quality: I firmly believe that quality is remembered long after the price is forgotten.

Politics and Politicians: No comment.

Responsibility: From Goethe, *"Was du ererbt von deinen Vätern hast, erwirh es, um es zu besitzen,"* which translated reads "What you have inherited from your father, you must earn in order to possess."

Index

Borge, Victor, 220
Bousquet, Marie Louise, 300
Boussac, Marcel, 102, 301
Bowles, Charles, 207
Boys Town of Italy, 214
Brader, Betty, 140
Bramley, Norman William, 227, 352–353
Braque, Georges, 282, 290
Bricard, Madame, 301
Bro, René, 286
Broadway-Hale Stores, Inc., 356–357
Brooks, Donald, 309
Brown, Myra, 29
Brown University, 157
Buchwald, Art, 142
Buffet, Bernard, 210
Bullock's Wilshire, 51
Business Week, 167
Byrd, D. Harold, 247

Cagli, Corrado, 214
Calder, Alexander, 287
Callas, Maria, 192–193
Camerino, Giuliana (Roberta), 214–215
Canton Trade Fair, 341
Cantrell, Mary. *See* Marcus, Mrs. Stanley (Mary Cantrell, "Billie")
Capitol News, 312
Cardin, Pierre, 309
Carlebach, Julius, 281–282
Carlson, Maurice, 366
Carnegie, Hattie, 79, 100, 137
Carpenter, Elizabeth, 266
Carson, Pirie, Scott and Company (Chicago), 141
Carter, Amon, 26
Carter, Edward W., 356–357
Cartier, 141
Casals, Pablo, 253
Cashin, Bonnie, 308–309
Cerf, Bennett, 119–120
Chagall, Marc, 283
Chanel, Coco, 299–300, 304, 305, 307
Channing, Carol, 232
Charles of the Ritz, 182, 303, 314
Chase, Edna Woolman, 74–75, 100
Chez Point, 330–331
Chicago Civic Opera Company, 26
Chicago Confidential (Lait and Mortimer), 349

Chronicle, The (Houston), 133
Clark, Edward, 218
Coca-Cola, 4
Code Duello, 326
Collier's, 78–79
Colt, Alvin, 222, 352, 354
Commercial (Pine Bluff, Arkansas), 253
Committee for the Acquisition of Paintings for the White House, 253
Confrèries des Chevaliers du Tastevin, 329–330
Connally, John C., 343
Consolidated Foods, 288, 357
Cooper, Gloria Vanderbilt (Mrs. Wyatt), 220
Cooper, John Sherman, 265
Cooper, Wyatt, 220
Corbitt, Helen, 181–182, 353
Côte d'Or, 331
cotton: in World War I, 23; and Texas economy, 243–246
Coudert Frères, 267
Courrèges, André, 303
Cowles, Gardner, 319, 338
Cronkite, Walter, 228
Crume, Paul, 68
Cullen, Moira, 6, 24, 31, 82, 103; ability as buyer, 61–63; customer requests, 63; training of Lawrence Marcus, 135–136; and ready-to-wear, 11
Cummings, Nathan, 288–289, 357

Daché, Lilly, 79
Daily Telegraph (London), 333
Daily Telegraph Magazine of London, 68
Dallas, 12; history and growth, 25–27; effect of oil discoveries on, 71, 246–247; Texas Centennial, 74–75; politics in, 153–156; McCarthy era in, 156, 249–250; Kennedy assassination, 253–259; long hair episode, 261–268; racial desegregation in, 368–371
Dallas Art Association, 153, 156
Dallas Citizens Council, 256
Dallas Civic Auditorium, 250
Dallas Civic Opera Company, 192–193, 213
Dallas Garden Center, 159